# I WANT TO KNOW CHRIST

## Weekday Reflections
## for Liturgical Year 2018/2019

**MARTIN HOGAN**

First published 2018 by Messenger Publications

Extracts from The New Jerusalem Bible reproduced with kind permission
of Darton, Longman and Todd

ISBN 978 1 788120 08 1

Designed by Messenger Publications Design Department
Typeset in Times New Roman & DIN Condensed
Printed by Johnswood Press Ltd

Messenger Publications,
37 Lower Leeson Street, Dublin 2
www.messenger.ie

# INTRODUCTION

In his letter from prison to the church of Philippi, Paul says, 'I want to know Christ'. It often struck me as a strange thing for Paul to say. It is evident from this wonderful letter, and from the letters Paul had written before he wrote to the Philippians, that he knew Christ intimately. Indeed, a few verses before making this statement, Paul declares, with reference to his previous life as a zealous Pharisee, 'I regard everything as loss because of the surpassing value of knowing Christ Jesus my Lord'. Paul had tasted the 'surpassing value of knowing Christ Jesus my Lord' and, yet, he could say, 'I want to know Christ'. He realised that the journey of coming to know Christ, with one's head and heart, would never be complete in this life. As he declared to the church in Corinth, 'now we see in a mirror, dimly, but then we will see face to face. Now I know only in part; then I will know fully, even as I have been fully known'. The letter to the Ephesians speaks of knowing 'the love of Christ that surpasses knowledge'.

We are all travelling this same journey of coming to know Christ who surpasses knowledge. It is the adventure of a lifetime. The more we come to know him, the more we realise how much more there is to know. We can only truly know those we love. In the fourth Gospel, it is the beloved disciple, the disciple who is closest to Jesus in love, who has the deepest insight into Jesus, recognising before others did his presence in the empty tomb and on the shore of the Sea of Galilee. It is in giving our heart in love to Jesus that we come to know him more fully. Our love for Jesus is always a response to his love for us. One of the privileged ways we encounter the Lord's love for us is in and through the pages of the four Gospels. In prayerfully reflecting on the words of the gospels we can experience the Lord's love for us and be moved to grow in our love and knowledge of him. Jerome, one of the earliest biblical scholars in the history of the Church, declares that 'ignorance of Scripture is ignorance of Christ'. Within the Scriptures, it is above all in and through the gGospels that we come to know and love Christ, the human face of God.

The gospel readings of the weekdays of the Liturgical Year present us with a large proportion of all four Gospels. The Gospels of Mark, Matthew and Luke each have a significant block within Ordinary Time. The Gospel of John features prominently in the seasons of Christmas, Lent and, especially, Easter. In prayerfully reflecting upon the weekday gospel readings for the liturgical year we are responding to Paul's call in his letter to the Colossians to 'let the word of Christ dwell in you richly'. The following pages contain a reflection on each of the gospel readings, with occasional reference to the first reading, for the liturgical year 2018/19. It is my hope that people will find these reflections a helpful companion on their own personal journey of coming 'to know the love of Christ that surpasses knowledge'.

## 3 December, Monday, First Week of Advent

*Matthew 8:5–11*

The Roman centurion in today's gospel reading displays an awareness of the power of his own word. As a centurion, he has one hundred soldiers under his command, and he has only to say a word and his soldiers will obey him, 'Go … Come here … Do this'. Yet, he recognises that the power of his word is but a pale reflection of the power of Jesus' word. He has such faith in Jesus' word that he believes that Jesus could heal his servant at a distance by speaking a word, without Jesus, a Jew, having to come into his pagan household. Jesus is amazed that a pagan, a non-Jew, could display such faith, such trust in his word: 'nowhere in Israel have I found faith like this'. In the first reading, we find a similar recognition of the value and the power of God's word on the part of pagans. The pagan nations are envisaged by the prophet Isaiah as streaming to Jerusalem because it is there that God will teach them his ways; it is from there that the Law of God, the oracle or word of the Lord, goes out. Both readings present us with pagans who show a deep appreciation for and trust in the value and power of the Lord's word. We, the Lord's disciples, can be expected to value his word even more. Advent is a time when we try to listen more attentively to the Lord's word to us, especially as it comes to us through the Gospels and the other documents of the New Testament. The word of the Lord is alive and active. The risen Lord continues to speak to us. Advent is a time to open ourselves to the Lord's life-giving word, after the example of the Roman centurion in today's gospel reading.

## 4 December, Tuesday, First Week of Advent

*Luke 10:21–24*

In today's gospel reading, Jesus speaks of the unique relationship he enjoys with God, his Father: 'No one knows who the Son is except the Father, and who the Father is except the Son'. Only God knows Jesus, his Son, thoroughly, and only Jesus knows God, his Father, thoroughly. The knowledge that God the Father and Jesus have of each other is a knowledge born of love. It is true even at the level of human relationships that we can really only know those we love. Yet, even though God and Jesus have a unique relationship, it is not a closed relationship. At the beginning of the gospel reading, Jesus blesses God for revealing 'these things' to mere children, and at the end of the gospel reading he declares to his disciples, 'Happy the eyes that see what you see'. God has made himself known to us through his Son Jesus and, as a result, we have come to see what prophets and kings in the Jewish Scriptures wanted to see and never saw. Although we may not know God as Jesus does, Jesus has made God known to us in a wonderful way. To that extent, Jesus invites us to share in his own relationship with God and with God's relationship with him. If that is to happen, we need to become what the gospel reading calls 'children'. We need something of the openness, receptivity and trust of children in our relationship with Jesus, so that he can look upon us, as he looked upon his disciples in the gospel reading, and declare us blessed or happy for seeing what we see.

## 5 December, Wednesday, First Week of Advent

*Matthew 15:29–37*

In the first part of today's gospel reading, Jesus heals the broken, and the crowds who witness it are astonished at Jesus' life-giving work, and praise God because of it. Jesus appears to be working on his own. Immediately after this time of ministry, Jesus attends to the needs of the crowds. Noticing how hungry they are, he has compassion for them, and sets himself the task of feeding them. However, on this occasion, he doesn't work alone, he involves his disciples very directly: he shares his concern for the crowds with his disciples, he questions them about the resources of food to be found among the crowds and he involves them directly in feeding the crowds from these resources. Perhaps there is an image here of how the Lord works today. There are times when he engages very directly with people who come to him in their need, as in the first part of the gospel reading. There are other times when he needs his disciples to minister to people in the way he wants. He needs us to give expression to his own compassion for people, just as he needed the disciples in the second part of the gospel reading. Like them, we may feel inadequate before the task the Lord seems to set us: 'Where could we get enough bread in this deserted place to feed such a crowd?' Yet, today's gospel reading shows us that the Lord can work powerfully through what look to us to be very inadequate resources. Our equivalent of the seven loaves and the few fish can be enough for the Lord to do his work, if we entrust those resources to him and create space for him to do his life-giving work through them.

## 6 December, Thursday, First Week of Advent

*Matthew 7:21, 24–27*

There are many images of God in the Jewish Scriptures. All such images are simply that, images. They give a very small window onto God. They attempt to express some element of God's reality which, in itself, is always beyond our full comprehension. We find one such image in today's first reading. Isaiah speaks of God as 'the everlasting rock'. There is very little in our created world that could be considered 'everlasting'. Yet perhaps rock comes close to being an exception to that rule. There is something about rock that is clearly enduring and reliable. When Isaiah speaks of God as an everlasting rock, he is expressing his conviction that God is someone who is enduring and reliable and, therefore, to be trusted. We step on rock knowing that it will hold us up. We can trust rock. Isaiah in that reading calls on his hearers to 'trust in the Lord forever' because he is an 'everlasting rock'. Jesus is the one who reveals God to us in a way that no other human has ever done or could ever do. It is not surprising, then, that Jesus uses the image of rock with reference to himself. In the gospel reading he declares that those who listen to his words and live by them are like builders who build a house on rock. We live in a world in which so much is disposable, so little lasts, in which the rate of change is constantly progressive. We often feel the need to find some solid ground that endures, that can be trusted and relied upon. Jesus declares himself to be that solid ground and he calls to us to build our lives on him by allowing his words to shape us.

## 7 December, Friday, First Week of Advent
*Matthew 9:27–31*
The persistence of the two blind men in today's gospel reading is very striking. Jesus is walking somewhere in Galilee. These two blind men keep following him, even though Jesus appears to be ignoring them. When Jesus reaches the house towards which he has been journeying, they come up to him. At that point, Jesus finally takes notice of them. He turns around and asks them, 'Do you believe I can do this?' The blind men are not put off by Jesus initially appearing to ignore them. They keep following and shouting until he engages directly with them. Before Jesus grants their request and heals their blindness, they follows him in darkness, without knowing whether or not their prayer will be heard. There are times when we find ourselves in a spiritual darkness of some kind. At such times, we have to keep following the Lord, like the two blind men, even though the temptation can

be strong to walk away because he seems remote from us. At such times we need to keep faithful to prayer, even though we are tempted to give up on prayer. The blind men believed while in the darkness. 'Do you believe … ?' Jesus asked them, to which they replied, 'We do'. There are times when we have to go on believing while in the darkness, trusting that the Lord remains aware of us and will lead us through that darkness to the light of his presence.

## 8 December, Saturday, Solemnity of the Immaculate Conception

*Luke 1:26–38*

Children's games have become a lot more sophisticated in recent years, especially those that are computer based. Such digital games will be purchased as Christmas presents in the weeks to come. Many of them are very expensive. Yet there are some games that never seem to go out of fashion with children and have no financial cost attached to them. One such game is that of hide-and-seek. A child hides some-where and other children have to find them. There are times when we might be tempted to think that God is playing hide-and-seek with us. We seek God but we struggle to find God. God appears to be in hiding.

In today's first reading, however, it is God who asks the question, 'Where are you?' It is God who is seeking Adam and Adam who is hiding from God. There is a sense in which the story of Adam and Eve is the story of every human being. We may, at heart, be people who seek God continually. Yet, there are times when we hide from God and God becomes the seeker, crying out to us, 'Where are you?' In the case of Adam, it was shame and guilt that caused him to hide from God. The sense that all is not well in our relationship with God can cause us to hide from God too. We are reluctant to face God. Yet, the first reading suggests that whenever we hide from God out of shame or guilt, God continues to seek us out. God continues to pursue us in his love. God's question, 'Where are you?' springs from a heart of love. Jesus, Mary's Son, revealed this seeking heart of God to the full. He said of himself that he came to seek out and to save the lost. There are times in our lives when we simply need to allow ourselves to be found by God. God is always calling on us to step out into the light of God's love and to open our hearts to God's light which continues to shine upon us through Jesus.

Today's feast celebrates the good news that Mary was always open to the light of God's love, from the first moment of her conception in the womb of her mother. At no point did Mary ever hide from God, because she had no reason to do so. God never had to address the question to her, 'Where are you?' In today's gospel reading, God seeks out Mary through his messenger, the angel Gabriel. Mary does not hide from God's messenger. Yes, we are told that she was 'deeply disturbed' by Gabriel's greeting. Yes, her response to Gabriel's subsequent message was initially a questioning one, 'How can this come about?' God's presence will always be, to some extent, a disturbing experience; it will always leave us with questions. Yet, despite these uncomfortable feelings, Mary stood her ground. She remained open to God's presence. She surrendered to God's desire for her life: 'Let what you have said be done to me', thereby allowing God's desire for all humanity to come to pass. On this, the feast of the Immaculate Conception, we ask Mary to pray for us sinners now, so that we may be as open and responsive as she was to God's searching presence and to God's desire for our lives.

## 10 December, Monday, Second Week of Advent

*Luke 5:17–26*

The men who carried the paralysed man to Jesus were, in a sense, a little community of faith. The gospel reading says that when they lowered the paralysed man down through the roof to Jesus, he immediately recognised the faith of these men: 'seeing their faith, he said … ' The paralytic man was carried to Jesus by the faith of his friends, as much as by their physical strength. There is an image here of the Church. We are a community of faith. Part of our calling is to carry each other to the Lord through our faith. The faith of any one of us helps everyone else on their journey towards the Lord. Faith is personal to each one of us, but it is never purely private. Faith always has a communal dimension. Our relationship with the Lord impacts on everyone else in the community of faith. As we grow in our faith, we help everyone else to grow in theirs, even though we may not be consciously aware of doing so. We need the faith of others on our own journey of faith. There are times when we are like the paralysed man in the gospel reading; we need the faith of others to carry us to the Lord and to open us up to hearing the Lord's healing and life-giving word. There are other times when we are like those carrying the paralytic person; our own faith helps to carry others to the Lord who may be struggling to get there on their own. We journey together towards the Lord, carrying others by our faith and being carried by the faith of others. This is the essence of what it means to be Church.

## 11 December, Tuesday, Second Week of Advent
*Matthew 18:12–14*

There is an unusual mixture of images at the end of today's first reading. Isaiah speaks of the Lord coming with power, almost in the guise of a military leader who triumphs over his enemies. However, this somewhat war-like image immediately gives way to the tender image of a shepherd feeding his flock, gathering lambs in his arms and holding them against his breast, while leading the ewes to their rest. Shepherds were not powerful people in that culture. It turns out that the Lord's power finds expression in tender loving care. It is not the power of domination associated with war but the power of love associated with protecting the most vulnerable and needy. Jesus picks up this image of the shepherd in the parable he speaks in the gospel reading. The shepherd's priority is the most vulnerable member of the flock, the one who has strayed from the others, who is without the protection of the flock. The power of Jesus showed itself in the care of the most vulnerable, the sick, the excluded, the spiritually and materially poor. The image of the Lord as shepherd suggests that the Lord is always with us in a life-giving way at those moments of greatest vulnerability in our lives. In the words of Paul, the Lord's power is made perfect in our weakness. The parable Jesus speaks also announces to us that the most powerful people among the Lord's disciples are the most caring, those who have an eye and an ear to the most vulnerable, after the Lord's example.

## 12 December, Wednesday, Second Week of Advent
*Matthew 11:28–30*
There is a close correspondence between the image of God in the first reading and the image of Jesus in the gospel reading. In the first reading God speaks of himself as someone who never grows tired or weary and, because of that, can give strength to the wearied and strengthen the powerless. In the gospel reading Jesus speaks of himself as someone who gives rest to those who labour and are overburdened. As a result, he calls on all those who labour and are overburdened to come to him. The message of both readings is that the Lord has a special ministry to those who are tired and weary, to those who are labouring and weighed down by burdens of one kind or another. The end of that first reading says, 'Young people may grow tired and weary; youths may stumble'. How much more is that the case with those of us who no longer quite qualify as young. We can easily grow tired and weary, and tired and weary also of serving others. The reading declares that 'those who hope in the Lord renew their strength, they put out wings like eagles'. We need to keep

drawing on the Lord's strength if we are to give his strength to others. At the heart of our relationship with those we serve is our own relationship with the Lord. Advent is a good season to come before the Lord in our weakness, perhaps in our tiredness, and to ask him to fill us with his strength, so that we can be channels of his life-giving strength to others, especially to those who are overburdened.

## 13 December, Thursday, Second Week of Advent
*Matthew 11:11–15*

In today's gospel reading, Jesus has high praise for John the Baptist. He is greater than all the children born of women. Yet, for all his greatness, John the Baptist pointed to someone greater than himself, Jesus. He did not live to witness Jesus' death and resurrection, and the coming of the Holy Spirit at Pentecost which flowed from those events. He knew nothing of the Church, what Paul calls the body of Christ. That is why Jesus says of him that the least in the kingdom of heaven, which Jesus proclaimed and inaugurated, is greater than John. We have all been more privileged than John the Baptist. What John pointed towards we look back on and, indeed, experience in the here and now. In and through the Eucharist, the death and resurrection of Jesus are present to us sacramentally. The Spirit of God's Son has been poured into our hearts through Baptism and Confirmation. We possess the written Gospels, the letters of Paul and the other documents that make up the New Testament, all of which we venerate as the living word of the Lord and none of which John the Baptist knew. We have indeed been greatly blessed. As Jesus says to his disciples at one point in the Gospels, 'Blessed are the eyes that see what you see!'. It is a beatitude that embraces us all. Having been so greatly graced, we are called to appreciate and value the graces we have received and to allow those graces to shape us and make us graceful and grateful people, so that our lives may bless others as we have been blessed.

## 14 December, Friday, Second Week of Advent

*Matthew 11:16–19*

Children have started to get very excited about Christmas. They are beginning to look forward to the presents they will get from Santa. Some of those presents will consist of games that will amuse the children for hours. Yet children also have a way of making up their own games. When I was young, one of the games children played involved entering into different roles. We might play at being a doctor or a nurse or a pilot or a firefighter or whatever it might be. Today's gospel reading suggests that children weren't all that different in Jesus' day. Jesus alludes to the ways that they played at being at a wedding or even a funeral. They played the pipes associated with the celebrations at a wedding, and they sang dirges as if at a funeral. Jesus noticed, however, that there were other children who didn't want to join in these games. They were spoilsports, which is why the others complained to them, 'we played the pipes for you and you wouldn't dance, we sang dirges and you wouldn't be mourners'. This scenario reminded Jesus of how many of his contemporaries responded to his ministry and the ministry of John the Baptist. They were unmoved both by the solemn message and lifestyle of John and the much more celebratory message and lifestyle of Jesus. Many dismissed Jesus as someone who ate food and drank wine with sinners. We, however, rejoice that Jesus has brought the good news of God's merciful and faithful love to sinners, among whom we can all count ourselves. We spend our lives trying to live in harmony with the joyful tune of God's love for all that Jesus continues to play today as risen Lord.

## 15 December, Saturday, Second Week of Advent

*Matthew 17:10–13*

When Jesus says in today's gospel reading, in response to a question from his disciples, that 'Elijah has come already', he is referring to John the Baptist. He was the Elijah figure, the prophet whom the Jewish people expected to come just prior to the coming of the Messiah. Jesus says of John the Baptist that 'they did not recognise him but treated him as they pleased'. By this stage in Jesus' ministry, John the Baptist had been beheaded by the ruler of Galilee, Herod Antipas. Jesus is saying that people did not appreciate who John the Baptist really was; he was indeed the prophet who was expected to come just before the Messiah. Because they did not recognise him for who he was, they treated him shamefully. Jesus was very aware that the fate of John the Baptist would be his own fate too. Many people would fail to recognise who Jesus really was, would fail to appreciate his true significance, and, as a result, they would do to Jesus what they pleased, treating him shamefully. The failure to appreciate others, to recognise their true significance, often leads to their being treated badly. Treating others with respect begins with the recognition of their full significance and dignity before God. How we see others will often impact on how we relate to them. Today's gospel reading suggests that the way people see others can be very limited, so how they treat them can leave a lot to be desired. The Gospels keep challenging us to refine our seeing, so that we see others in all their God-given dignity and relate to them accordingly.

## 17 December, Monday, Third Week of Advent

*Matthew 1:1–17*

Today we begin the octave of Christmas. The readings for these eight days are very specially chosen. The first reading invariably consists of one of the great Messianic promises in the Jewish Scriptures. The gospel acclamation on each of these eight days is also very significant. Each one is a beautiful prayer, a variation on the simple 'Come Lord Jesus'. In today's Mass it is 'Wisdom of the Most High; ordering all things with strength and gentleness, come and teach us the way of truth'. The gospel readings for these eight days are all taken from the first chapter of the Gospel of Matthew and the Gospel of Luke. Today's gospel reading consists of the opening seventeen verses of Matthew. It is an unusual gospel reading; it is tempting to ask, 'What is the point of that long list of names?' What was Matthew doing by beginning his Gospel in this particular way? He wanted to show that Jesus was rooted in the Jewish people; his family tree included Abraham and Isaac, David and Solomon, and many others. Jesus was hewn from the rock of Abraham, like the remainder of the people of Israel. We are being reminded that the deepest roots of our own Christian faith are to be found in the story of the people of Israel. That list of names is anything but a list of saints, there are plenty of people whose lives left a lot to be desired – we only have to think of David. Yet, Matthew is saying that in some mysterious way, God worked through all of those characters to bring Jesus to humanity. Matthew is reminding us that God can bring great good out of human sin and brokenness. That realisation is not an encouragement to sin, rather it gives us hope that even when we fall short of our calling the Lord's saving purpose continues to work itself out.

## 18 December, Tuesday, Third Week of Advent

*Matthew 1:18–24*

Today's gospel reading is Matthew's account of the annunciation of the birth of Jesus. In Luke's Gospel, the annunciation of Jesus' birth is made to Mary; in Matthew's Gospel, it is made to Joseph. Artists have tended to depict Luke's version of the annunciation to Mary much more often than Matthew's version of the annunciation to Joseph. In both accounts, the angel announces that Mary is to conceive her child through the Holy Spirit. In both accounts there is a rich description of the unique identity of the child. Matthew's account of the annunciation highlights two aspects of the identity of Mary's child. He is to be named Jesus, a name which means in Hebrew 'the Lord saves', because he is to save God's people from their sins. He is also to be named Emmanuel, which in Hebrew means 'God is with us'. Combining these names indicates that Jesus is the presence of the loving mercy of God. When we look upon this child, we are looking upon God with us, or, as Paul says in his letter to the Romans, God 'for us', working to reconcile us to himself. Jesus was born, lived, died and was raised from the dead to reconcile us to God, to lead us back to God. At the last meal Jesus had with his disciples before his death, the Last Supper, he said, 'this is my blood of the covenant, which is poured out for many for the forgiveness of sins'. It is because Jesus is the face of God's mercy that we celebrate his birth with such gladness and hope. He has shown us that nothing need come between us and the love of God.

## 19 December, Wednesday, Third Week of Advent

*Luke 1:5–25*

Yesterday's gospel reading from Matthew was the story of the annunciation to Joseph of the birth of Jesus. Today's gospel reading from Luke is the story of the annunciation to Zechariah of the birth of John the Baptist. Joseph was a carpenter in the small village of Nazareth in Galilee. Zechariah was a priest who was carrying out his duties in the Temple of Jerusalem. The Lord spoke to both of these men as they went about their very different tasks. The Lord always meets us where we are, wherever that is. Although a priest, familiar with the world of the sacred, Zechariah's response to God's messenger was one of disbelief. As the angel Gabriel declared to him, 'you have not believed my words'. Zechariah was rendered dumb, as if to indicate that this experience left him speechless. It was such a mysterious experience that he could convey nothing about it to anyone. Some months later when his child was born and he had started to come to terms with the mystery of it all, he would speak, and, how he would speak! He would burst forth in the praise of God, in the wonderful prayer that we have come to call the *Benedictus* and that has become part of the morning prayer of the Church. Sometimes, the Lord can touch our lives in very mysterious ways that leave us speechless. We struggle to put words on the experience. Paul once referred to some mystical experience in which 'he heard things that are not to be told, that no mortal is permitted to repeat'. Silence is often the only response we can make to the Lord touching our lives in some mysterious way. Like Zechariah, it is only over time that we may find words to proclaim such experiences to God in prayer and to others as gospel.

## 20 December, Thursday, Third Week of Advent

*Luke 1:26–38*

In yesterday's gospel reading, there was something lacking in the response of Zechariah to the message of the angel Gabriel that his wife, Elizabeth, is to give birth to a son. In today's gospel reading, there is nothing lacking in Mary's response to the message of the angel Gabriel that she is to give birth to a child, who will be called the Son of God. Yes, Mary was initially very disturbed by Gabriel's words of greeting, and she went on to question Gabriel: 'But how can this come about, since I am a virgin?' However, she eventually submitted completely to God's will for her life: 'I am the handmaid of the Lord, let what you have said be done to me'. She thereby joined a long line of women in the Jewish Scriptures who placed themselves at the disposal of God's purpose for their lives and the life of his people. The word 'handmaid' that Mary uses might suggest weakness or passivity. However, Mary's response to God's will for her life as revealed by Gabriel, God's messenger, was strong and active. She actively cooperated with what God was asking of her. This required great inner strength for the remainder of her earthly life. It was a strength that had its origins in the Holy Spirit who came upon Mary, and whose power overshadowed her, in the words of Gabriel. Mary's 'yes' was an adult and courageous response to a God who wanted to do something amazingly new. We need something of Mary's spiritual strength in these days. We need the kind of spiritual strength that leaves us standing at the foot of the cross, if necessary. We need the Holy Spirit to overshadow us, so that we can keep making a strong, adult, active response to God's desire for our lives and our world, as Mary did.

## 21 December, Friday, Third Week of Advent
*Luke 1:39–45*

According to today's gospel reading, Mary set out on a journey to visit her older cousin Elizabeth to be with her in her pregnancy, and she stayed with Elizabeth for three months. This was a visit that seemed to bring out the best in both women. Because of Mary's visit, Elizabeth was filled with the Holy Spirit and the child in her womb leapt for joy, and Mary herself was moved to pray the great prayer that we know as the Magnificat. Both women, the visitor and the one visited, were the better for Mary's visit. The journey and the visit are very much part of our own celebration of Christmas. Some members of your own family may have already arrived to visit you for Christmas after making a long journey. Others may be setting out in the next few days and their visits are eagerly anticipated. Our airports, ports, bus and train stations will be very busy places over the next few days. As Mary visited Elizabeth in the gospel reading and that visit was joyfully received by Elizabeth, so the act of visiting and the receiving of visits will be at the heart of our lives over the coming days. Mary's visit brought the Lord to Elizabeth. Her generous welcome was matched by Elisabeth's generous welcome, a welcome that recognised Mary's worth and celebrated her goodness. If Mary shows us how to visit, Elizabeth shows us how to receive a visit. We welcome our visitors by recognising the good that is in them, by recognising the ways the Lord is working in their lives.

## 22 December, Saturday, Third Week of Advent
*Luke 1:46–56*

Mary's great prayer, the Magnificat, is set within the context of Elizabeth's visit to her. Her visit was a real blessing for Mary. When Elizabeth greeted Mary, she declared Mary blessed because of the child she had conceived and also because, prior to her conceiving, she had believed the message spoken to her by the angel Gabriel. Mary's response to this visit of Elizabeth and to the blessing it brought her was to praise God: 'My soul magnifies the Lord, and my spirit rejoices in God my Saviour'. Her prayer sprung from an event in her life, the visit of her relative. This can be true of our prayer too. Our prayer, like Mary's, tends to be rooted in our lives. It is often the case that our prayer is rooted in the pain and struggle of our lives. We find ourselves in some dark or difficult situation, and we cry to God for help. In a sense, that was the prayer of Hannah in the first reading today. She was childless and she prayed to God out of her need. However, Mary's prayer teaches us that the blessings that come our way in life can also be an occasion for prayer – not the prayer of petition but the prayer of praise and thanksgiving. Someone might visit us or we might visit someone, and we sense that something good has come from this meeting for both of us. Such encounters are real opportunities to give thanks and praise to God. It can be good at the end of our day to look back over the day and to notice the blessings that have come our way in the course of the day and to thank and praise God for them. Whenever we are blessed by someone, in no matter how small a way, it is always the Lord who stands behind such blessing, and it is to him that our praise and thanks is due.

## 24 December, Monday, Fourth Week of Advent

*Luke 1:67–79*

In today's first reading, King David had in mind to do something worthwhile for God. He was going to build an impressive dwelling place to house the Ark of the Covenant. However, he came to understand through the prophet Nathan that this was not what God wanted. God had much bigger plans. Nathan declared to David that God would make a house for David, rather than David making a house for God. God would establish David's house, in the sense of David's household, David's lineage. God would see to it that one of David's descendants would rule forever. God would relate to this descendant as father to son. The early Church understood this prophecy to have been fulfilled with the birth of Jesus, who was a descendant of David through Joseph. What God intended was so much more than David could have foreseen. Zechariah, the father of John the Baptist, made this same discovery. When Gabriel announced to him that his wife Elizabeth would bear him a son who would prepare a way for the Lord, he refused to believe it. He couldn't come to terms with the magnitude of God's purpose for his life. However, like David, he eventually surrendered to this greater purpose of God, and when his son John was born he sung that wonderful hymn which is today's gospel reading. It has come to be known as the *Benedictus* and is now part of the morning prayer of the Church. Both readings remind us that God's purpose for our lives is always much more wonderful than anything we could ask for or imagine, and this is good news for all of us.

## 26 December, Wednesday, St Stephen

*Matthew 10:17–22*

In the gospel reading, Jesus is very clear about what his followers can expect from the world into which he is sending them. Jesus' warnings soon come to pass with the stoning of Stephen, the first Christian martyr, whose feast we celebrate today. Yet, Jesus' warnings are accompanied by a reassuring promise. He tells his followers that when people do their worst to them, the Holy Spirit will come to assist them and will speak through them. This reassuring promise also comes to pass when Stephen is put on trial. The first reading declares that the Spirit prompted what Stephen said, and that, at the moment of greatest hostility towards him, he was filled with the Holy Spirit and had a vision of God the Father and his risen Son. At the end of the gospel reading, Jesus says that the disciple who stands firm to the end will be saved. Stephen certainly stood firm to the end, and so he came to share in the Lord's risen life. Both readings today inspire us to stand firm in our faith in the Lord to the end. They assure us that whenever witnessing to our faith proves demanding and difficult, we will not be left to our own resources. The Holy Spirit will be present to us as our helper, our advocate. That first reading also suggests that our courageous witness to our faith can have a powerful impact on others. It is said in that reading that when Stephen was being stoned, his clothes were placed at the feet of a young man named Saul, who, at the time, approved of the killing of Stephen. Perhaps Stephen's courageous witness to his faith, unto death, left its mark on Saul or Paul and helped to sow the seed for Saul's future transformation from persecutor of the Church to tireless apostle to the pagans. We can never underestimate the impact on the faith of others of our own courageous witness to our faith in the Lord.

## 27 December, Thursday, St John, Apostle and Evangelist
*John 20:2–8*

Today we celebrate the feast of the fourth evangelist, traditionally identified as John the son of Zebedee. It is this evangelist who, at the beginning of his Gospel, gives us the statement that expresses in a very succinct way the meaning of the feast of Christmas, 'the Word became flesh and dwelt among us'. The Word who was with God in the beginning and who was God at a certain moment in history became flesh and dwelt among us in the person of Jesus, son of Joseph from Nazareth. The Word was now Word in human flesh. According to the fourth evangelist Jesus was none other than God in human form. This child, this adult, was the fullest revelation of God possible in a human life. John had a very profound insight into who Jesus was and he witnessed to this insight in his preaching, his teaching and in the Gospel that he wrote, so that we too might see what he saw, and might come to believe what he believed. The gospel reading for this feast focuses on the capacity of this beloved disciple, as he is often called, to see deeply and clearly. Mary Magdalene, Simon Peter and the beloved disciple all came to the tomb on the first Easter Sunday and found it empty, but it was only the beloved disciple who 'saw and believed'. He saw more deeply than the other two; he alone saw the true significance of the empty tomb and the arrangement of the burial cloths. Jesus had been raised from the dead. Today we pray for something of this disciple's insight into Jesus; we pray that we might see as he sees, believe as he believes and witness to what we see and believe as fully as he did.

## 28 December, Friday, Feast of the Holy Innocents
*Matthew 2:13–18*
Matthew's story of the birth and early childhood of Jesus is painted in much darker colours than the story that Luke tells. It is Matthew who reminds us that Jesus was born into a world where the powerful people of the land, men like King Herod, abused their power, even to the point of shedding innocent blood. Herod the Great, who tried to do away with the child Jesus, would find his counterpart in Pilate, who put the adult Jesus to death. The first reading says that 'God is

light'. Yet Jesus, God-with-us, was born into and lived in a world where darkness was much in evidence, especially within those who exercised political power. Jesus came as light into darkness, as God's light into a darkened world. He came as a revelation of God's love into a world where the darkness of hatred and sin often reigned. He remains a light in our darkness to this day; his life, death and resurrection continue to shine as a beacon in our world, which often seems shrouded in darkness. He promises that whoever follows him will never walk in darkness. We look to him to enlighten and guide us, to show us the way we need to walk if we are to be true to our deepest identity as people made in God's image. We can also rely on him to scatter the darkness that resides in all of our lives. The first reading assures us that 'if anyone should sin, we have our advocate with the Father, Jesus Christ ... the sacrifice that takes our sins away'. We often say that it is better to light a candle than to curse the darkness. In sending his Son into the world, God has done more than light a candle; he has kindled a fire within our darkness, the fire of his love, which will never die away.

## 29 December, Saturday, Fifth Day in the Octave of Christmas

*Luke 2:22–35*

Simeon is one of those very attractive people who feature in the opening chapters of Luke's Gospel. He is described in the gospel reading as an 'upright and devout man'. In other words, he related well to other people ('upright') and to God ('devout'). Just as Mary and Joseph were bringing their newborn child to the Temple, Simeon was prompted by the Holy Spirit to go there. The Holy Spirit led Simeon to Jesus, and being the man that he was, Simeon responded to the prompting of the Holy Spirit. That is the role of the Holy Spirit in all of our lives, to lead us to Jesus. In John's Gospel, Jesus says that the Paraclete (from the Greek, meaning 'advocate') will lead you to the complete truth, and the complete truth is none other than Jesus himself who declared, 'I am the truth'. Simeon was a seeker; he spent his life seeking the Christ of the Lord. On a certain day, the Spirit led him to the one he had been seeking. We are all seekers: we seek and long for truth, goodness, love and light, all of which are to be found in the person of Jesus. In seeking the Lord, we are not left to our own devices. The Spirit is with us, leading us to the Lord, prompting us to take paths that will bring us to the Lord. Simeon was so overjoyed to see Jesus that he was ready for God to call him out of this earthly life. 'Now, Master, you can let your servant go in peace … because my eyes have seen … '. We too have seen the Lord with the eyes of faith. What the adult Jesus will say to his disciples, he says to all of us who believe in him, 'Blessed are the eyes that see what you see'. The Holy Spirit has led us too to see Jesus. We look forward in hope to seeing him face to face.

## 31 December, Monday, Seventh Day in the Octave of Christmas
*John 1:1–18*
This is New Year's Eve. At midnight, a new year begins. It is a time of new beginning. The gospel reading for this New Year's Eve is itself a beginning, the opening verses of the Gospel of John. The first verse of that gospel reading, the first verse of the fourth Gospel, speaks of a beginning. 'In the beginning was the Word'. Before all things came into being, before anything was created, the Word was. This Word was God's self-communication, a self-communication that was so complete and perfect that it was itself God, 'the Word was God'. It was this Word that became flesh, according to our gospel reading. This self-communication of God became human in the person of Jesus of Nazareth. We celebrate the birth of Jesus because we recognise in this child the fullest possible self-communication of God. Jesus is the fullest Word that God could have spoken to us. We speak, we

communicate, not just by our words but by the way we relate, by the way we live and, even, by the way we die. God spoke to us through the life of Jesus, and through his death and resurrection. God has said everything he wants to say to us through the life, death and resurrection of Jesus, his Word. God and his Son, together, have sent us the Holy Spirit to help us plumb the depths of all God has said to us through Jesus. As Jesus will later declare in this fourth Gospel, the Holy Spirit 'will guide you into all the truth … he will take from what is mine and declare it to you'. The Holy Spirit enables us to keep hearing the Word that is Jesus in all its richness, to hear it as a word for us here and now. At the beginning of this new year, we invite the Spirit to open us up more fully to the truth of this Word that God spoke in the beginning and that became flesh in the person of Jesus.

## 1 January, Tuesday, Mary, the Holy Mother of God
*Luke 2:16–21*

I am very fond of that blessing of Aaron that is to be found in the first reading. I often find myself praying it for someone who needs prayers. It is a lovely prayer of intercession. The last line of the prayer is, 'May the Lord uncover his face to you and bring you peace'. It strikes me that this prayer has been fulfilled in a wonderful way through the birth of Jesus, Mary's son. In and through this child, God was uncovering his face to us and bringing us peace. When we look upon the face of Mary's child, we are looking upon the face of God. This is why we can venerate Mary, not only as the mother of Jesus, but also as the mother of God. Mary was proclaimed Mother of God at the Council of Ephesus in modern-day Turkey in the year AD431. The council was expressing its conviction that Mary's son was not only fully human but was also fully divine. In the frailty and vulnerability of this newborn child, God was uncovering his face. God was being revealed in a way that was profoundly new. Jesus was not only Mary's son but

God's Son. In the words of Paul in today's second reading, 'When the appointed time came, God sent his Son, born of a woman'. There was so much more to this newborn child than met the eye.

The rich identity of this baby had been revealed to the shepherds by an angel as a 'Saviour, who is Christ, the Lord'. According to the gospel reading, the shepherds repeated to Mary what the angel had said to them about her child. We are told that Mary treasured the words of the shepherds and pondered them in her heart. It was as if Mary was trying to come to terms with who her child really was. The feast of Christmas, the celebration of the birth of Jesus, gives us all much to treasure and much to ponder in our hearts. God is uncovering his face to us through Jesus; God is drawing near to us through Jesus, the same Jesus who is now the risen Lord in our midst. We are invited to go on treasuring and pondering this good news, like Mary, and to continue glorifying and praising God for it, like the shepherds.

## 2 January, Wednesday before Epiphany

*John 1:19–28*

At the end of today's gospel reading, John the Baptist declares to those who question him, 'There stands among you, unknown to you, the one who is coming after me'. Jesus, God's Son, the Word made flesh, was standing among them, but they were unaware of his significance. John knew who Jesus really was. He could see more deeply than those who were questioning him. He wanted to open the eyes of his contemporaries so that they could see Jesus as he saw him and come to know him as he knew him. Jesus was close to them, standing among them. Yet, he was also remote from them, because they were blind to who he was. God was present to them through Jesus, but they were unaware of it. John the Baptist could use the same phrase with reference to us today, 'there stands among you, unknown to you'. Jesus, now risen Lord, stands among us. He is as present to us as he was to his contemporaries. Yet, he often stands among us, unknown to us. We do not always recognise his presence. We fail to appreciate the significance of his presence to us. We can sometimes live our lives as if he was not standing among us. We often need a John the Baptist figure to help us to see the Lord who is at the heart of our lives. We all need the guidance of other people of faith who see more deeply than we do. Others can help us to see the Lord who stands among us, but we can also help ourselves. We can learn to become more attentive to the Lord standing among us. We can become more responsive to the Lord's daily invitation to 'come and see'.

## 3 January, Thursday before Epiphany

*John 1:29–34*

Some of the words of Scripture have become a fixed part of the language of the Church's liturgy. The opening words of today's gospel reading are a good example of that. The words of John the Baptist, 'Look, there is the lamb of God that takes away the sin of the world' are more or less the words the celebrant speaks at Mass just before Communion, when he holds up the host. Jesus came among us, according to John's Gospel, to take away the sin of the world, the sin of us all. Yet John's Gospel shows that Jesus could not take away the sin of those who had no awareness of their sin. In the story of the man born blind, the religious leaders reject Jesus and they cast out the man Jesus has healed. They consider that they have nothing to learn, nothing to receive, either from Jesus or from the man he has healed, because, as they claim in the course of that story, 'We know God spoke to Moses'. That is all the light they need; they are not open to any further light. That is why at the end of that story Jesus says to them, 'Now that you say, "we see", your sin remains'. Jesus could not take away their sin because they had no sense of their own need to see more clearly or more deeply. The Lamb of God has come to take away the sin of the world. We need to acknowledge the ways in which we have been tainted by the sin of the world, the ways in which we are still blind, if we are to experience the enlightenment and the freedom that Jesus has come to give.

## 4 January, Friday before Epiphany

*John 1:35–42*

Today's gospel suggests that our coming to Jesus is often in and through each other. John the Baptist directs two of his disciples to Jesus with the words, 'Look, there is the Lamb of God'. Jesus goes on to call these two disciples personally, saying, 'Come and see', but it was John the Baptist who put them in the way of that call. According to the gospel reading, one of these two disciples of John the Baptist was Andrew. He directs his brother, Simon, to Jesus with the words, 'We have found the Messiah'. Jesus goes on to call Simon personally with the words, 'You are to be called Cephas', but it was Andrew who put Simon in the way of that call. The Lord uses all of us in different ways to put others in the way of the call of Jesus. He uses us as intermediaries to bring people to him. We cannot make people respond to the call of Jesus, no more than John the Baptist could have made his disciples respond to the call of Jesus or Andrew could have made Simon respond to Jesus' call. We can only do so much. We can find ourselves very frustrated at how little we can do. Yet, we can all do something. As we strive to grow in our faith and in living that faith to the full we will inevitably have opportunities to put people in the way of the call of Jesus. We then have to step back and allow the mysterious dialogue between the Lord and others to unfold and take its course, just as John the Baptist and Andrew had to step back, having played their part.

## 5 January, Saturday before Epiphany

*John 1:43–51*

Nathanael's initial assessment of Jesus was rather negative, 'Can anything good come from Nazareth?' Yet, this was not to be his final assessment of Jesus. By the end of the gospel reading he exclaims, 'Rabbi, you are the Son of God, you are the King of Israel'. Nathanael needed time to see that there was more to Jesus than met the eye, that, in reality, there was a goodness in Jesus that was unique. Unlike Nathanael's initial assessment of Jesus, Jesus' initial assessment of Nathanael was very positive, in spite of Nathanael's earlier dismissive comment: 'There is an Israelite who deserves the name incapable of deceit'. Jesus did not need time to see the good in Nathanael; he saw it immediately. The gospel reading suggests that whereas most people need time to see the good in others, the Lord sees the good in us immediately. The Lord is more attuned to the goodness in ourselves and in others that we are. Realising that is both consoling and challenging. It is consoling to know that the Lord recognises the goodness in us that others may not recognise and that we may not even recognise ourselves. It is challenging in that we are called to see others with the Lord's eyes, to recognise the good qualities that are there, even though they may not be obvious or expected.

## 7 January, Monday after Epiphany

*Matthew 4:12–17, 23–25*

We are still at the beginning of the new year, and the gospel reading today is Matthew's account of the beginning of the ministry of Jesus in Galilee. Matthew describes the beginning of Jesus' ministry as the dawning of a great light on a people living in darkness, in the land of the shadow of death. Most of us like the light; we are pleased to know that the days are gradually getting longer, even if it is not very perceptible yet. We look forward to the bright evenings in a few months' time when we can go for late walks if we choose to. Too much darkness can get us down. Light helps us to feel more alive; it lifts our spirits. We often meet people who have the same effect on us. They lift our spirits and leave us feeling more alive. Jesus was such a person to a unique degree. He proclaimed good news, in the words of today's gospel reading. He was and is good news. The heart of his good news was, 'the kingdom of heaven is close at hand'. God is powerfully present to us. Jesus was announcing that in and through his ministry God is present as power in our weakness, as life in our death, as light in our darkness. That remains good news for all of us today. It is because God is powerfully present to us in this way, through his risen Son, that Jesus calls on us to repent, to turn towards God more fully, which means turning towards Jesus who is Immanuel, God-with-us. It is only after we have heard the good news that the call to repent, to turn towards the one who embodies that good news, makes any sense. We pray that we would hear the good news afresh this coming year and respond with renewed energy and enthusiasm.

## 8 January, Tuesday after Epiphany
*Mark 6:34–44*

There is a striking difference in the gospel reading between the response of Jesus and the response of his disciples to the phenomenon of a large number of hungry people in a deserted place. Jesus' disciples see only an insurmountable problem. They want Jesus to send the crowd away and, when Jesus suggests to his disciples that they begin to address the problem themselves, they respond with a despairing question: 'Are we to go and spend two hundred denarii on bread for them to eat?' Jesus' response to the situation is much more hopeful and energised. Jesus insists that the disciples bring him whatever food is to be found among the crowd. Then, having prayed to God in thanksgiving for the food that was brought to him, he somehow manages to satisfy the hunger of everyone present. Perhaps at the root of the different responses of Jesus and the disciples is the fact that the disciples behaved as if they had to deal with the situation on their own. Jesus, however, knew that he was not on his own but that God was with him. That is why he turned in prayer to God before feeding the crowd with the resources that came to him. Jesus knew that God can work powerfully through what may seem like weak and inadequate resources, such as five loaves and two fish, if only we call on God in our need. We can be tempted to respond to difficult situations like the disciples, in a discouraging and even despairing spirit. Jesus, however, invites us to look upon such situations with the eyes of faith, recognising that God can do more than we could ever imagine, if only we place our resources, small as they may seem, at his disposal.

## 9 January, Wednesday after Epiphany

*Mark 6:45–52*

In the Gospels, Jesus often goes off to pray after a busy period of ministry. We see this pattern in today's gospel reading. Jesus has fed the multitude in the wilderness with bread and fish. He now sends his disciples away in a boat across the Sea of Galilee and he then sends the crowd away. Alone as evening falls, he goes off into the hills to pray. This was a moment of personal communion with God. Yet, while Jesus' prayer removed him physically from others, it did not remove him spiritually from them. According to our gospel reading, while at prayer, Jesus became aware of his struggling disciples, worn out with rowing against a strong headwind. The gospel reading says that Jesus could 'see' them. It was as if his prayerful communion with God sharpened his vision of his disciples and allowed him to enter more fully into their struggles. From his prayer he came to them with reassuring words: 'Courage! It is I! Do not be afraid'. When he got into the boat with them, the wind dropped; somehow the journey was no longer the struggle for his disciples that it had been. The gospel reading reminds us that the risen Lord's prayerful communion with his heavenly Father does not remove him from us. Rather, he is highly attuned to our particular situation and he is constantly coming to us in our moments of struggle and weakness.

While living forever to intercede for us with God the Father, he is also our constant companion on the way. When we find ourselves struggling with life's demands, he is there saying to us, 'Courage! It is I! Do not be afraid'. We are also being reminded that our own prayer need not remove us from others but can make us more fully present to them. As we open ourselves in prayer to the Lord, we are caught up into his loving concern for others, especially those for whom life is a struggle and a battle.

## 10 January, Thursday after Epiphany
*Luke 4:14–22*

Many of us have our favourite passages of Scripture. When we have a bible in our hands, we are inclined to open it at one of those passages, because they have spoken to us in the past and continue to speak to us today. We feel an affinity with these texts. They feed our spirit, encouraging us or, at times, challenging us. Jesus, too, seems to have had his favourite passages of Scripture. We sense that The Psalms spoke powerfully to him, since he often quotes them. In today's gospel reading, when Jesus returns to his home synagogue in Nazareth for the first time after setting out on his public ministry, the synagogue attendant hands him the scroll of the prophet Isaiah. Jesus was led by the Spirit to go to one particular passage in that wonderful scroll, a passage that must often have spoken to him very powerfully. It helped him to put words on what his public ministry was about. Like Isaiah before him, but in a strikingly new way, he would proclaim the good news of God's favour to those who were desperately in need of a gracious word from God, such as the poor, those in any form captivity, those who were physically or spiritually blind and the downtrodden. We all belong there in that broad category of needy people. We all need the gracious word of God's favour to enrich us in our poverty, to free us in our captivity, to enlighten us in our blindness and to lift us up when we feel downtrodden for whatever reason. Jesus assures us that this powerful grace, this divine favour, is available to us, 'today', this very day, if we only acknowledge our need for it and seek it out.

## 11 January, Friday after Epiphany

*Luke 5:12–16*

There seems to have been some doubt on the part of the leper in today's gospel reading as to whether or not Jesus would want to heal him: 'If you want to, you can cure me'. He didn't doubt Jesus' power to heal him, but he was unsure of Jesus' desire to do so. Perhaps he was so used to being treated as an outcast, living on the margins, that he doubted whether anyone would have wanted to change his situation for the better, even if they were able to. There was no hesitation in Jesus' reply to the leper. He stretched out his hand and touched him and said, 'Of course I want to! Be cured'. Jesus wanted to touch the untouchables.

A short while earlier in the synagogue of Nazareth, Jesus had announced that he had come to proclaim the year of the Lord's favour, especially to the poor and the captive, those like the leper who approached him to implore his help. There can be times in our own lives when, like the leper, we might wonder if the Lord really wants to help us. We wonder if we are significant enough for the Lord to give us his personal attention and become involved with our lives. If we feel like that, the Lord would say to us what he says to the leper in today's gospel reading, 'Of course I want to'. When we approach the

Lord with the same urgency as the leper, he will not fail to respond to us in a life-giving way. In the words of the first letter of John, in today's first reading, 'anyone who has the Son, has life'.

## 12 January, Saturday after Epiphany
*John 3:22–30*

There is a striking contrast in today's gospel reading between the attitude of John the Baptist's disciples towards Jesus and the attitude of John the Baptist himself towards Jesus. John's disciples view Jesus as unwelcome competition, declaring that Jesus 'is baptising now, and everyone is going to him'. The implication of what they say is that everyone is not going to John the Baptist. John himself, however, has a totally different response to this emerging situation. John recognises that Jesus is the bridegroom, the earthly representative of the heavenly bridegroom. The bride, God's people, belongs to him. John is happy to be the friend of the bridegroom and he rejoices to hear the bridegroom's voice. He is very clear that he, the friend of the bridegroom, should grow smaller and that the bridegroom should grow greater. In the fourth Gospel, John the Baptist is a model for all believers. Like John, we are all called into friendship with Jesus; we are all friends of the bridegroom. At the Last Supper in this gospel, Jesus will say to his disciples, 'I do not call you servants any longer ... I have called you friends'. We show ourselves to be friends of Jesus by loving one another as he has loved us, by allowing his love to be in us, or, in the words of John the Baptist in today's gospel reading, by allowing Jesus to grow greater in us and allowing our own selfish and competitive selves to grow less. Such growth of Jesus within us is, ultimately, the work of the Holy Spirit to which we are invited to surrender. When Jesus grows within us, then, with Paul, we will be able to say, 'It is no longer I who live, but it is Christ who lives in me'.

## 14 January, Monday, First Week in Ordinary Time

*Mark 1:14–20*

This is the first week of Ordinary Time. What the Church calls 'Ordinary Time' is distinguished from those other times in the Church's year which are special for one reason or another, the seasons of Lent, Easter, Advent and Christmas. Yet 'Ordinary Time' is not really ordinary at all, because all time has the potential to be special. At Christmas we celebrated the good news that the Word became flesh. The Word entered the realm of space and time, and having done so, has never left that realm. The Word is with us in every time, in all the times that go to make up our human living. The risen Lord promised his disciples and us that he would be with us until the end of time. In the gospel reading Jesus proclaims the good news that the kingdom of God is close at hand. The kingdom of God, the reign or rule of God, continues to be close at hand, in every time, through the risen Lord who journeys with us and the Holy Spirit who dwells within us. That continuing good news calls for a continuing response. We are to repent and believe the good news. We are to keep recognising the good news of God's presence with us in and through Jesus and the Holy Spirit, and to keep turning towards that good news and living our lives on the basis of it. When we turn towards that good news, we will hear the call of the Lord to follow him, to walk in his ways, to live by his values. If we respond to that call, as Andrew, Peter, James and John did, then we will experience all time as special, as charged with the Lord's presence.

## 15 January, Tuesday, First Week in Ordinary Time

*Mark 1:21–28*

It is probably true to say that the word 'authority' has had something of a bad press in recent times. In contrast, the word 'freedom' is very much in vogue and some would see authority as undermining freedom, and as being a threat to it. That perception may well have a basis in reality. The misuse of authority by authority figures has had serious negative consequences for individuals and whole societies. In today's gospel reading, the people of Capernaum have a very positive experience of authority through their meeting with Jesus. Mark writes that Jesus' teaching made a deep impression on them because he taught them with authority. Having watched Jesus heal a man with an unclean spirit, the people exclaim, 'Here is a teaching that is new and with authority behind it'. Jesus' teaching, his word, was powerful in a life-giving sense. He exercised authority in a way that enhanced the lives of others. Authority in itself is neither good nor bad, it can be a power for good or a power for harm. It can enhance human freedom or it can damage it. When we submit to Jesus' authority, to his lordship, we become more alive, more fully human; we move closer towards what Paul calls the glorious freedom of the children of God. It is in and through our union with the Lord that we too can exercise authority in life-giving ways.

## 16 January, Wednesday, First Week in Ordinary Time
*Mark 1:29–39*

In today's gospel reading we have the first clash between Jesus and his disciples in Mark's Gospel. After a very busy day healing the sick in Capernaum, Jesus withdrew to a lonely place for a time of prayer. Whereas people greatly appreciated Jesus' healing ministry and wanted more of it, they didn't seem to appreciate his going off on his own to find time and space for prayer. Jesus' own disciples didn't seem to appreciate this either, because Simon Peter and his companions went out in search of him, and when they found him they rebuked him, saying, 'Everybody is looking for you', as much as to say, 'What are you doing out here on your own when there are so many needy people in Capernaum looking for you?' Jesus, however, did not go back to Capernaum, in spite of the pressure put upon him by all. After his prayer, he went on to other villages and towns. Activity is often more appreciated than prayer, and that is as true of our own time as it was of Jesus' time. Yet, Jesus shows us that the kind of activity which is an expression of God's work must always be rooted in prayer. In prayer we open ourselves to God's activity, and that helps to ensure that our activity is in harmony with God's desire for ourselves and for others.

## 17 January, Thursday, First Week in Ordinary Time
*Mark 1:40–45*

In today's gospel reading, Jesus heals a leper. In the gospels Jesus often heals people by means of his word. In healing the leper, however, Jesus not only spoke to him, he touched him. In touching the leper Jesus did what no one else would have done. For the sake of communal hygiene, if for no other reason, people kept lepers at a distance, and lepers were expected to keep their distance from others. Jesus, however, kept no one at a distance, not even lepers. No one was beyond his reach; no one was untouchable in his eyes. He came to touch our lives, all of our lives, in a very tangible way, regardless of our condition. The leper did not doubt Jesus' power to heal him, but he wasn't sure whether Jesus wanted to heal him, as is clear from his opening words to Jesus, 'If you want to, you can cure me'. Jesus showed how much he wanted to heal this leper by touching him. Jesus wants to touch all of our lives, because he wants to bring life to us all. Nothing we do or fail to do, no circumstance in which we find ourselves, need place us beyond his life-giving reach. As Paul says in his letter to the Romans, 'nothing can come between us and the love of God made visible in Christ Jesus'. The Lord touches our lives, where we are, as we are. All we need is something of the leper's daring initiative in approaching Jesus.

## 18 January, Friday, First Week in Ordinary Time

*Mark 2:1–12*

There may very well come a time in our lives when we need to be carried in one way or other, whether it is physically or emotionally or spiritually. Hopefully, if that time comes along for us, we will find people who are willing and able to carry us. Some of us may be doing or have done such carrying of others, or perhaps we have experienced being carried ourselves. In today's gospel reading the paralytic person needed to be carried physically. He needed others to help him to get where he wanted to go. Fortunately, he was a man who had good friends. When he desperately wanted to be placed before Jesus, his friends stopped at nothing to make sure that happened, even going as far as creating a hole in a perfectly good roof. The energy of those friends was the energy of love. It was also the energy of faith. The gospel reading comments on Jesus seeing their faith. The energy of their faith and love created a space for this man to pass over into a fuller life, through the power of Jesus. We can never underestimate the power for good that resides within our energy of love that is rooted in our faith. The Lord can work powerfully through our faith-filled love for the well-being of others. In his letter to the Galatians Paul declares, 'the only thing that counts is faith working through love'. Today's gospel reading gives a graphic description of such faith.

## 19 January, Saturday, First Week in Ordinary Time

*Mark 2:13–17*

Jesus did not hesitate to call people from a great variety of backgrounds to follow him. Having called a group of fishermen, he went on to call a tax collector, someone who collected tolls on behalf of the Roman administration. Such a person would not have been judged religious at the time. Along with a lot of other people, tax collectors were considered to be sinners. The gospel reading suggests that those considered 'sinners' were drawn to Jesus in a special way. The professionally religious of the time found this scandalous and asked the question, 'Why does this man eat with tax collectors and sinners?' The reason why those considered sinners and those who thought of themselves as sinners were drawn to Jesus was because he revealed God's merciful love. Jesus was the doctor who came for the sick; his mission was to bring God's merciful and healing love to the sinner. One of the great themes of Pope Francis's pontificate is the availability of God's mercy to sinners. In a very revealing interview, in response to the question of the interviewer, 'Who are you?' Francis replied very simply, 'I am a sinner'. Only someone who had a personal experience of and conviction about God's mercy could give such an answer. He knows himself to be a forgiven sinner. We are all forgiven sinners, and it is to forgiven sinners that the Lord says what he said to Levi, the tax collector, in today's gospel reading: 'Follow me'.

## 21 January, Monday, Second Week in Ordinary Time
*Mark 2:18–22*

There is a reference to the death of Jesus in each of today's readings. In the gospel reading, Jesus alludes to his passion and death, declaring that 'the time will come for the bridegroom to be taken away from them'. Jesus will be forcibly and violently taken from his closest associates. In the first reading from the letter to the Hebrews, the author seems to allude to Jesus' distraught prayer in the Garden of Gethsemane: 'During his life on earth, he offered up prayer and entreaty, aloud and in silent tears, to the one who had the power to save him out of death.' In the gospel reading, Jesus refers to the newness of his ministry and message, relative to what was already there within the religious tradition of his time. He brings new wine, which the old wineskins struggle to contain. It was the very newness of his ministry that led him to an early and violent death on a cross. The instinct of many was to protect the old wineskins and to reject the new wine. Taking a new direction can often be painful. Jesus' renewing work continued beyond his death. As risen Lord, he continues to call on us to keep renewing our old wineskins so they can contain the new wine of the Spirit. The Lord's body, the Church, needs to be open to continuing renewal. Such work of renewal can be painful and disconcerting. It will often entail a way of the Cross, as it did for Jesus, yet we can be assured that the Lord is with us on this difficult journey of ongoing renewal and will provide us with all the resources we need if we entrust ourselves to him.

## 22 January, Tuesday, Second Week in Ordinary Time
*Mark 2:23–28*

When Jesus says at the end of today's gospel reading that 'the Son of Man is master even of the Sabbath', he is making quite a claim for himself. He is stating that he is not simply subject to the Law of the Sabbath like other men and women, but he is over the Law of the Sabbath. He is its authoritative interpreter. As master of the Sabbath, he tells those who criticise his disciples for plucking ears of grain on the Sabbath that the Sabbath is there to serve God's people and not the other way around. God's people are more important than God's Law, and if God's people are hungry on the Sabbath, then no Sabbath Law can prohibit them from satisfying their hunger. Jesus is declaring that people's basic needs must take priority over human institutions, even an institution as sacred and venerable as the Sabbath Law. Every so often the guardians of institutions have to ask themselves, 'Whose needs are being served here, those of the institution or those of the people it claims to serve?' We can substitute various nouns for the word 'Sabbath' in Jesus' saying, 'The Sabbath was made for humanity, not humanity for the Sabbath', such as, 'The Church was made for humanity, not humanity for the Church', or 'The national parliament is there for the people, not the people for the national parliament'. Jesus, who declared of himself that he came not to be served but to serve, is always prompting us to put the fundamental needs of our fellow human beings before all else.

## 23 January, Wednesday, Second Week in Ordinary Time
*Mark 3:1–6*

In some ways, the portrait of Jesus in Mark's Gospel is the most human of all the portraits by the four evangelists. Mark is never slow to ascribe human emotions to Jesus. In today's gospel reading, Mark says of Jesus that he was grieved at some people's hardness of heart, and that he looked angrily round at them, before healing the man with the withered hand on the Sabbath. Grief and anger are two emotions we all experience from time to time. We know too that they can be difficult emotions to deal with; their impact on us can be very significant. Grief can drag us down; anger can make us say and do things that we subsequently regret. In the gospel reading, however, Jesus shows us that those difficult emotions can be harnessed for good. It was in grief and anger that Jesus gave new life to the man with the withered hand. Jesus channelled those emotions in the service of God's kingdom. Paul says in his letter to the Romans that 'all things work together for good, for those who love God'. Paul is saying there that if God is our first love, God can work in a life-giving way through all things, even in and through those emotions, those events, that we might judge to be negative and of little value or worth.

## 24 January, Thursday, Second Week in Ordinary Time
*Mark 3:7–12*

One of the most reassuring verses in the New Testament opens today's first reading. It refers to Jesus as 'living forever to intercede for all who come to God through him'. We are given an image of the risen Lord praying for all who come to God through him. Paul, in his letter to the Romans, expresses this same conviction. He refers to 'Christ Jesus, who died, yes, who was raised, who is at the right hand of God, who indeed intercedes for us'. Jesus interceding for all who come to God through him is reflected in today's gospel reading. Mark tells us that great crowds from a very wide area came to God through Jesus.

Their longing for God brought them to Jesus because they recognised Jesus as one in whom God was present and through whom God was powerfully at work. When they came to God through Jesus they discovered Jesus to be someone who was working on their behalf, healing their afflictions. The letter to the Hebrews today is reminding us that the same Jesus, now risen Lord, continues to work on our behalf, interceding for all who come to God through him. His continual prayer for us is prior to our prayer to him. His working on our behalf is prior to our working on his behalf. His prayer for us, his work for us, are givens, and all our own prayer and work are always located within that graced initiative of the Lord towards us.

## 25 January, Friday, Conversion of St Paul

*Mark 16:15–18*

One of my favourite paintings is the depiction of the conversion of Saul by Caravaggio. The original is in a side chapel of the church of Santa Maria del Popolo in Rome. It depicts Paul on the ground beside his horse with his arms open in surrender to the heavenly light of the risen Lord. Perhaps the word 'conversion' is not the best one to describe this experience. Paul did not convert from a life of sin to a life of virtue. As he set about the work of persecuting the followers of Jesus, he did not think he was doing anything wrong.

On the contrary, he thought he was doing God's will. He was being zealous for God's Law. Paul did not convert from one religion to another, he did not think of himself as leaving Judaism to become a Christian. Rather, he came to see his faith in Christ as the full flowering of his Judaism. It is perhaps better to speak of the call of Saul or Paul. This is the language Paul himself uses when he looks back on this moment. He speaks of God who 'set me apart before I was born and called me by his grace'.

Paul's relationship with the God of Israel underwent a deepening, a transformation, through his encounter with the risen Jesus. He came to see that Jesus was the Son of the God of Israel and that the God whom he had always tried to serve was the Father of this Jesus who had been crucified and was now risen from the dead. Because of this moment of grace, Paul came to see everything in a new light. On our faith journey, we can all have an experience comparable to Paul's. At any moment in our lives, our relationship with God and with his Son, Jesus, can be transformed.

Like Paul on the ground with his open arms in Caravaggio's painting, there can come a point in our lives when we open our hearts more fully to God's purpose for our lives. God is always calling us by his grace into a deeper relationship with himself, through his Son, as a result of which we come to see everything in a new light. As with Paul, this call can come at a time and place when we are least expecting it.

## 26 January, Saturday, Memorial of Ss Timothy and Titus
*Luke 10:1–9*

The feast of Ss Timothy and Titus always comes on the day after the feast of the conversion of Paul. The Lord called Paul on the road to Damascus to become an apostle to the pagans. However, in this very important mission he needed others to work alongside him, and Timothy and Titus were two of his closest co-workers. He had several other co-workers, men and women. In his letter to the Philippians, he mentions two women by name, Euodia and Syntyche, declaring that 'they have struggled beside me in the work of the gospel'. At the end of his letter to the Romans, he mentions a married couple, Prisca and Aquila, and says of them that they 'work with me in Christ Jesus', and that they 'risked their necks for my life'. A few verses later, he mentions another married couple, Andronicus and Junia, 'who were in prison with me', and then says of them that 'they are prominent among the apostles'. It is clear that Paul greatly appreciated all his co-workers. His appreciation of Timothy is very evident from today's first reading. For all his exceptional gifts, Paul was aware that he needed people to work alongside him. Paul reminds us that when it comes to the work of the Lord, we are all interdependent. That is why in the gospel reading, Jesus sends out the seventy-two in pairs, not singly. Labourers in the Lord's harvest need to labour together. We need each other's gifts if the Lord's work is to be done in today's world. Each of us has some gift of the Spirit to give to others, and each of us has much to receive from the gifts of the Spirit in others. In that first reading, Paul encourages us to 'fan into a flame' whatever gift God has given us, because, as Paul goes on to say, whatever gift God has given us is never a 'spirit of timidity' but always a 'Spirit of power, and love, and self-control'.

## 28 January, Monday, Third Week in Ordinary Time

*Mark 3:22–30*

It may strike us as strange to hear Jesus speak in today's gospel reading of 'an eternal sin', a sin that 'will never have forgiveness'. Surely there is no sin that is beyond the scope of God's forgiveness? Jesus was referring to the sin of blaspheming against the Holy Spirit. It was the sin of those opponents of Jesus who declared that the Spirit that was at work in the ministry of Jesus was, in reality, an evil spirit. They were claiming that the power revealed in the life and ministry of Jesus was not the power of God but the power of Satan. There were affirming that all the good Jesus was doing had its origin in an evil power. Jesus was saying that those who are so hostile to him as to consider him to be an agent of Satan will be incapable of receiving the gift of God's forgiveness. God forgives all but his forgiveness has to be received. Receiving God's forgiveness requires some minimal openness to Jesus, the one through whom God was seeking to reconcile the world to himself. Those who reject Jesus because they see him as an instrument of Satan show that they lack such minimal openness. In that sense they are guilty of an eternal sin; they have placed themselves beyond the reach of God's forgiveness. The consoling word in the gospel reading is Jesus' declaration that, apart from this eternal sin, 'all people's sins will be forgiven and all their blasphemies'. Even the smallest openness to Jesus, the revelation of God's mercy, is all that is needed for God's forgiveness to become effective in our lives and for us to find ourselves at peace with God.

## 29 January, Tuesday, Third Week in Ordinary Time

*Mark 3:31–35*

This is the only scene in Mark's Gospel where the members of Jesus' family feature. Reference is made to Jesus' mother, brothers and sisters. There is no reference to Jesus' father. Joseph never appears in the context of Jesus' public ministry in any of the Gospels. This may suggest that Joseph was already dead by the time Jesus began his public ministry at the age of thirty or so. It seems as if the family of Jesus on this occasion want to take Jesus away with them; this was their will. Yet, Jesus does not go with them. Instead he declares that his disciples, seated in a circle around him, are his new spiritual family. Anyone who seeks to do God's will, as Jesus reveals it, can become a member of this new spiritual family. It must have been a struggle for Jesus' blood family to let him go to this new family he was forming, the family of his disciples, which came to be called the Church. We have been baptised into this family. As members of Jesus' spiritual family, we are called to do the will of God as Jesus has revealed it to us, through his teaching, his life, his death and resurrection. We spend our lives trying to discern what the Lord's will for our lives is, and then trying to grow in the freedom to do that will. For Jesus' mother and his family, doing God's will entailed renouncing control over Jesus, letting go of their own will for him, which did not come easily to them. Doing the will of God does not come easily to us either. Yet, with the help of the Holy Spirit, our will can be gradually conformed to God's will for our lives. This is the journey we are asked to be faithful to until the end of our earthly lives.

## 30 January, Wednesday, Third Week in Ordinary Time

*Mark 4:1–20*

There are times when our efforts to do something worthwhile don't appear to get very far. The opening lines of the parable of the sower in today's gospel reading reflect that reality. Much of the seed that the sower scattered produced nothing; it was taken by the birds of the air, choked by thorns, scorched by the sun. Yet, some of what the sower sowed produced a wonderful harvest. In spite of much frustration and failure, there was a great crop at the end of the day. The Lord appears to be saying to his disciples through that parable that his own efforts, his words and his deeds, would eventually bear great fruit, in spite of many setbacks, including misunderstanding, rejection and, eventually, crucifixion. The parable is a word of encouragement to those who might be tempted to lose faith in him, because all does not appear to be moving as they had expected. It is also a word of encouragement to all of us today as we try to share in the Lord's work and mission. It is as if Jesus is saying to us, 'if the seed is good, the crop will be good, in spite of setbacks and failure'. We do have good seed, the good seed of the gospel. We can be confident that in scattering that seed, in witnessing to that gospel by what we say and do, the Lord will work powerfully through us. The failures and setbacks we experience in living and witnessing to the gospel need not leave us discouraged because the Lord will give the growth in the end.

## 31 January, Thursday, Third Week in Ordinary Time
*Mark 4:21–25*

The verses we have just heard come immediately after the parable of the sower and its interpretation. That parable sought to reassure Jesus' disciples that the word Jesus proclaimed would bear fruit in people's lives, in spite of the many obstacles working against that word, such as the cares and pleasures of this life and the persecution that the word can bring. The verses that make up today's gospel reading remind us that we have our part to play in the word bearing fruit. Jesus says, 'if anyone has ears to hear, let him listen', and he says further, 'take notice of what you are hearing'. We need to become good listeners to the word. Jesus goes on to say that the more we invest ourselves in that attentive listening to the word, the more we will be given, 'the amount you measure out is the amount you will be given'. In that sense, 'the one who has will be given more'. As we give of ourselves to the word, we discover that we keep receiving more. On the other hand, 'from the one who has not, even what he has will be taken away'. If we don't make the effort to hear the word and receive from its riches, our spiritual understanding of the word diminishes. We can never underestimate the power of the Lord's word, but today's gospel reminds us that its power can be rendered ineffective if we do not make the effort to hear it.

## 1 February, Friday, Feast of St Brigid

*Luke 6:32–38*

St Brigid was born around AD454. When she was young, her father wished to make a suitable marriage for her, but she insisted on devoting her life completely to God. She probably received the veil and spiritual formation from Mel and stayed for a period under his direction in Ardagh. Others followed her example and this led her to found a double monastery in Kildare with the assistance of Bishop Conleth. She died in AD524 and her cult is widespread, not only throughout Ireland but in several European lands. As well as being a person of deep prayer, she was renowned for her hospitality, her almsgiving and her care of the sick. That is why the Church has chosen the reading from Paul's letter to the Romans as an option for her feast day. The reading concludes by calling on us to 'contribute to the needs of the saints; extend hospitality to strangers'. Brigid did both. She served the members of the Church, the saints, and she also showed hospitality to strangers, those who were not part of the Church. In the language of that first reading, she discovered her gift, the particular grace given to her, and she placed that gift at the service of others. We have all been given some particular grace; our gifts will differ according to the grace that has been given to us. Our calling is to try to discern our own particular gifts, the unique way that the Holy Spirit has graced us, and to place those gifts at the service of the Lord, and of others, both those who are part of the Church, the 'saints' and those who are not, 'strangers'.

## 2 February, Saturday, The Presentation of the Lord

*Luke 2:22–40*

In today's first reading, the prophet Malachi announces that the Lord will one day enter his Temple in Jerusalem as the refiner and purifier of his people, so that their worship will be as the Lord desires it. In

John's Gospel, Jesus declares that he will enable people to worship God as God wants to be worshipped, a worship in spirit and truth. Jesus is referring to a worship of God that is inspired by the Spirit of Truth, the Holy Spirit. This worship of God, inspired by the Spirit of God, is not confined to a religious building, a church. The Spirit inspires us to worship God not only with our lips, as in the liturgy, but with our lives. Paul in his letter to the Romans refers to our spiritual worship, by which he means a worship which embraces all of our lives. He calls on us to present our bodies, our embodied selves, as a living sacrifice, holy and acceptable to God. This is the worship of our lives. Each day we are to offer our lives to God. This was the kind of worship that characterised the life of Jesus. In the gospel reading, Mary and Joseph came to the principal place of worship for Jewish people, the Temple. They come not just to worship but to present their son to God. As an adult, Jesus lived out that presentation of himself to God that was made by his parents at this time. Throughout his adult life, Jesus presented himself as a living sacrifice to God, in the words of Paul. He lived his life with a clear focus on God at all times. Jesus calls on us to have that same focus. Because Jesus is the full revelation of God, to live our lives with a clear focus on God means living our lives with a clear focus on Jesus, our risen Lord. Today's feast encourages us to keep presenting ourselves, our hearts, minds and bodies, to the Lord. We are to keep our relationship with the Lord to the fore in all we say and do. In that way, our whole lives will be a worship of the Lord

## 4 February, Monday, Fourth Week in Ordinary Time
*Mark 5:1–20*

This is one of the most graphically narrated of Jesus' miracles. Jesus is on the far side of the Sea of Galilee, mostly pagan territory. The man at the centre of the story is a very disturbed person. A powerful storm is raging within him. The community's response to him is to chain him among the tombs outside the town. They consider him as good as dead, and consign him to live among the dead. Yet, his spirit will not be chained. Although he continues to live among the tombs, he has broken free of his chains. When he sees Jesus at a distance, he runs to him and throws himself at the feet of the life-giver. We are given a picture of someone who is desperately trying to move beyond his situation of enslavement and death. Through his encounter with Jesus, the storm within him is calmed. The community who were so determined to enslave him, and to be rid of him now find him sitting at the feet of Jesus, clothed and in his right mind. The Lord invites us all to come before him in our need, with whatever storm may be brewing within us. If we open ourselves to the Lord's life-giving presence, as we do in prayer, he will calm us as he calmed the storm; he will restore us to ourselves and to others. There is a striking contrast between the reaction of the man's neighbours to what had happened and the reaction of the man himself. The neighbours implored Jesus to leave; the man begged to be allowed to stay with Jesus. The neighbours found Jesus' presence disturbing; he had restored someone to the community who had been judged not to belong there. The man found Jesus' presence calming. We are being reminded that the Lord can both disturb the calm and calm the disturbed. It is striking that Jesus would not allow the man to go with him as he requested. Having received the gift of wholeness from Jesus, he now had a mission among his own people, the very people who had treated him so badly. He was to proclaim in this pagan region the gospel of the Lord's mercy to the broken. Whenever we receive the Lord's mercy, he sends us out as messengers of his mercy to others.

## 5 February, Tuesday, Fourth Week in Ordinary Time

*Mark 5:21–43*

There are two stories in today's gospel reading. There is the story of Jesus healing the daughter of Jairus, the synagogue official, and the story of the healing of the woman with a flow of blood. The woman's condition not only cost her a lot of money for physicians but leaves her on the margins of the community. In virtue of her condition she is considered ritually unclean and is not able to attend the synagogue. On his way to the house of Jairus, Jesus is interrupted by this name-less woman who furtively touches the cloak of Jesus and, as a result, experiences healing of her condition. Although he is interrupted while on an important mission to heal Jairus's daughter, Jesus looks to engage this woman in a very personal way. She simply wants the most secretive and impersonal of contacts, the touching of Jesus' cloak. Jesus wants more. He senses a woman of faith has touched him and has opened herself to the life-giving power of God's kingdom at work within him. Jesus wants to acknowledge this woman's faith publicly and he wants her to witness publicly to her own faith in him. When she comes forward to do so, Jesus assures this woman who had been excluded from the community to which she belongs; he addresses her as 'daughter'. She is as much a daughter of Abraham as anyone else. Jesus also acknowledges that while many people were touching him, her touching him was an act of faith that was life-giving for her. When we are heading somewhere and we are interrupted, the interruption can be just as important as the destination. Jesus shows us that the interruption can often be an opportunity to reach out to someone in a way that leaves them with a greater sense of belonging.

## 6 February, Wednesday, Fourth Week in Ordinary Time

*Mark 6:1–6*

The people of Nazareth were slow to recognise the implications of the great wisdom Jesus possessed and the power for good that was at work through him on behalf of the sick and suffering. They should have concluded from all of this that God must be working through this man in a special way. Instead, they would not accept him: in the words of Jesus, they despised him. He was too familiar to them; they knew his mother and his family. He was one of their own; he was too ordinary. He could not possibly be all that different from everyone else in Nazareth. It is a clear case of familiarity breeding contempt. The reading suggests that we can sometimes be slow to recognise the presence of God in the ordinary and the familiar. We don't have to go long distances, or encounter extraordinary phenomena, to make contact with the wisdom and the power of God. The Lord's presence is all around us in the near and the familiar, in the humdrum and in the ordinary, if we have eyes to see and ears to hear. The gospel reading invites us to see the familiar and the ordinary with new eyes, with the eyes of faith. The failure of the people of Nazareth to see in this way inhibited what Jesus could do among them: 'he could work no miracle there'. In contrast, our seeing with the eyes of faith gives the Lord space to work among us in new and surprising ways.

## 7 February, Thursday, Fourth Week in Ordinary Time

*Mark 6:7–13*

In the gospel reading Mark shows how, early into his ministry ,Jesus sent out the Twelve that he had chosen to share in his work. He sent them out to do what he had been doing, to preach the gospel and to heal the sick. Jesus understood that he needed the help of others to do the work he had been sent to do. He continues to need us to do his work today. We are to be his eyes, his ears, his hands, his feet and his voice. As risen Lord he wants to work in and through us. Paul understood this very clearly. He understood the Church to be the body of Christ in the world. He was very clear that every member of Christ's body had a vital role to play.

The body of Christ could not be all Christ wants it to be unless everyone plays the role they are called and equipped to play through their Baptism. Each one of us has a unique contribution to make to the life of Christ's body, the Church, and, thereby, to the work of the Lord in the world today. Each one of us is indispensable and necessary. The first reading from the letter to the Hebrews puts it very simply. In the Church everyone is a 'first-born child' and a 'citizen of heaven'. There are to be no second-class citizens in the Church. Each of us is a vital member of Christ's body, uniquely graced by the Lord for his work and mission in the world.

## 8 February, Friday, Fourth Week in Ordinary Time
*Mark 6:14–29*
Today's gospel reading from Mark is one of the more gruesome stories in the Gospels, outside of the story of the passion and death of Jesus. A banquet celebrating the birthday of Herod Antipas becomes the occasion for the summary execution of someone Jesus described as 'more than a prophet'. Herod comes across as a person who acts contrary to his own better judgement and instincts. He knew John to be a good and holy man and liked to listen to him, yet he had John thrown into prison because it was what his wife, Herodias, wanted. Then, at his birthday celebration, he ordered the beheading of John, even though it left him deeply distressed. Having made a rash promise to his stepdaughter, he felt obliged to keep his promise because it was what his guests would have expected of him. His honour was at stake. Neither action, throwing John into prison and ordering his execution, came from deep within Herod. He did both under pressure,

from his wife and from his guests. The portrait of Herod in today's gospel reading reminds us that we can all do things under pressure from others that we are not at peace about. Like Herod, we can take paths that are not true to what is best in us, to please someone or to protect our position in the eyes of others. The gospel calls on us to be true to our deepest and best values, to the Lord's call which resounds through them. There may be some loss for us in doing so, but, as Jesus says elsewhere in the Gospels, 'those who lose their life for my sake, and for the sake of the gospel, will save it'.

## 9 February, Saturday, Fourth Week in Ordinary Time
*Mark 6:30–34*

The image of the shepherd links today's first reading, responsorial psalm and gospel reading. The first reading speaks of God raising our Lord Jesus from the dead to become the great Shepherd of the sheep. The responsorial psalm is the much-loved psalm, 'the Lord is my shepherd'. On the lips of the Jewish people who prayed that psalm, 'the Lord' referred to the God of Israel. As Christians, we instinctively think of Jesus when we say, 'the Lord is my shepherd'. He is, in the words of the first reading, 'our Lord, Jesus'. In the gospel reading, Jesus looked out upon the crowd of people who had so unexpectedly disrupted his plans for rest with the eyes of a shepherd. He had compassion for them, because he recognised that they were like sheep without a shepherd. Jesus would become their shepherd, which is why he immediately set himself to teach them at some length. He went on to feed them with bread and fish as a shepherd feeds his flock. The risen Lord continues to look upon us with the eyes of a shepherd. He feeds us with his teaching, with his word, which we hear in the Scriptures. He feeds us with the bread of life, his body, in the Eucharist. He looks to us to feed the physically and spiritually hungry, as he did. Jesus was not disturbed by the crowd who interrupted his plans for some rest for himself and his disciples, because his instinct was always that of the shepherd. It remains his instinct as risen Lord. His deepest desire is to feed and nourish us. He has no times that are out of bounds. It is always timely for us to turn to him in our hunger and allow him to feed us with his presence, so that we can be good shepherds to each other.

## 11 February, Monday, Fifth Week in Ordinary Time
*Mark 6:53–56*
Today's first reading consists of the opening nineteen verses of the Bible. It is a poetic expression of the people of Israel's understanding of God as Creator of the universe. There are a number of little refrains in that very poetic text. One of the refrains that has always struck me is 'and God saw that it was good'. There is a conviction coming through in the author of this text that the created world is essentially good. In some way, all of created reality reflects the goodness of God. In these times when we can be so aware of and so preoccupied with evil, it is good to be reminded of that truth. When it comes to God's creation of the human person on the sixth day, the author declares not only that 'it was good' but that 'it was very good'. The human person has the potential to be a much fuller revelation of God's goodness than anything else in all creation. Jesus was the fullest revelation of God's goodness. In the gospel reading, Mark portrays great human goodness. It is said that in the countryside people brought the sick on stretchers to wherever they heard Jesus was present and that in the villages, towns and farms they laid down the sick in the open spaces, so that the sick could touch even the fringe of Jesus' clock. The sick, who could not come to Jesus by themselves, were carried and brought to Jesus by the healthy. There is an image here of what is best in human nature, with the strong looking out for the weak and the healthy for the sick. We are all capable of great good, and, with the help of the

Holy Spirit, we can live as that unique image of God's goodness that we were created to be.

## 12 February, Tuesday, Fifth Week in Ordinary Time

*Mark 7:1–13*

In today's gospel reading, Jesus confronts the Pharisees because their various traditions, about which they are so zealous, are not always in harmony with the word of God. As Jesus says to them, 'You make God's word null and void for the sake of your tradition which you have handed down'. Jesus is reminding us that not every religious tradition is worth holding on to. Every tradition has to be measured against the word of God. We have to keep asking if this or that tradition is really in keeping with God's will for our lives as revealed in the Scriptures. That is why it is so important for us to keep listening to the word of God. Pope Francis is very keen that, in particular, we listen to the Gospels on a regular basis. More than once he has encouraged people to keep a small copy of the Gospels in their pocket and to read from it every day. It is above all in the Gospels that we encounter the Word who was with God in the beginning and who became flesh and dwelt among us. Jesus not only speaks God's word but he is God's word in human flesh. In listening to God's word, present in Jesus, we are helped to assess the value of our traditions, including our religious traditions. Such traditions are the wineskins that need to keep changing if the always new wine of God's word is to be heard afresh in every generation.

## 13 February, Wednesday, Fifth Week in Ordinary Time

*Mark 7:14–23*

In the gospel reading Jesus is responding to those who pay too much attention to external ritual, external observance, and not enough attention to what is going on within, in their heart, their inner core.

Jesus declares that it is from within, from people's hearts, that evil intentions emerge. Our inner core, what the Gospel calls our 'heart', can be a reservoir for good, but it can also be a reservoir for evil. Jesus seems to have been very aware that we are capable of great evil as well as great good. He wanted people to have hearts that were the wellspring of all that is good, wholesome and life-giving. You may recall one of the beatitudes he spoke, 'Blessed are the pure in heart, for they shall see God'. He was declaring blessed those whose heart is in the right place, as we might say today, those whose heart is fixed on God, whose intention is centred on what God wants, on God's will, God's desire for our lives and our world. It is from such a heart that great good comes. Only harm can come from a heart that is fixed on self, centred on its own comfort and pleasure. We need to keep calling on the Holy Spirit to fill and renew our hearts, so that we are as pure in heart as Jesus was, as focused on God's will for our lives as he was.

## 14 February, Thursday, Feast of Ss Cyril and Methodius
*Luke 10:1–9*

Today we celebrate the feast of Ss Cyril and Methodius, brothers from Macedonia in Greece. In the ninth-century they preached the Gospel in Moravia, the modern-day Czech Republic, as well as in modern-day Slovakia and Hungary. In their efforts to communicate the Gospel they translated the Scriptures and the liturgical texts into the local Slav language. They understood that if they were to communicate with the local people, these important texts would need to be in the vernacular. Because of opposition, they had to leave their mission in the Slavic lands and, at the invitation of the Pope, they travelled to Rome. There Cyril became a monk, and he is buried in the Irish Dominican church of San Clemente, where an ancient fresco depicts his funeral. Methodius returned to Moravia where he continued to preach the Gospel in spite of great opposition, including opposition from local bishops, who objected to his use of the vernacular. Cyril and Methodius were labourers in the Lord's harvest. In today's gospel reading, Jesus sends out seventy-two such labourers, and he calls on them to ask God to send more labourers to the harvest. Jesus was aware that God needed an abundance of labourers in God's harvest. Seventy-two would not be sufficient, much less the twelve, who had been sent out earlier. God needs each one of us. We are all called to be labourers in the Lord's harvest in one way or another. We may not be asked to travel far from our homes, like Cyril and Methodius. We can labour for the Lord wherever we find ourselves. The Lord will always provide us with opportunities to make his kingdom values present to others. We each have some unique gift that the Lord needs if his work is to get done in our time.

## 15 February, Friday, Fifth Week in Ordinary Time
*Mark 7:31–37*

In the gospel reading, when Jesus was asked by people to heal a deaf man who had a speech impediment, he listened to their request and he responded to it. After Jesus healed the man, he asked those same people not to tell others about what he had done. However, the people who had brought the deaf and dumb man to Jesus did not listen to Jesus' request. In fact, the more Jesus insisted that they say nothing to anyone about the healing he had performed, the more widely they published it. Even though Jesus listened to their request, they did not listen to his. The man the people brought to Jesus did not listen because he could not listen; he was deaf. Yet, we know from our experience of ourselves and of others that good hearing does not always make for good listening. Our failure to listen can often have an impact on what we say and how we say it. It is striking that when Jesus restored the deaf man's hearing, he was able to speak clearly for the first time. His hearing and speech were closely associated. Listening and speaking are also closely associated. The more we truly listen to someone, the more likely it is that the words we speak to them will build them up and bring them life.

## 16 February, Saturday, Fifth Week in Ordinary Time
*Mark 8:1–10*

Different people react in different ways to the same situation. In the gospel reading  today, there is quite a difference between the reaction of Jesus and the reaction of the disciples to the sight of a large hungry crowd in the wilderness. The disciples' question, 'Where could anyone get bread to feed these people?' suggests that they wanted Jesus to send the crowd away. Jesus' question to his disciples, 'How many loaves have you?', suggests that he wanted them to make some effort to feed the crowd. Jesus got them to bring the little food they could find to him. Then, with that little, with those few resources of seven loaves, the Lord fed the crowd, with the help of his reluctant disciples. The gospel reading suggests that the Lord will always encourage us to take on some service of others, even when we may feel that our resources are inadequate. If we are generous with those few resources, the Lord will then work with them and through them in ways that will surprise us. The Lord can work wonders through the very ordinary and sometimes unpromising looking resources and gifts that we possess. We have to do our bit, like the disciples in the gospel reading, but the Lord always does much more. Yet, if we are not willing to do the little we can with what we have, the Lord's own capacity for ministry to others is curtailed. The Lord needs our resources, small and inadequate at they may seem, to continue his good work among us and in the world.

## 18 February, Monday, Sixth Week in Ordinary Time
*Mark 8:11–13*

Mark's Gospel gives us the most human portrait of Jesus of all the Gospels. Mark makes more frequent reference than any of the other evangelists to the human emotions of Jesus. In today's reading, Mark states that Jesus responded to the Pharisees' request for a sign from heaven 'with a sigh that came straight from the heart'. That sigh issued forth in a question: 'Why does this generation demand a sign?' We can almost sense the frustration and weariness of Jesus in that phrase, 'with a sigh that came straight from the heart'. The religious quest often takes the form of a search for heavenly signs, a longing for the extra-ordinary and unusual.

The Jesus of the Gospels, however, will always redirect us towards the ordinary, such as the sower who goes out to sow his field, the woman who looks for her lost coin, the care given to a stranger on the road from Jerusalem to Jericho, the poor day labourer who unexpectedly finds treasure in his field, the rich merchant who finds the pearl of great price he has always been looking for, children playing games in the marketplace. It is in the ordinary events of daily life that the mystery of God's kingdom is to be found, because God's good creation is full of God's glory.

## 19 February, Tuesday, Sixth Week in Ordinary Time
*Mark 8:14–21*

In today's gospel reading Jesus seems very frustrated with his disciples. They misunderstand what Jesus says to them about the yeast of the Pharisees and the yeast of Herod, thinking that Jesus is referring to the fact that they have forgotten to bring bread. In reality, in that culture yeast was often a negative symbol, and Jesus was trying to warn his disciples against the evil intentions of the Pharisees and of Herod. Jesus addresses his disciples as people without perception. It is likely that Jesus can be just as frustrated with us at times. Like the first disciples we, too, can demonstrate a lack of perception, a failure to hear what Jesus is really saying to us, a failure to see what Jesus is trying to show us.

We need to keep coming before the Lord in the awareness that we do not see as he wants us to see or hear as he wants us to hear. Our eyes and our ears need opening, and, perhaps, the times when we think we see and hear well are the very times when we are most blind and deaf. We need the humility, the poverty of spirit, which keeps us praying, 'Lord, that I may see', 'Lord, that I may hear'.

## 20 February, Wednesday, Sixth Week in Ordinary Time
*Mark 8:22–26*

In both of today's readings, we find a progression towards a state that is sought after and longed for. In the first reading, Noah lives in hope that the waters of the flood will be dried up from the earth. He sends out a dove and, finding nowhere to perch, it returns to him in the ark. Then he sends out the dove a second time, and again the dove returns to the ark. However, on this occasion, the returning dove has a new olive branch in its beak, indicating that the waters were beginning to recede. When Noah sends out the dove the third time, it does not return to the ark, showing that the flood has receded and that creation is being renewed. In the gospel reading, Jesus works to heal a blind man who had been brought to him. After Jesus put spittle on the man's eyes and laid his hands on him, the blind man began to see. He could see people but they looked like trees walking about. When Jesus laid his hands on the man's eyes again, he could see clearly. Noah needed to be patient, and so did Jesus. In both readings, God's creative work is afoot, but it happens slowly and gradually. Some processes cannot be rushed. At the beginning of his letter to the Philippians Paul prays that God who has begun his good work in the community would bring it to completion. God's good work in our lives will only be brought to completion in eternity. Here and now we try to cooperate with God's ongoing creative work within us and among us, learning to be patient with its seemingly slow progress in ourselves and in others.

## 21 February, Thursday, Sixth Week in Ordinary Time
*Mark 8:27–33*

We probably all find it easier to tell people who we think they are than listen to people tell us who they really are. In particular, we can struggle to hear the story of someone's brokenness, especially if our picture of them has been one that doesn't allow for that. In today's gospel reading, Peter wasn't able to hear Jesus talking about himself as a broken, failed, rejected Messiah. It was really only after the resurrection that Peter and the disciples were able to come to terms with such brokenness, such failure. It can be a struggle for us to accept failure and brokenness in others and, also, to accept our own brokenness. Jesus could accept his own failure, his own brokenness, because he trusted in God as one who would make him whole. Because he could accept his own failure, his own brokenness, he was at home with the failure and brokenness of others. The broken, the failures of this world, flocked to him, and in his presence they became whole. We will more easily accept our own brokenness and failures if we know in our heart of hearts that we too can approach the Lord as one who can make us whole. The Eucharist has been described as bread broken for a broken people. The Lord who was broken on the cross for us is present in the Eucharist as our life-giver. We approach the Lord in the Eucharist in our own brokenness asking to be made whole and asking also for the grace to be able to sit with others in their brokenness.

## 22 February, Friday, Feast of the Chair of St Peter

*Matthew 16:13–19*

In the Jewish culture of Jesus' time it was customary for the teachers of the Law to sit when teaching. At the beginning of the Sermon on the Mount, Matthew depicts Jesus as being seated. 'When Jesus saw the crowds, he went up the mountain, and after he sat down, his disciples came to him. Then he began to speak, and taught them, saying … '. The feast of the Chair of St Peter commemorates the teaching authority of the bishop of Rome, the vicar of Christ. In Matthew's Gospel, from which today's gospel reading is taken, Jesus is the great teacher. He is the authoritative interpreter of God's will for our lives because he teaches as Emmanuel, God-with-us. In today's gospel reading, Jesus is portrayed as passing on his teaching authority to Peter. The image of 'keys' suggests authority and responsibility. The reference to binding and loosing specifies the nature of this authority and responsibility. The experts in the Jewish Law bound and loosed the Law; by their teaching they showed what was binding in the Law and what could be taken more loosely. In Matthew's Gospel, it is Jesus who performs this teaching role. He declares authoritatively when the Law is binding and when it could be interpreted more loosely than was customary at the time. When Jesus passes on his teaching authority to Peter, it is not the Jewish Law that Peter is to bind or lose, but Jesus' own teaching. Peter is being given the role of interpreting the teaching of Jesus for the Church that will be formed beyond the death and resurrection of Jesus, declaring what is binding there and what can be taken more loosely. As Roman Catholics we believe that the teaching role that Jesus entrusted to Peter now resides with the bishop of Rome, the pope. We look to him to give the lead in interpreting the teaching of Jesus for the Church and beyond. At a time when authority, at so many levels and in so many institutions, has been weakened, today's feast invites us to renew our confidence in the teaching authority of the pope, whom we believe to be guided by the Spirit of the risen Lord.

## 23 February, Saturday, Sixth Week in Ordinary Time

*Mark 9:2–13*

In today's gospel reading, Mark describes what must have been a very memorable moment in the lives of Peter, James and John. This experience of Jesus transfigured on the mountain came to them as a sheer gift. They had done nothing to make it happen. It was Jesus who took the initiative to lead them up a mountain where they could be alone with him. They had no hand or part in the transformation that came over Jesus on the mountain. They were simply the recipients of this extraordinary grace. In Mark's Gospel, this experience came just after that difficult moment when Jesus revealed himself to his disciples as the Son of Man who must suffer and die, much to their consternation, and Peter's consternation in particular. Beyond this experience lay the way to Jerusalem where Jesus would undergo his passion and the disciples would know the pain of denial and flight. Here on the mountain they were given the grace of seeing the deeper reality behind all the suffering to come, the love of the Father for the Son, the love of the Son for the Father, and the Father's gift of the Son to all, 'Listen to him'. We, too, can be unexpectedly graced by the Lord on our life's journey, sometimes even in the midst of struggle and suffering. Such graces can take many forms, but they all leave us saying, with Peter, 'it is wonderful for us to be here'. Often it is not what we work for but what is given to us that touches us most deeply and enduringly.

## 25 February, Monday, Seventh Week in Ordinary Time

*Mark 9:14–29*

Sometimes we can find ourselves helpless before certain situations. It seems as if there is nothing we can do to resolve them. This is the situation the disciples find themselves in according to today's gospel reading. A father brings his very disturbed son to them for healing, but there is nothing they can do for the boy, much to the father's upset. He says to Jesus, 'I asked your disciples to cast it out and they were unable to'. Jesus went on to do what the disciples were unable to do; he restored the boy to his senses, and to his father. When the disciples asked Jesus why they could not drive out the demon that had enslaved the boy, Jesus replied, 'this is the kind that can only be driven out by prayer'. Jesus suggests that there are some situations that only God can resolve and all we can do is pray. The disciples had done their best to heal the boy but their efforts were never going to be enough. Sometimes our efforts are never enough, and all we can do is give the situation over to the Lord in prayer. Jesus is suggesting to his disciples that sometimes prayer can accomplish something that our efforts cannot. In a similar vein, in the first reading James declares that there is a certain kind of wisdom that only comes down from above. It cannot just come from us; we need to open ourselves to it in prayer. The father of the disturbed boy did pray to Jesus. Many have identified with his prayer ever since: 'I do have faith. Help the little faith I have'. He recognised the truth of what Jesus went on to say, that all we can do before some situations is pray.

## 26 February, Tuesday, Seventh Week in Ordinary Time
*Mark 9:30–37*
In Mark's Gospel the disciples seem to be often 'off message', as we say today. They don't quite seem to grasp the fundamental message of Jesus; their concerns are often a long way from his concerns; their priorities are often in conflict with his priorities. We should be slow to judge those first disciples of Jesus because we can all go 'off message' in the same way from time to time. In today's gospel Jesus announces to his disciples that the day is drawing near when he will

be delivered into the hands of men and put to death; he will become one of the least. In response, the disciples immediately begin to argue among themselves as to which of them is the greatest. It is hard to imagine a more incongruous response to what Jesus has just said to them. Their concern about which of them is the greatest, as to who stands where in the pecking order, is a very human preoccupation. However, it is certainly not the preoccupation of Jesus. To convey his preoccupation, Jesus takes a little child, a symbol of the least in that culture, someone without status, position or influence, and he identifies himself fully with the child. He declares that anyone who welcomes one such child welcomes him. Jesus was great in God's eyes, yet on the cross he was the least of the least. The message of Jesus is that true greatness, greatness in God's eyes, tends to be at odds with what the world considers greatness. It shows itself in the service of the least.

## 27 February, Wednesday, Seventh Week in Ordinary Time
*Mark 9:38–40*

Today's gospel reading is taken from a section of Mark's Gospel where the disciples consistently show themselves to be at cross purposes with Jesus. After Jesus communicates to his disciples the painful truth that he is to be betrayed into human hands, they immediately begin to argue among themselves as to which of them is the greatest, earning a rebuke from Jesus. When parents were bringing children for Jesus for him to bless them, the disciples turn them away, and Jesus has to rebuke his disciples again. In today's gospel reading, which comes between those two incidents, the disciples try to prevent others doing good in Jesus' name simply because they do not belong to Jesus' circle of disciples; they are 'not one of us'.

Again, Jesus has to rebuke his disciples. Where the disciples saw unwelcoming competitors, Jesus saw potential co-workers. It is tempting to look upon them with very critical eyes, yet the disciples in Mark's Gospel represent us all. We all find ourselves at cross purposes with the Lord from time to time. Our way of seeing and the actions that flow from such seeing will not always be in harmony with the Lord's way of seeing and acting. We, too, can be unfairly dismissive of the good others are doing because they are 'not one of us'. We need to keep growing more fully into the Lord's generous vision and way of being.

## 28 February, Thursday, Seventh Week in Ordinary Time

*Mark 9:41–50*

I have often been struck by those words of Jesus at the beginning of today's gospel reading: 'If anyone gives you a cup of water to drink because you belong to Christ, then I tell you solemnly, he will most certainly not lose his reward.' Giving a cup of water to someone seems a very small gesture indeed. Yet, for someone who is really thirsty, a cup of water could be the greatest gift imaginable. Jesus is reminding us that the smallest gesture of kindness towards someone has enormous value in the sight of God. We can sometimes get discouraged because we may feel that we are not doing enough. Yet, Jesus is suggesting that God does not measure success in the way that the world tends to measure success. The love which is the fruit of the Holy Spirit can express itself in ways that are seemingly small and insignificant by normal human standards. Jesus noticed the two small coins that the widow put into the Temple treasure, because in giving so little, she was giving her all. Today's gospel reading encourages us never to underestimate the significance and life-giving impact of even the smallest of loving gestures. If the Lord can work powerfully through a young boy's few loaves and fish, feeding a multitude with them, he can work powerfully through our own gestures of loving kindness, no matter how small they may seem to ourselves and others.

## 1 March, Friday, Seventh Week in Ordinary Time

*Mark 10:1–12*

In today's gospel reading, Jesus presents God's vision of marriage, as found in the Book of Genesis, involving a man and a woman coming together and giving themselves to each other for life, so that their two lives become one life. In Jesus' own day there were reservations about this vision of married life. Some would have seen it as too idealistic and not taking sufficient account of the reality of people's lives. Yet, Jesus reiterates the teaching of the Book of Genesis. There is resistance to this vision today as well, of course, and some would want to define marriage in much broader and looser terms. Marriages certainly break down. We all know that from our own experience. I suspect many of us have family members whose marriages have not lasted. Yet, we need to hold on to the vision that Jesus gives us in today's gospel reading, because it corresponds to God's understanding of marriage. Jesus regarded marriage as a relationship of love between a man and a woman that reflected God's loving relationship with his people. The early Church came to understand marriage as a relationship of love between a man and a woman that reflected Christ's loving relationship with his Church. The love of husband and wife in marriage is a special expression of Christ's love for his Church and for the world. That vision is worth fighting for, especially in a culture that is often unsympathetic to it. It is worth fighting for because it is worthy of what is best and deepest in people.

## 2 March, Saturday, Seventh Week in Ordinary Time

*Mark 10:13–16*

Today's gospel reading is one that I usually select for the baptism of a child. Just as people were bringing children to Jesus for him to bless them, parents bring their children to Jesus when they present them for baptism. In and through the sacrament of Baptism, the Lord touches the lives of the children in a very blessed way. He receives them into his body, the Church, pouring the Spirit of God's love, the Holy Spirit, into their lives. They join a worldwide family which looks to God as Father, Jesus as brother and Mary as mother. In the gospel reading, Jesus' own disciples were turning the children away from Jesus, preventing people from bringing them to him. In response to this, the evangelist Mark describes Jesus as 'indignant', the only time that indignation is ascribed to Jesus in the Gospels. The risen Lord must be equally indignant whenever we do anything to hinder children from being brought to the Lord to receive his many blessings. Rather than blocking children from coming to the Lord, we are to learn from them how to approach the Lord. Jesus reminds his misguided disciples that they have much to learn from children about receiving the gift of God's kingdom. Like children, we are to recognise that we are beggars before God. We are to approach God, trusting that he gives generously to those who recognise their dependence on him and come to him with an open and receptive heart.

## 4 March, Monday, Eighth Week in Ordinary Time
*Mark 10:17–27*

We all ask questions in the course of a week, even a day. Most of these questions get answered and we move on from them. However, there are other bigger questions in life that remain with us all our lives. These are questions that keep us seeking and asking. We find one of these big questions on the lips of the man who approached Jesus in today's gospel reading: 'What must I do to inherit eternal life?' He was asking, 'What is the path of life that I need to take?' It is a question we can all identify with, because it is a fundamental human question. In response to his question, Jesus directed him to the core teaching of his own Jewish religious tradition, in particular, to the ten commandments, quoting six of those commandments. Our own religious tradition is the first place we often turn to when trying to answer the big questions of life. Indeed, it is the search for the answer to the big questions of life that has given rise to the various religious traditions in the world. Our own religious tradition has the capacity to speak to each one of us in a very personal way. After quoting the tradition, Jesus then spoke to this man in a very personal way; he gave him a very personal calling on the basis of that tradition: 'Sell everything you own ... then, come, follow me'. Jesus did not insist that everyone who followed him should sell everything they owned. Mary and Martha, who provided hospitality for Jesus, were certainly among his followers, but it seems they were not asked to sell their home. The Lord's general call to us from our religious tradition takes on a very personal form for each one of us. Within the broad path we are all called to take, the Lord has a very particular path for each of us. In so far as we try to listen for that very personal call and try to respond to it, we will find that path of life which the man in the gospel reading was looking for and which we are all seeking.

## 5 March, Tuesday, Eighth Week in Ordinary Time
*Mark 10:28–31*

Today's gospel reading begins with a question from Peter, 'What about us? We have left everything and followed you'. Peter and the other members of the Twelve had given up a great deal to become followers of Jesus. They may have been wondering if it was really worth it all. We too have responded to the Lord's call, although not in the same very radical way that those intimate associates of Jesus did, who had left livelihood and family for a very uncertain future. Perhaps on our off days we might be tempted to ask a question similar to Peter's: 'Is it worth the effort, this following of Jesus, this struggle to live by the values of the Gospel day in and day out'.

The answer of Jesus to Peter and to us all is, 'Yes, it is worth the effort'. Jesus promises us in that gospel reading that when we respond to his call, when we give of ourselves for his sake, we will receive far more than we will give. In particular, he says that we will gain a new experience of family, far beyond the confines of our blood family, the family of believers. We will find ourselves co-travellers with others who are trying to take the same path as ourselves; we will experience the richness of the Church, the community of the Lord's followers. That community embraces not only those of us still on our pilgrim way but all who have passed beyond this life, including the saints, that great 'cloud of witnesses', in the words of the letter to the Hebrews.

## 6 March, Ash Wednesday
*Matthew 6:1–6, 16–18*

We often think of Lent as a time when we do something worthwhile to grow in our relationship with the Lord. We might think in terms of the three practices that Jesus mentions in the gospel reading: prayer, fasting and almsgiving. We decide to pray a little more or we decide to fast from something that we like or that we are too attached to, or we resolve to give more generously to others out of our resources and gifts. This is a very valid way of looking at Lent. As well as thinking of Lent as a time when we do something worthwhile for the Lord, we could also think of Lent as a time when we allow the Lord to do something worthwhile for us. Lent is as much about God's work for us as it is about our work for God. In today's second reading, Paul says, 'we beg you once again not to neglect the grace of God that you have received'. Paul is reminding us that God has already graced us. He has already been at work in our lives, and he continues to do his work in our lives. Lent could be understood as a time when we give God more space to do God's good work in our lives. The goal of our lives as Christians is, in the words of Paul in that reading, to be-come the goodness of God. This is predominantly God's work in our lives through his Son and the Holy Spirit. Writing to the Philippians, Paul says to them, 'I am confident of this, that the one who began a good work among you will bring it to completion by the day of Jesus Christ'. God has begun a good work in our lives. That good work of God is always ongoing. It will be brought to completion when we become the goodness of God. Lent is a time when we allow God to do his good work in our lives more easily, more freely.

## 7 March, Thursday after Ash Wednesday
*Luke 9:22–25*

The call of Moses in today's first reading is 'Choose life'. Earlier in that reading, Moses called on people to 'love the Lord your God and follow his ways'. To choose life is to choose love, the love of the Lord and the love of all whom the Lord loves. One way of checking whether or not we are choosing life is to ask, 'What is the most loving thing I can do here?' 'How do I choose love in this situation?' 'What does it mean to give expression to my love of the Lord at this moment?' In the gospel reading, Jesus declares that 'anyone who loses his life for my sake, that person will save it'. Jesus implies that choosing life, for ourselves and for others, often means losing our lives for his sake. It is in dying to ourselves, out of love for the Lord and others, that we find life. This is what it means to choose life. Choosing love, and the life which flows from love, will often mean losing our lives in the sense of dying to ourselves, denying ourselves. Jesus himself lost his life because he chose love, but in choosing love he found life. God raised him to new life. Jesus' teaching and his whole existence shows us that when we chose the kind of self-emptying love that Jesus embodied, we will be choosing life. Our choice to love will always be life-giving for ourselves and for others. Choice is not a value in itself. Its value, or disvalue, is determined by what is chosen, the object of our choice. Jesus wants us to keep choosing love and, in so doing, to keep choosing life. We are always choosing, whether we are aware of it or not, because not to choose is to choose. The important question is 'What do we chose?'

## 8 March, Friday after Ash Wednesday

*Matthew 9:14–15*

There are only two days of fast and abstinence in Lent, Ash Wednesday and Good Friday. Yet, many people chose to fast from some form of food or drink for the season of Lent. According to the gospel reading, Jesus' disciples were criticised by the disciples of John the Baptist for not fasting in the way they did. John the Baptist was a more austere man than Jesus. Jesus once referred to John the Baptist as one who had come eating no bread and drinking no wine, and to himself as the Son of Man who came eating and drinking. It seems that neither Jesus nor his disciples were as much into fasting as John the Baptist and his disciples. There was something more celebratory about Jesus' ministry in comparison to the ministry of John the Baptist. In the gospel reading, Jesus speaks of himself as the bridegroom and his disciples as the bridegroom's attendants. Jesus' life and ministry had something of the celebratory quality of a wedding, and who fasts at a wedding?

Yet, Jesus also acknowledges that a time will come when fasting will be appropriate: 'the time will come ... '. Jesus is looking ahead to the time of the Church. When we fast from some food or drink, we are showing that it is not vitally important to us, that we are not dependent upon it. What really matters to us is our relationship with the Lord. We fast so as to as to grow in our relationship with the Lord. In the first reading, Isaiah links fasting to our relationship with those in greatest need. We fast so as to be freer to respond to the call of those who most need our help. Fasting is always in the service of our love of the Lord and our love of others. If fasting is a saying 'no' to something, it is always with a view to our making a more generous 'yes' to the Lord and his people.

## 9 March, Saturday after Ash Wednesday

*Luke 5:27–32*

When I read the Gospels, I am often struck by the questions that people ask. Jesus himself asks many questions in the pages of the Gospels, as do many of the other characters who appear in them. In today's gospel reading, the scribes and Pharisees ask Jesus' disciples, 'Why do you eat with tax collectors and sinners?' As far as they were concerned, to eat with tax collectors and sinners was to risk being contaminated by them. They would have argued that it was better to keep yourself separate from such people in order to preserve your moral health. However, Jesus did not share this concern. Rather than the sin of others infecting him, he knew that his goodness, God's goodness in him, would transform others. The Lord is never diminished by our failings; rather, we are always ennobled and enriched by his holiness. That is why the Lord does not separate himself from us, even when we might be tempted to separate ourselves from him, because of what we have done or failed to do. The Lord is always ready to sit with us, to share table with us, to enter into communion with us, in order that in our weakness we might draw from his strength and in our many failings we might draw from his goodness and love. He has not come to call the virtuous but sinners to repentance and we are all sinners in need of his merciful love.

## 11 March, Monday, First Week of Lent

*Matthew 25:31–46*

The last line of today's first reading from the Book of Leviticus is well known to us from the gospels: 'You must love your neighbour as yourself'. Jesus quotes this verse in response to a question he is asked regarding the first commandment in the Jewish Law. Having given the first commandment, to love God with all one's heart, soul, mind and strength, he then quotes this verse from Leviticus, 'You shall love your neighbour as yourself', and identifies it as the second commandment, thereby giving it a really important standing. We are to show our love of God by loving our neighbour as if they were an extension of ourselves. In today's gospel reading, Jesus goes further than this second commandment. Jesus declares that not only are we to see our neighbour as an extension of ourselves but we are to see our neighbour as an extension of himself. It is almost as if the first commandment and the second commandment have become one. In loving our neighbour, Jesus declares that we are loving him, and we know from elsewhere in Matthew's Gospel that in loving Jesus we are loving God, because Jesus is Emmanuel, God with us. Whenever we render loving service to our fellow human beings, especially those in greatest need, we are rendering loving service to Jesus and to God. The opposite is also true. Whenever we neglect to love our neighbour in need, we are neglecting to love the Lord. This is the case whether or not we are aware of it. It is striking that, in the gospel reading, both groups were unaware that they were serving the Lord in love or neglecting to do so. Jesus suggests that there is a great deal more going on in our dealings with each other than we often realise, especially in our dealings with the most vulnerable.

## 12 March, Tuesday, First Week of Lent

*Matthew 6:7–15*

Some people have difficulty with that petition in the Lord's Prayer: 'Lead us not into temptation'. It seems to imply that God would deliberately lead us into temptation. The translation of that phrase in today's gospel reading is 'Do not put us to the test'. Perhaps that sounds like a more acceptable petition. We are asking God not to let us be tested beyond our limits, not to allow our faith in him to be tested beyond what we can endure. Whichever way this petition is translated, there is a second part to it which explains the first part, 'deliver us from evil' or, in the translation of today's gospel reading, 'save us from the Evil One'. No one could have a difficulty with that prayer. We are asking God to keep us faithful when evil or the evil one puts us to the test or tempts us. This is the true meaning of the petition, 'Lead us not into temptation'. We are asking God to strengthen us for that time when our faith in him will be severely put to the test, when we will be tempted to turn away from God's will for our lives. Simon Peter was tempted in this sense, and he failed the test when it came, denying Jesus and his own discipleship publicly. That petition in the Lord's Prayer is very realistic. It acknowledges that it isn't always easy to be true to our baptismal calling, to our relationship with the Lord. In making that petition, we can be confident that the Lord will hear our prayer and will keep us strong when such testing moments come. As Paul declares in his first letter to the Corinthians, 'God is faithful, and he will not let you be tested beyond your strength'.

## 13 March, Wednesday, First Week of Lent
*Luke 11:29–32*

In the gospel reading Jesus addresses his contemporaries as people who fail to appreciate him; they do not recognise the significance of his person, his presence, someone greater than Jonah, greater even than Solomon. If the people of Nineveh responded to Jonah, and if the Queen of the South responded to Solomon, how much more should Jesus' contemporaries respond to him. The same Jesus who was present to his contemporaries is present to us as risen Lord. We, too, can fail to appreciate the Lord who stands among us. Like Jesus' contemporaries, we can look for signs without recognising the powerful signs of his presence that are all around us. The greatest sign of the

Lord's presence, a sacred sign or sacrament, is the Eucharist. In the Eucharist the Lord is present to us under the form of bread and wine, saying to us, 'This is my body ... This is my blood'. In coming to the Lord in the Eucharist we are coming to someone greater than Jonah or Solomon. The Lord is present to us in other ways also. We take his presence seriously by responding to his call and following in his way, as the people of Nineveh responded to Jonah's call. Having been graced by the Lord's presence, we are to respond to his presence by living in a graced way.

## 14 March, Thursday, First Week of Lent

*Matthew 7:7–12*

The teaching of Jesus in the Sermon on the Mount is very demanding. We might be tempted to get discouraged by its challenging call. It is in that demanding context, towards the end of the Sermon on the Mount, that today's gospel reading is to be found. Jesus encourages us to seek God's help, without which we will not be able to live out Jesus' teaching. We are to come before God in prayer, asking, seeking and knocking. We are to do this not just occasionally but repeatedly. The sense of what Jesus says is, 'keep on asking', 'keep on seeking', 'keep on knocking'. We are to keep looking for the help that only God can give. It is God who enables us to live in the way Jesus calls us to live, as God desires us to live. At the end of his first letter to the Thessalonians, Paul prays, 'May the God of peace sanctify you entirely', and then immediately declares, 'The one who calls you is faithful, and he will do this'. God, who calls us through Jesus, will make it possible for us to answer the call. Our response to the Lord's call is always a graced response. We need to acknowledge our dependence on God for the strength to live according to God's will for our lives as revealed by Jesus. That is why we need to keep on asking God, to keep on seeking God and to keep on knocking on God's door.

## 15 March, Friday, First Week of Lent

*Matthew 5:20–26*

Today's gospel reading comes from the beginning of Jesus' Sermon on the Mount. Throughout this Sermon, Jesus is presenting us with what he calls a virtue that goes deeper than that of the scribes and Pharisees. In other words, the kind of virtue or virtuous life that Jesus is presenting in the Sermon, while based on the Jewish Law, goes further than is called for by the Jewish Law. We are all familiar with the fifth of the Ten Commandments in the Jewish Law: 'You must not kill'. In today's gospel reading, Jesus takes that commandment and goes beyond it. He recognises that prior to the action of taking someone's life, there is a set of attitudes and emotions that underlie this action. The underlying emotion is often anger. The underlying attitude is often one of disrespect for the person, expressed, for example, in labelling someone a 'fool', or worse. It is this kind of emotion and attitude that concerns Jesus in today's gospel reading. Anger is a normal human emotion. We cannot avoid it. Sometimes our anger is very justified. Jesus himself was angry at how the Temple in Jerusalem was being run, yet he was very aware of how destructive anger can be. It can often find expression in speaking disrespectfully to others or about others, or in acting disrespectfully towards them. The ultimate disrespectful action towards another person is to take their life away. Today's gospel reading encourages us to become more aware of the emotion of anger in our lives and of its potential to be destructive of others. It is an emotion we can bring to prayer, asking the Lord to help us to express it in ways that serve God's purposes for our world.

## 16 March, Saturday, First Week of Lent

*Matthew 5:43–48*

We tend to use the terms 'perfect', 'perfection' and 'perfectionist' in a very particular way. When we say of someone that he or she is a 'perfectionist' we mean that they want everything to be right in every respect. There must be no room for mistake or error of any kind. We tend to think that perfectionists can be difficult to live with or work with because they are so demanding of themselves and of others. When Jesus uses the term 'perfect' in today's gospel reading, he uses it in a rather different sense. When Jesus says to his disciples 'be perfect just as your heavenly Father is perfect', he is using the term 'perfect' in a different way from how we tend to use it. Sometimes there is more than one version of a saying of Jesus in the Gospels. Today's gospel reading is from Matthew, but Luke's version of that saying of Jesus goes as follows: 'Be merciful, just as your Father is merciful'. God's perfection consists in his merciful love. To be perfect as God is perfect is to be merciful in the way that God is merciful. A merciful person has a different connotation for us than a perfectionist. The merciful love that Jesus calls for is a love without limits. It is an inclusive love to the point of including those who are our enemies, those who wish us ill, who seek to damage us. Jesus declares that this is nothing less than a divine love. We might ask, 'How could Jesus ask humans to love in a divine way?' We need a divine resource to love in a divine way, and that divine resource is the Holy Spirit. Paul refers to the Holy Spirit as the Spirit of God's love. It is only the Spirit who can empower us to love as God loves, to be merciful as God is merciful, to be perfect as God is perfect.

## 18 March, Monday, Second Week of Lent

*Luke 6:36–38*

There is a striking tone of 'confession' in today's first reading from the Book of Daniel. It was in fact a communal prayer of confession. The whole people are acknowledging their sinfulness before God. 'We have sinned, we have done wrong, we have acted wickedly, we have betrayed your commandments … we have not listened to the voice of the Lord our God'. This public act of confession on the part of the people of Israel is one that we, the Church, can easily make our own. We know that we too have failed, as individuals and, especially, as a community of believers. Yet, it is to such individuals and to such a community that the Lord issues the challenging invitation in today's gospel reading: 'Be compassionate as your Father is compassionate'. Jesus is calling on us to be nothing less than God-like. He knows of what we are made; he knows that we are prone to sin, and, yet, he keeps calling us towards the highest ideals. He continues to give us a calling in keeping with our identity as people made in the image of God. He pays us the complement of putting a noble calling before us, in spite of our repeated failures. He also gives us the means to respond to that calling, by pouring the Holy Spirit into our hearts. He gives us a great resource as well as a great calling. We are invited to draw on that resource in a special way this Lent so that we may be faithful to our calling.

## 19 March, Tuesday, Feast of St Joseph

*Luke 2:41–52*

Luke's portrayal of the twelve-year-old Jesus sitting among the doctors of the Law in the Temple is a striking one. It doesn't say that Jesus was teaching these doctors of the Law, rather, he was listening to them and asking questions. He was receptive to what they were saying. No doubt Jesus was also receptive to what Joseph said to him.

In the Jewish family, the father was the one responsible for passing on the religious tradition to the children. Joseph may not have been a doctor of the Law, but he was a teacher within his own home. Yet, the gospel reading suggests that, at twelve years of age, Jesus was moving on from receiving the wisdom of his superiors to taking his own path in life. Having travelled with his family from Nazareth to Jerusalem for the feast of Passover, he decided not to travel back with them, without informing any member of his extended family. Mary and Joseph decided to head back to Jerusalem where they eventually found him in the Temple. Their disappointment in Jesus and the distress he caused them is very evident in the question Mary put to him. Yet, his answer to their question caused them a different kind of distress. 'Did you not know that I must be busy with my Father's affairs?' They didn't understand what he meant. By 'my Father's affairs', the boy Jesus was not referring to his father Joseph but to his heavenly Father, God. If Jesus was learning from the doctors of the Law, Joseph had his own lesson to learn from his young son. He was beginning to realise that his influence on his son would have to take second place to God's influence. He and his wife, Mary, would have to learn to let Jesus go to God's purpose for his life. We can learn from Joseph that gentle art of letting go, of surrendering those we cherish to God's purpose for their lives, even though it may leave us with a great sense of loss. Joseph learned to allow God to be God in his own life and in the life of his Son. We pray for something of that same generosity of spirit that Joseph clearly had.

## 20 March, Wednesday, Second Week of Lent
*Matthew 20:17–28*

Mothers always want the best for their children. In today's reading, the mother of James and John asks Jesus for the best places in his kingdom for her two sons. She interceded with Jesus on behalf of her sons. However, her request, her prayer, was not one that Jesus could respond to. Jesus did not respond to every request that was made of him; not every prayer we make is heard. Instead of responding to the mother's request, Jesus made a request of his own to her two sons: 'Can you drink the cup that I am going to drink?' Jesus was asking James and John if they were ready to follow him, even though it would mean travelling the way of the Cross. The question that Jesus asked James and John is one that he addresses to us all. He asks how committed we are to his way of life, to the values he lived by and died for. Like the mother of James and John, we often ask the Lord for something in prayer. Today's gospel reminds us that the Lord also asks us for something; he asks us for nothing less than ourselves; he asks us to give ourselves to him as he gave himself to us on the cross. What the Lord asks of us should shape our prayer of petition to him.

## 21 March, Thursday, Second Week of Lent
*Luke 16:19–31*

There is one point where the description of Lazarus in today's parable overlaps with the depiction of the rebellious son in the parable of the Prodigal Son. It is said to Lazarus that he '*longed to fill himself* with the scraps that fell from the rich man's table'. It is said of the rebellious son that he '*longed to fill himself* with the pods that the pigs were eating'. Both men were destitute – Lazarus, through no apparent fault of his own, and the son because of his own selfish decision to leave his family and head out to spend his inheritance on himself. There was one crucial difference between the two men. Lazarus had nowhere to go. He sat at the gate of a rich man, but he could never get beyond the gate. The rebellious son did have somewhere to go. He could go home. When he drew near to the gate of his wealthy father, his father was moved with compassion for him, ran to him, put his arms around him, kissed him and brought him into the house where a feast was prepared for him. There was no feast for Lazarus, not even the scraps that fell from the rich man's table. Even though Lazarus and the rebellious son had much in common, the people they looked to for help, both rich men, were polar opposites. The self-absorption of the rich man in today's parable stands in sharp contrast to the compassionate generosity of the rich father in the parable of the Prodigal Son. The rich man is an all too human figure; the father is a God-like figure. When we listen to these two parables in relation to each other, they call on us, whenever we are faced with the broken and destitute of our world, to become less like the rich man in today's parable and more like the father in the parable of the Prodigal Son.

## 22 March, Friday, Second Week of Lent

*Matthew 21:33–43, 45–46*

The experience of rejection is to be found in both readings today. Joseph is rejected by his brothers, who were jealous of Joseph because their father loved him more than any of his other sons. They intended to kill Joseph, but, in the end, they threw him into a well and sold him on to some foreigners who were heading to Egypt. Joseph, the rejected one, rose to a prominent position in Egypt. He went on to become the saviour of his brothers. At a time of great famine in the land of Canaan, later the land of Israel, his brothers had to go to Egypt for food and it was Joseph who was in charge of Egypt's food supply at the time. The story of Joseph is an expression of the image that Jesus uses in today's gospel reading, drawn from one of the psalms: 'it was the stone rejected by the builders that became the keystone'. The parable that Jesus tells is also a story of rejection. The landowner sends his servants to collect the vine harvest from his tenants, and the servants are rejected and killed by the tenants. Finally, the landowner sends his son to collect the harvest, fully expecting that his son would be treated with respect. On the contrary, he is rejected in the most brutal way, thrown out of the vineyard and killed. Jesus must have seen himself in the person of the landowner's son. He was thrown out of the city of Jerusalem and crucified outside the city walls. Yet, like Joseph, but to an even greater extent, this rejected son became the saviour of those who rejected him. The stone rejected by the builders became the keystone. The crucified Jesus rose from the dead and became the keystone of a new community of believers which was open to all, including those who rejected him. Both readings suggest that God is always at work to bring good out of the suffering people experience because of the hostility of others. God works in a life-giving way in even the most unpromising of situations. This gives us hope as we try to come to terms with our own painful and difficult experiences of rejection and hostility.

## 23 March, Saturday, Second Week of Lent

*Luke 15:1–5, 11–32*

Today's gospel reading gives us one of the most memorable of Jesus' parables. It has inspired artists through the ages. The moment in the story that artists tend to depict is the meeting between the younger rebellious son and his father. The memorable artistic depiction by Rembrandt has the son on his knees before his father who has his hands open in welcome. It is the moment in the story that speaks not just to artists but to all of us. Jesus' depiction of the father in this story is really a portrayal of God the Father, as well as being a portrayal of his own ministry. Jesus portrays a God who welcomes those who turn back to him when they stray. Indeed, Jesus reveals a God who seeks out the lost and the straying, just as the Father sought out his lost son by running to him while the son was still a long way off. Jesus was saying to his critics, 'if God is like the father in this story, then I must seek out tax collectors and sinners and eat with them'. Yet the story does not end with that memorable moment of the father's welcome of his rebellious son. There is a second son. He is the dutiful son, but his sense of duty has also made him resentful. Why, he must have wondered, should his father show such hospitable love to a son who has brought shame and dishonour on the family? The subsequent meeting between the father and this older son is a much tenser affair than the father's earlier meeting with his younger son. It is the same father reaching out in love towards a son. Whereas the younger son, in his brokenness, received his father's love, we are left to wonder whether the older son, in the end, received the father's love. The parable suggests that God the Father's love is never in doubt. What is in doubt is our openness to receive this love which transcends all human loves.

## 25 March, Monday, Feast of the Annunciation
*Luke 1:26–38*

For the evangelist Luke, who gives us the story of the annunciation of the angel Gabriel to Mary, this moment is the beginning of the Gospel. The Gospel is proclaimed for the first time by Gabriel to Mary. Gabriel announces to Mary the good news that she is to conceive by the power of the Holy Spirit and give birth to Jesus, who will be called Son of God. He will be a king who will reign over Israel and his kingdom will have no end. Mary, according to Luke, is the first to hear the Gospel. She is the first to have the opportunity to respond to the preached Gospel. According to Luke, after some understandable perplexity and questioning, she responded with all her being to the word of the Gospel that Gabriel preached to her: 'I am the servant of the Lord, let what you have said be done to me', or, in another translation, 'let it be with me according to your word'. Luke invites us to look to Mary as the one who made not only the first response to the preached Gospel, but also the most complete response. Every time the Gospel is preached, every time we hear the Lord's word, we can do no better than say with Mary, 'let it be with me according to your word'. She allowed her life to be shaped by God's word, by God's will and purpose as expressed in the word of the Gospel. In this way, she anticipated her adult son's response to God's word, to God's will and purpose. Jesus' response is expressed in today's second reading: 'God, here I am! I am coming to obey your will'. Mary followed her Son before he was conceived; we are called to follow him as risen Lord in the same complete way that she did.

## 26 March, Tuesday, Third Week of Lent

*Matthew 18:21–35*

The first reading today is one of the great prayers for forgiveness in the Jewish Scriptures. The prayer reflects the experience of exile, after the overthrow of the king and the destruction of Jerusalem and its Temple. 'We have at this time no leader, no prophet, no prince, no holocaust, no sacrifice, no oblation, no incense, no place where we can offer you the first fruits'. The Temple, where people traditionally looked for and received God's forgiveness, is gone. Yet the person praying is not despondent. He or she may not be able to offer sacrifices in the Temple, but can offer another, more significant sacrifice, which doesn't require a Temple, namely 'the contrite soul, the humbled spirit'. This sacrifice of a contrite soul and humble spirit gives the person praying confidence that God's forgiveness will be forthcoming: 'Those who put their trust in you will not be disappointed'. The mood of this prayer is very close to the message of Jesus. He came to reassure people, as God's Son, that those who put their trust in God's mercy, those who look to God for forgiveness with a contrite spirit and heart, will receive God's mercy in abundance. God does not withhold his mercy from those who seek it. That message finds expression in story form in the parable Jesus speaks in today's gospel reading. The servant who owed an unpayable debt to his master has that debt cancelled because the servant pleaded with the master with a contrite soul and heart. If the first part of the parable has that consoling message, the second part has a more challenging message. We are to give to others, as we have received from God. We are to forgive others, when forgiveness is asked of us, just as God forgives us when we ask to be forgiven.

## 27 March, Wednesday, Third Week of Lent

*Matthew 5:17–19*

Jesus was often critical of the religious tradition to which he belonged. He had heated arguments with the religious leaders of his own tradition. Yet, he did not reject his own Jewish religious tradition, even though it was not perfect. In today's gospel reading he declares that he has come not to abolish the Jewish law or the teaching of the Jewish prophets but to bring them all to completion. He wanted to renew his own religious tradition rather than cast it aside or walk away from it. He came to prune what needed pruning in his religious tradition and to bring what was good there to completion. That remains the work of the risen Lord in the Church today. In spite of its failings, the Lord does not reject the Church, just as he did not reject his disciples who failed him. Rather, he works to renew the Church, to prune away what needs pruning in its traditions and to bring what is good there to completion. He does that work in and through all of us, the members of his body. He needs us to be willing instruments of the Lord's renewing work in his Church and in the world. If that is to happen, we need to be open to the Lord's renewing work in our own lives. He works to prune what needs pruning in our lives and to bring to completion what is good there.

## 28 March, Thursday, Third Week of Lent

*Luke 11:14–23*

In today's first reading, God, speaking through the prophet Jeremiah, complains that his people have not been listening to him; they have not been paying attention to what he has been saying to them. Listening to the Lord is always at the core of our relationship with him. In the words of today's responsorial psalm, 'O that, today, you would listen to his voice'. In the gospel reading, Jesus encounters the same resistance that God complains of in the first reading. On this occasion, the resistance takes the form of a refusal to see rather than a refusal to listen. Jesus had been healing the sick. Some of the people were amazed at what Jesus was doing, seeing it for what it was, a sign of God's presence. However, there were others who saw what Jesus was doing as the work of Satan rather than the work of God. 'It is through Beelzebul, the prince of devils, that he casts out devils'. They looked at what Jesus was doing but they did not see it for what it really was. Instead, what they saw was the polar opposite of what it actually was. When it comes to our relationship with the Lord, seeing is as important as listening. The Lord is always engaging with us, communicating with us, in different ways. He speaks to us and he shows himself to us in a whole variety of ways. We constantly need a listening ear and a seeing eye in the Lord's regard. We need ears and eyes that are open to the many ways in which the Lord communicates with us. We might pray for such open eyes and ears this Lent.

## 29 March, Friday, Third Week of Lent

*Mark 12:28–34*

In today's gospel reading, a scribe asks Jesus an important question, 'What is the first of all the commandments?' He wanted Jesus to help him find the one commandment that really mattered amid the 600 or so commandments in the Jewish Law. We all find ourselves asking at times, 'What is it that really matters in life?' 'What is really worth pursuing?' Jesus answered the scribe's question by giving him the two most important commandments, not just the first but the second as well. What these two commandments have in common is the call to love. They differ in the object of our love and in the totality of our love. In the first commandment it is God who is to be loved; in the second it is the neighbour. It is only God who is to be loved with all our heart, soul, mind and strength. Jesus declares to the scribe that what matters most in the Jewish tradition is love, the love of God with all one's being, overflowing into a love of those whom God loves, the neighbour. When the scribe agrees with Jesus' answer, Jesus declares that this scribe is not far from the kingdom of God. Any Jew who lives by these two commandments of love is on the cusp of the kingdom of God that Jesus came to proclaim. Love is at the heart of the Jewish faith and it is at the heart of the Gospel that Jesus preached and lived. Love, as Jesus embodied it, is at the heart of our Christian faith today. Pope Francis's 2016 apostolic exhortation is entitled *The Joy of Love*. The essence of our faith is love, God's love for us in Jesus, our love for God in return, overflowing into a love of all whom God loves, all human life.

## 30 March, Saturday, Third Week of Lent

*Luke 18:9–14*

In both readings today, there is a contrast between what God wants and what people bring him. In the first reading, the people bring sacrifices and burnt offerings to God in the Temple, but in response God, speaking through the prophet Hosea, says, 'What I want is love, not sacrifice; knowledge of God, not holocausts'. God wants the love of his people, a love that finds expression in the love of others. In the parable Jesus speaks in the gospel reading, the Pharisee lists what he brings to God. He fasts twice a week; he pays tithes on all he gets;

he is not grasping, unjust or adulterous. All of that is true. However, what he brings to God is not accompanied by love, in particular, love of others. While telling God in prayer what he offers him, he is, at that very moment, looking down on a fellow worshipper, the tax collector. Indeed, he is despising him. He hasn't been listening to God's word spoken through the prophet Hosea: 'What I want is love'. His prayer is not the kind of prayer that God wants. The prayer of the tax collector is much simpler but more authentic, 'God, be merciful to me, a sinner'. There is no lack of love towards others in his prayer. His focus is on his own failure to do what God wants, his sin. In the language of today's responsorial psalm, he prays with a 'contrite spirit, a humbled, contrite heart'. This is one expression of what God does want. 'A humbled, contrite heart you will not spurn'. We can all make our own that simple prayer of the tax collector, 'God, be merciful to me, a sinner'. We can pray that prayer in the knowledge that such a prayer is always acceptable to God. It always corresponds to what God wants.

## 1 April, Monday, Fourth Week of Lent
*John 12:1–11*

We are familiar with the saying, 'seeing is believing'. The disciple Thomas in John's Gospel refused to believe unless he saw the risen Lord. In today's gospel reading, Jesus says to the court official from Capernaum, 'So you will not believe unless you see signs and portents'. Yet, this court official turned out to be someone who did not need to see signs and portents to believe. He pleaded with Jesus to come to his home and cure his son. When Jesus said to him, 'Go home, your son will live', the man believed the word of Jesus, without waiting to see whether or not his son was healed. He believed without seeing. He believed on the basis of the word of Jesus alone. The faith of this royal official is representative of the faith of us all.

We, too, believe without having seen. We have not seen with our eyes the signs and wonders that God worked through Jesus during Jesus' public ministry. Unlike Thomas, we have not seen the risen Lord with our eyes. Like the court official in today's gospel reading, we believe on the basis of Jesus' word to us. Our faith is based on the Lord's presence to us in his word. The Lord's presence to us in the sacraments, especially the Eucharist, is also foundational to our faith. Yet, without the Lord's word to us, we would not be aware of his presence to us in the sacraments and in other ways. Today, we give thanks for the great blessing of the Lord's word. Like the court official who believed Jesus' word and then started on his way, we are invited to allow the Lord's word to guide and direct us on our way.

## 2 April, Tuesday, Fourth Week of Lent

*John 5:1–3, 5–16*

The Dead Sea in the Judean wilderness is a very strange sea. Its salt content is so great that nothing can live in it. The Dead Sea is referred to in today's first reading from the prophet Ezekiel, although not by name. The water that pours out of the Temple in Jerusalem is described as flowing 'east down to the Arabah and the sea', that is, down to the Judean wilderness and the Dead Sea. The impact of this water from the Temple on the Dead Sea is very striking: 'it makes its waters wholesome … all living creatures teeming in it will live'. In a very imaginative way, Ezekiel is declaring that God's presence in the Temple is life-giving for all. God is a God of the living. In John's Gospel, from which our gospel reading is taken, Jesus is portrayed as the new Temple of God, where God is uniquely present in a life-giving way. In the gospel reading, we find Jesus giving a new lease of life to a paralysed man whose paralysis had lasted for thirty-eight years. The real mission of Jesus in John's Gospel is to bring people to a share in God's own life, the life from above, eternal life. If that is to happen, people need to believe in him. Jesus declares more than once in John's Gospel that those who believe in him already share in the life of heaven, the life of God. To believe is to allow Jesus to draw us to himself. It is not clear whether the man Jesus healed in today's gospel came to believe in him. After his healing, he appears to betray Jesus to the Jewish authorities, who then proceed to plan Jesus' death. Yet, even from the cross, especially from the cross, Jesus continues to draw us to himself so that we may believe in him and, thereby, come to share in God's own life.

## 3 April, Wednesday, Fourth Week of Lent

*John 5:17–30*

One of the most striking images of God as mother is to be found at the end of today's first reading. 'Does a woman forget her baby at the breast, or fail to cherish the child of her womb? Yet, even if these forget, I will never forget you.' A mother's love for the child of her womb is tender and life-giving. A mother loves her child as she loves herself because for nine months her child was an integral part of herself. Speaking through the prophet Isaiah, God declares that his love for his people is even stronger than a mother's love for her child. What an extraordinary statement! Surely the Jewish Scriptures come close here to that profound declaration in the first letter of John, 'God is Love'. In today's gospel reading, Jesus speaks of God as 'my Father' in a way that is typical of this fourth Gospel. Yet, it is the Father as life-giver that Jesus highlights in speaking of God: 'the Father raises the dead and gives them life … For the Father, who is the source of life, has made the Son the source of life'. Jesus is saying that such is the communion between himself and God that he is as much the source of life as God. Jesus is the life-giver. He came that we may have life to the full. This 'life' in its fullness will only be ours in eternity, but we can begin to live with this life here and now, insofar as we listen to the words of the Son and live by them. Whenever we allow the Lord's word to make a home in us, shaping our lives, we will not only draw life from him, but our lives will become life-giving for others.

## 4 April, Thursday, Fourth Week of Lent

*John 5:31–47*

In today's gospel reading, Jesus refers to John the Baptist as a lamp alight and shining and declares that for a time people were content to enjoy the light that he gave. Jesus will go on to say in the Gospel of John, 'I am the light of the world. Whoever follows me will never walk in darkness but will have the light of life'. John the Baptist may be a lamp who gives off some light, but only Jesus is the true light. People like John the Baptist have brought something of God's light to others, but Jesus alone is the light of God. We all need lamps as we go through life, people like John the Baptist who reveal the light of God's presence to us in some way. We are all called to be a lamp in that sense. If we are to be a lamp for others, we need to keep turning towards Jesus, the true light. This activity of turning to Jesus, the true light, lasts a lifetime. In various ways we can turn away from this light of God that shines so brilliantly through the person of Jesus. We can turn towards the darkness, in some form or other, just as in today's first reading the people of Israel turned from God and worshipped a golden calf that had been made by human hands. This is the human story; it is often our personal story. When that happens, we need to keep turning back towards Jesus, the true light who is always turned towards us. Only then can we live out our calling to be a lamp alight and shining. When we keep turning towards the light, we can become a light for others.

## 5 April, Friday, Fourth Week of Lent

*John 7:1–2, 10, 25–30*

We often ask others what part of the country they are from or, if they live in the city, what part of the city they are from. We sense that if we know where people are from, we have information that might help us to understand them. It is not surprising that people often return to where they are from, if only to visit it. They know they are getting in touch with their roots. In the gospel reading, the people of Jerusalem say of Jesus, 'We all know where he comes from'. They were aware that he came from a very different kind of place from Jerusalem, a small village far to the north of Jerusalem, in the region of Galilee. Jesus acknowledges that, in one sense, the people of Jerusalem know where he comes from, but, in a deeper sense, they do not know where he comes from. As Jesus declares, 'there is one who sent me, and I really come from him, and you do not know him'. Jesus speaks as one who, ultimately, comes from God, and the people of Jerusalem do not know God as well as they think. It is as if Jesus were saying, 'my place of upbringing does not explain who I am'. That is true of us all. We cannot be fully understood on the basis of our place of origin. It is even truer of Jesus.

He was not simply the son of a carpenter from Nazareth in Galilee. He was also the Son of God. If there is more to each of us than meets the eye and ear, that is true to a much greater extent of Jesus. There is such a depth to the mystery of Jesus' identity that we are always only coming to know him. Part of the adventure of faith is coming to know the Lord more and more. I have always liked the prayer associated with a thirteenth-century English bishop: 'O most merciful redeemer, friend and brother, may I know thee more clearly, love thee more dearly and follow thee more nearly, day by day'.

## 6 April, Saturday, Fourth Week of Lent

*John 7:40–52*

Several questions are asked by a variety of people in today's gospel reading. The question that stands out for me is the one asked by Nicodemus: 'Surely the Law does not allow us to pass judgment on a man without giving him a hearing and discovering what he is about?' It raises the question for us all, 'On what basis do we make a judgement about someone?' Do we make a judgement after giving someone a hearing with an open heart and mind and after seeking to discover what he or she is really about?' It seems that Nicodemus's fellow Pharisees were ready to make a judgement about Jesus without giving him a proper hearing or making a serious effort to discover what he is really about. Nicodemus was prepared to stand up against the emerging consensus among his peers, a consensus that wasn't well thought through or based on a genuine search for truth. Nicodemus's independence of mind and spirit earned him the dismissive comment, 'Are you a Galilean too?' From the perspective of Jerusalem, where many of Nicodemus' peers were based, Galilee was a marginal area whose residents could be dismissed as rabble who knew nothing about God's Law. The figure of Nicodemus encourages us to think for ourselves, especially when it comes to our faith. He invites us to give Jesus a hearing and to discover what he is about, even when such a path is unfashionable. When it comes to witnessing to our faith or to our emerging faith, as was the case with Nicodemus, we will often need something of his independence of mind and spirit, something of his courage.

## 8 April, Monday, Fifth Week of Lent

*John 8:1–11*

There are three characters in today's gospel reading, Jesus, the woman and a group of male experts in the Jewish Law. The group of men brought the woman to Jesus to test him. They were using her against him. It was Jesus who was in their sights rather than the woman they claimed was caught in the act of adultery. They were of the view that if Jesus was to be faithful to God's Law, he should condemn the woman. If he didn't condemn her it would confirm their view of Jesus as someone who broke God's Law and was, therefore, a sinner. Jesus did not fall into their trap. He gave himself time by writing distractingly on the ground with his finger. When the group persisted, Jesus issued that striking challenge: 'If there is one of you who has not sinned, let him be the first to throw a stone at her'. They had brought the woman to Jesus as a sinner; they were of the view that Jesus himself was a sinner. Now Jesus faced them with the reality of their own sin. Their walking away was their acknowledgement that there was no one among them who had not sinned. We are all sinners; we just sin in different ways. We can never set ourselves up as the moral superior of others. Jesus did not condemn the woman, yet he did call her to live in a new way. 'Go away, and don't sin any more'. Earlier in John's Gospel Jesus said, 'God did not send the Son into the world to condemn the world, but in order that the world might be saved through him'. The Lord's instinct is not to condemn, but to call us and empower us to take the path that will lead us to a share in God's own life, both now in this earthly life and in eternity.

## 9 April, Tuesday, Fifth Week of Lent

*John 8:21–30*

In the gospel reading, people ask Jesus the question, 'Who are you?' It is a question that is often asked about Jesus in the gospels, in one form or another. 'Who is this?' There was something about Jesus that left people wondering as to his real identity. There is something of a mystery to every human person. When it comes to the person of Jesus, that sense of mystery is greatly magnified. In his answer, Jesus suggests that the question, 'Who are you?' can only be answered when he is lifted up on the cross. 'When you have lifted up the Son of Man, then you will know that I am he'. When he is lifted up on the cross, Jesus reveals himself most fully. He reveals himself as God among us. In the language of Paul, the death of Jesus reveals God 'for us'. The death of Jesus reveals God's unconditional love for sinners. The early Church came to recognise the paradox of the cross. At this hour of greatest darkness, the light of God's loving presence shone most brightly. That is why we will venerate the cross on Good Friday. With the eyes of faith, we see beyond the human sin that crucified Jesus, we see beyond Jesus' great physical suffering. We recognise a divine light that the darkness cannot overcome, a divine love that human hatred cannot extinguish. It is only when Jesus is lifted up on the cross, and in glory, that we can answer the question, 'Who is this?'

## 10 April, Wednesday, Fifth Week of Lent
*John 8:31–42*

In today's gospel reading, Jesus speaks of himself as the source of true freedom. He says, 'If you make my word your home ... you will learn the truth and the truth will make you free'; and, again, 'If the Son makes you free, you will be free indeed'. Some people see religion, and Christianity in particular, as a threat to freedom, as undermining of human freedom. Yet, Jesus declares that if we make his word our home we will be free. If we allow our lives to be shaped by the word of Jesus we will experience what Paul in his letter to the Romans calls 'the glorious freedom of the children of God'. If we allow the Lord's word to shape our lives we will begin to love one another as the Lord has loved us and, then, we will be truly free with the freedom of the Holy Spirit.

In the teaching of Jesus, and in the New Testament as a whole, the free person is the loving person, the person who is free to love as Jesus loved. In his second letter to the Corinthians Paul declares, 'where the Spirit of the Lord is, there is freedom', and the fruit of the Spirit is love. Jesus was the freest person who ever lived because he was the most loving person, the fullest revelation of God's love. He calls us to share in his freedom through the power of the Holy Spirit.

## 11 April, Thursday, Fifth Week of Lent
*John 8:51–59*
In today's gospel reading from the fourth Gospel, Jesus is portrayed as making an extraordinary claim for himself: 'I tell you most solemnly, before Abraham ever was, I Am'. Jesus' statement can be understood against the background of the opening verse of this gospel, 'In the beginning was the Word, and the Word was with God, and the Word was God'. The evangelist is claiming that Jesus, the Word of God, was with God in that mysterious moment before the beginning of creation. If that is true, then Jesus is obviously before Abraham ever was.

The fourth Gospel makes claims for Jesus that go beyond those of any of the other three Gospels. It is the last and most recent one to be written and it represents the fruit of much reflection as to the identity of Jesus. It is perhaps not surprising that this Gospel ends with the statement that if everything Jesus did were written down, 'the world itself could not contain the books that would be written'. In other words, there is more to Jesus than a world full of books could express.

We might be tempted to think that there is less to Jesus than the Gospels give us. Perhaps they have exaggerated who Jesus is. However, it is certainly the conviction of the fourth evangelist, and probably of the other three evangelists, that their written Gospel is only a small window on to a mystery that cannot be fully expressed in words. Jesus is even more attractive, more mysterious, than the Gospels present him. We will only come to know the Lord in all his fullness when we encounter him in eternity. In the meantime, we are thankful to God for the Gospels, which give us such wonderful access to the Lord, God's Word in human form.

## 12 April, Friday, Fifth Week of Lent

*John 10:31–42*

As we draw near to Holy Week, the gospel readings highlight the growing hostility to Jesus. At the beginning of today's gospel, Jesus' opponents fetch stones to stone him. At the end of the reading, they want to arrest him. Jesus seems perplexed by their hostility, 'I have done many good works for you to see … for which of these are you stoning me?' Violence can often be mindless and irrational, as we know only too well. On this occasion, Jesus was able to escape from those who would do him harm. However, the time would come when they would have him arrested and put to death. In spite of the many good works Jesus did, he was put to death. In the first reading, Jeremiah speaks out of a similar experience to Jesus. He did God's work, he proclaimed God's word, and, for that, he was denounced by people who wanted to bring about his downfall. Jeremiah's reaction to this undeserved hostility from his opponents was a very human one. He prays to God, 'Let me see the vengeance you will take on them'. We could never imagine such a prayer on the lips of Jesus. Rather, Jesus revealed God's love even to his enemies. He washed the feet of his betrayer, Judas. He prayed for his executioners, asking God to forgive them. Jesus' passion and death, even more than his life, revealed a love that was constant even in the face of hostility and rejection. Jesus' passion and death reveals God's love for all humanity, a quality of love that is very different from any human love. That is why the Friday on which Jesus'passion and death is remembered is called Good Friday, and why the story of Jesus' passion and death is part of the larger Gospel story. It is gospel, good news, for us all.

## 13 April, Saturday, Fifth Week of Lent

*John 11:45–56*

In today's gospel reading, Caiaphas, the high priest, speaks at a meeting of the Jewish ruling council. The high priest at that time was closely associated with the Roman ruling power. The Roman governor gave the high priest a certain autonomy in running the affairs of the people, provided he was loyal to Rome and ensured that the people remained loyal. Caiaphas would have been concerned to ensure that the Romans were kept on side, so as to maintain his own position.

We can hear that concern in the words of Caiaphas in the gospel reading: 'If we let him [Jesus] go on in this way everybody will believe in him, and the Romans will come and destroy the Holy Place and our nation'. If Jesus starts to gain a large following, especially in Jerusalem, the Romans will take action and everyone will suffer. This leads Caiaphas to state his pragmatic solution that 'it is better for one man to die for the people, than for the whole nation to be destroyed'. The individual can be sacrificed to the perceived good of the collective. This is a way of reasoning that has always been with us and remains with us today. Individuals don't really matter; what matters is the nation, the people, the collective, the state, the institution. In the ministry of Jesus, the individual mattered a great deal. He related to each person with respect for their uniqueness and individuality.

It is above all the individual human being who is precious in God's sight and needs cherishing by others. The good of the collective can never be pursued at the expense of the individuals who make it up. Jesus was put to death for the people, to preserve the perceived good of the nation, to keep the status quo. For the evangelist, the irony is that Jesus did die for the people, but not in the sense Caiaphas intended. He died out of love for all, for each one, to gather together into one family of faith the scattered children of God. We are all members of that new family that was formed through the death of Jesus. As members of that family in which Jesus is our brother, we are called to relate to others with the same care for the individual as Jesus showed.

## 15 April, Monday in Holy Week

*John 12:1–11*

The story of Holy Week begins with the lovely scene in today's gospel reading. In a week when so many men let Jesus down or, worse, inflict terrible violence on him, a woman, Mary, the sister of Lazarus, shows him great respect and love. Jesus would go on to wash the feet of his disciples. Mary goes even further. She anoints the feet of Jesus with very costly ointment and wipes them with her hair, and the scent of her ointment fills the whole house. The love Jesus would show his disciples, she shows to him. To that extent, she is very much a Jesus figure. She is a beacon of light at the beginning of a very dark week for Jesus. Even though Jesus gave himself in love to all, he experienced deadly hostility from many. In a similar way, Mary's act of extravagant love for Jesus was met with hostility by one person in particular, Judas Iscariot. Judas saw Mary's gesture as a waste of money that could have been given to the poor. Jesus, however, saw it differently. He experienced Mary's gesture as an anointing to strengthen him for his passion and death that was imminent: 'She had to keep this scent for the day of my burial'. The scent that Mary's gesture created was the tangible expression of her faith in and love for Jesus, even in the face of hostility. We can learn from Mary to remain faithful and loving, even when the expression of our faith and love is misunderstood and criticised. In his second letter to the Corinthians, Paul says, 'we are the aroma of Christ to God'. Like Mary, the sister of Lazarus, we are to convey something of the aroma, the scent of Christ, by our faith in Jesus and the love of others that flows from our faith.

## 16 April, Tuesday in Holy Week

*John 13:21–33, 36–38*

Two of the disciples who gathered with Jesus for his Last Supper are mentioned by name in today's gospel reading, Judas and Simon Peter. Both of these disciples failed Jesus in the hour of his passion and death. At the beginning of the gospel reading, Jesus says, referring to Judas, 'I tell you most solemnly, one of you will betray me'. At the end of the gospel reading, Jesus says directly to Peter, 'I tell you most solemnly, before the cock crows you will have disowned me three times'. There is one significant difference between Judas and Peter. Judas is portrayed in the gospel reading as having already decided to betray Jesus. Having taken the bread from Jesus, he went out on his treacherous business into the night. Peter, on the other hand, had no intention of disowning Jesus. He says to Jesus, 'I will lay down my life for you'. His intention, his desire, was good. His heart was in the right place. It could be said of Peter that his spirit was willing but his flesh was weak, whereas it would be true to say of Judas that both his spirit and his flesh were weak. It is Peter more than Judas with whom we might find ourselves identifying. We know from our own experience that we do not always follow through on our good intentions. We don't always act out of our better desires. We want to be faithful to the Lord in all we say and do, but there are times when we go astray, when we disown the Lord. At such times, we need to remind ourselves that there is always a way back, as there was for Peter, when the risen Lord asked him, 'Do you love me?'

## 17 April, Wednesday in Holy Week

*Matthew 26:14–25*

There was light and darkness present at the Last Supper. Tomorrow, Holy Thursday, we reflect on the light that shone at that meal, through the loving actions of Jesus in washing the feet of his disciples and in giving them the gift of the Eucharist. In today's gospel reading the darkness is to the fore. While they are eating, Jesus solemnly announces, 'one of you is about to betray me'. As if to highlight the great tragedy of such an act, Jesus further specifies that his betrayer is 'someone who has dipped his hand into the dish with me'. In sharing the Passover Meal with his disciples, Jesus was entering into communion with them in a very solemn way. Yet, someone who shared in this communion was about to act in a way that would shatter the very communion being celebrated. Indeed, all of the disciples would soon break communion with Jesus, and Peter would do so in a more public way, denying Jesus three times before others. Judas's act of betraying Jesus to his enemies for money was the ultimate breach of communion with Jesus. Every time we celebrate the Eucharist, the Lord enters into communion with us and we enter into communion with the Lord. We are sent from the Eucharist to live out of that communion, to live in a way that reflects our communion with the Lord. Like the first disciples, we can fail to live out of that communion, in various ways. Holy Week assures us that the Lord remains in communion with us even when we fall out of communion with him. If we acknowledge our failure and turn to him we will discover that the Lord comes to our help, in the words of today's first reading.

# EASTER TRIDUUM: 18–20 APRIL

## 22 April, Easter Monday

*Matthew 28:8–15*

Money features in Matthew's story of the passion and death of Jesus and in his story of the resurrection of Jesus. The chief priests paid Judas thirty pieces of silver to betray Jesus to them. Judas subsequently regretted his actions and brought the money back to the chief priests, who used it to buy a field in which to bury foreigners.

In today's gospel reading, the elders of the people handed the soldiers a considerable sum of money to spread the story that Jesus' disciples came during the night and stole his body, and that is why the tomb was empty early on the first day of the week. The money given to Judas served its purpose. Judas betrayed Jesus to death. However, the money given to the soldiers did not serve its purpose. The story the soldiers were told to spread did not have the desired effect. The risen Lord appeared to his disciples on several occasions. They knew that the reason the tomb was empty was because Jesus had been raised from the dead, not because his body had been stolen. No amount of money could suppress the extraordinary work of God in raising his Son from the dead. Easter is God's 'Yes' to his Son's life and death. It is a 'Yes' that no human conniving or resistance can silence. Easter is also God's 'Yes' to all of us. Having sent his Son into the world, a world that crucified him, God then sent his risen Son into the world. To all who responded in faith to the gift of God's risen Son, God poured the Spirit of his Son, the Holy Spirit, into their hearts. Easter is the feast of God's faithfulness to his Son and to us all. Paul, in his second letter to the Corinthians, says of Jesus, 'the Son of God, Jesus Christ, whom we proclaimed among you … was not "Yes and No", but in him it is always "Yes". For in him every one of God's promises is a "Yes"'. It is because Easter is God's 'Yes' to us in Christ that it is the most celebratory season in the Church's year.

## 23 April, Easter Tuesday

*John 20:11–18*

At the beginning of today's gospel reading, we find Mary Magdalene weeping outside the tomb of Jesus. Not only has Jesus been crucified, but now it seems that some people have stolen his body. When someone dies tragically and the person's body is not found, it makes the grieving process for loved ones all the more difficult and complicated. The risen Lord was present to Mary in her grief, just as earlier in John's Gospel Jesus had been present to the grieving Martha and Mary in the wake of the death of their brother Lazarus. Yet, Mary Magdalene's grief blinded her to the presence of the risen Lord. The risen Jesus was no less present to his disciples than he had been during his public ministry, but his presence as risen Lord was of a different quality. He had been transformed through his resurrection from the dead and the mode of his presence to his disciples had also been transformed. The two disciples on the road to Emmaus did not recognise him in the stranger who journeyed with them. With the exception of the beloved disciple, the group of disciples in a boat on the Sea of Galilee after Easter did not recognise the Lord in the stranger who called out to them from the shore. Now Mary Magdalene imagines the risen Lord who speaks to her to be the gardener. We too often fail to recognise the many ways the risen Lord is present to us. He can be present to us in the gardener, or in the one who walks with us on our journey or in the one who calls out to us from the shore. The same kind of deep sadness that Mary Magdalene experienced can blind us to the Lord's presence to us in such dark times. Mary Magdalene recognised the risen Lord when he called her name, when he related to her in a very personal way. The Lord calls out to us by name too; he wants to enter into a deeply personal relationship with each of us. This Easter we are invited to allow ourselves to become more attuned to the Lord calling us by name, speaking a word of light and life into our own uniquely personal situation in life.

## 24 April, Easter Wednesday

*Luke 24:13–35*

Through his resurrection Jesus had undergone a transformation from earthly to risen life, and his presence to his disciples as risen Lord had a transforming effect on them. We can see that from today's gospel reading. The two disciples were burdened by sadness and a loss of hope. It is said of them that their faces were downcast and, in talking to the stranger, they said, 'We had hoped'. Now they hoped no longer. They were walking away from Jerusalem, the city of death, as they had come to experience it, away from the other disciples. In reality, Jerusalem was the city where life had triumphed over death and they should have remained there with the other disciples until the Holy Spirit came upon them. The risen Lord journeyed with them, even though they were heading in the wrong direction. His presence to them transformed their sorrow into joy and their despair into hope and, as a result, they turned around and journeyed back to Jerusalem, back to the gathering of the disciples. There they shared their Easter story and heard the Easter story of the others. We too can sometimes find ourselves going in the wrong direction, away from the community of believers, burdened by a sense of sadness and hopelessness. In such times, the risen Lord is journeying with us as he journeyed with the two disciples. He is present to us as our companion on the way, inviting us to share our story with him, speaking his word to us, just as he opened the Scriptures for his two disciples, and revealing himself to us as bread of life. If we open ourselves to the Lord's presence to us in these ways, we will be transformed as the two disciples were. Our sadness will turn to joy, our despair to hope, and we will begin to face again in the right direction. We will return to the gathering of the disciples, the community of believers, the Church.

## 25 April, Easter Thursday

*Luke 24:35–48*

At the beginning of today's gospel reading, the two disciples who were joined by the risen Lord as they walked towards Emmaus tell their story to the larger group of disciples. They were telling the story of their journey from darkness to light and from despondency to hope. The physical journey to Emmaus from Jerusalem turned out to be a profound spiritual journey because of the way the risen Lord was present to them in the stranger who opened the Scriptures and who then broke bread with them at table. These two disciples had quite a story to tell and they couldn't keep it to themselves. We all have some story to tell about our own spiritual journey. It can be a great service to others to share with them something of our own personal faith journey. According to the gospel reading, while the two disciples were still telling their story, the risen Lord stood among them. It was as if their telling of their story created a space for the risen Lord to be present to all who were gathered. When we share something of our spiritual journey, the risen Lord becomes present in a special way through us. When we share something of our Easter faith with others, the first Easter becomes real and tangible again. In the gospel reading, the presence of the risen Lord brought the larger group of the disciples from agitation and doubt to joy, a joy so great that they could hardly believe the risen Lord was present. Whenever we create a space for the risen Lord to be present among us, through the telling of our story, the primary fruit of his presence will also be a joy the world cannot give.

## 26 April, Easter Friday

*John 21:1–14*

There is something very evocative about the picture of the disciples at the beginning of the gospel reading. After Jesus' crucifixion in Jerusalem, they had returned to Galilee, back to their fishing. There they are, fishing all through the night on the Sea of Galilee and catching nothing. Their failure at what they know best is somehow symbolic of their failure to follow Jesus faithfully at the time of his passion and death. Yet, as dawn breaks over their fruitless labours, a more significant light is beginning to shine, although they are not yet aware of it. A stranger calls out to them from the shore, directing them to cast their nets again. This stranger was the one who, earlier in John's Gospel, had said of himself, 'I am the light of the world. Whoever follows me will never walk in darkness but will have the light of life'. It was only the disciple who was closest to Jesus in love who recognised the true identity of the stranger, identifying him to the others as 'the Lord'. The image of the Lord standing on the shore as his disciples floundered speaks powerfully to all of us of the Lord's faithfulness to us in our own times of weakness and failure. The Lord continues to stand on the shore of our lives even when we have not shown ourselves to be his faithful followers, even when we have failed to remain in his love. Having called out to his disciples from the shore, the Lord then took a further, more personal, step towards them. He called them to 'Come and have breakfast'. He invited them to share his table, as they had done many times before, as they had done at that last meal before he was crucified. He was calling them back into communion with him. That same call goes out to each of us at every Eucharist. The Eucharist is the sacrament of the Lord's faithfulness to us in our frailty and weakness. It is also the moment when we are invited to renew our faithfulness to him and to commit again to living it out in our daily lives.

## 27 April, Easter Saturday

*Mark 16:9–15*

Today's gospel reading is often referred to as the longer ending of Mark's Gospel. It was probably added to the end by someone other than Mark, to bring Mark's Gospel more into line with the ending of the other Gospels. This passage consists of a summary of the appearances of the risen Lord that are to be found in the other three Gospels.

There is mention there of Jesus' appearance to Mary Magdalene, which is found in the gospel of John, of Jesus' appearances to two disciples, which is found in Luke, and of Jesus' appearance to the disciples as a group, which is to be found in Luke and John. The mission the risen Lord gives to the disciples at the end of the reading, 'Go out to the whole world … ' reminds us of the commission the risen Lord gives to the disciples at the end of Matthew's Gospel, 'Go make disciples of all the nations'. Why did some early scribe think it necessary to make this addition to the ending of Mark? Probably because the way Mark had ended his Gospel seemed very unsatisfactory to him and to many others in the early Church: 'So they [the women] went out and fled from the tomb, for terror and amazement had seized them; and they said nothing to anyone, for they were afraid'.

Why, people must have wondered, end a Gospel on this note of fear-filled silence? Mark was sensitive to human failure and, in particular, to the failure of Jesus' disciples, including the women disciples who had been more faithful to Jesus than their male companions. Yet, he was all the more sensitive to the Lord's faithfulness to his failing disciples. Mark and his readers knew that the risen Lord met his failing disciples in Galilee, where he renewed their call. Even in today's gospel reading, the failure of the disciples is in evidence. They refused to believe either Mary Magdalene or the two disciples when they said that they had seen the risen Lord, yet it was to these somewhat obstinate disciples that Jesus entrusted his worldwide mission. The Lord continues to call us, weak as we are, to share in his work of proclaiming the Easter Gospel.

## 29 April, Monday, Feast of St Catherine of Siena
*Matthew 11:25–30*

Catherine was one of the great mystics of the Church. She was born in 1347 and died in 1380, at the age of thirty-three. At a young age, she decided to give herself to the Lord, and she resisted the attempts of her family to find her a good husband. Instead of joining a religious order, she became a Dominican tertiary. After a three-year period of prayer and seclusion she set about serving her neighbours, distributing alms to the poor, ministering to the sick and to prisoners. After a profound mystical experience, she had a sense of Christ calling her to serve the wider world and universal Church. She commenced her role as a public figure, dictating hundreds of letters to popes and monarchs, together with other letters of note. She also wrote her great work, *The Dialogue*, describing the contents of her mystical conversations with Christ. Catherine's mysticism did not withdraw her from the world; she was deeply involved in what was happening in Europe and in the Church in her time. She persuaded Pope Gregory XI to return to Rome from Avignon. She insisted that the pope's place was beside the bones of the martyrs. Shortly after his return, Pope Gregory died. He was succeeded by Pope Urban VI who turned out to be a disastrous pope. The cardinals regretted their decision and elected a second pope but could not persuade Pope Urban to retire.

The church now had two popes, one in Rome and one in Avignon, a situation that was to last for several decades. Catherine remained faithful to Urban, in spite of his faults, because he had been duly elected. She was convinced that the wound in the body of Christ could be healed only by great sacrifice. She prayed that she might atone for the sins of the Church, and shortly afterwards collapsed and died. Catherine stood out as a beacon of light in a dark time. That is the calling of each one of us. We are all called to be mystics to some degree. The Lord's invitation, 'Come to me, all who labour and are overburdened', is addressed to us all. He calls out to all of us to come to him, to know and love him as he knows and loves us. In calling us to himself he also sends us into the world afire with the flame of his love.

## 30 April, Tuesday, Second Week of Easter

*John 3:7–15*

The birth of a child is one of the greatest causes of joy in human experience, especially for the parents of the child. Life is never the same for a couple after the birth of their child. This new life has an extraordinary impact on their lives from the moment the child is born. There is something wonderfully mysterious about the birth of every child. We encounter something of the mystery of God in and through every human birth. The spontaneous response to such mysterious new life is thanksgiving. In today's gospel reading Jesus speaks to Nicodemus of a different kind of birth. He speaks to him of the need to be 'born from above', or 'born of the Spirit'. If human birth makes the child a son or daughter of his or her parents, birth from above, or birth of the Spirit, makes us sons and daughters of God, thereby giving us a share in Jesus' own relationship with God as Son. If there is something mysterious about every human birth, the kind of birth that Jesus speaks about is even more mysterious. Although a teacher in Israel, Nicodemus responds to Jesus' words about this kind of birth with the question, 'How can that be possible?' Yet, the good news is that Jesus came to draw us into his own relationship with God, and he makes this possible in and through the gift to us of his Spirit, the Holy Spirit. There is indeed much to ponder here and much to give thanks for.

## 1 May, Wednesday, Second Week of Easter

*John 3:16–21*

We can certainly notice a stretch in the evenings these days. All of a sudden it is bright beyond seven o'clock in the evening. Most of us like the light. We are pleased to know that the daylight is lengthening every day at this time of the year. Our heart sinks a bit when we re-alise that the days have begun to get shorter. Even though most of us like the light, the gospel reading declares that people have shown they prefer darkness to light. The evangelist is referring there not to daylight, but to the one who declares himself to be the light of the world. Our calling is to 'come out into the light', in the words of the gospel reading. Today's gospel reading makes the very generous statement that all who live by the truth come out into the light. All who seek the truth are already standing in the light of Christ, even though they may not be aware of it. The gospel reading suggests that people of faith, those who seek to be guided by the light of Christ, will always have something very fundamental in common with all who seek the truth with sincerity of heart.

## 2 May, Thursday, Second Week of Easter

*John 3:31–36*

In today's gospel, we are given words spoken by John the Baptist. In the verse just before this gospel reading begins, John the Baptist had said of Jesus, 'He must increase, but I must decrease'. He then goes on to speak of Jesus, in the opening line of our gospel reading, as 'the one who comes from above', and who, therefore, 'is above all others'. John was very aware that Jesus was above him. He goes on to say of Jesus, in the words of the gospel reading, that he 'comes from heaven', that 'the Father gives Jesus the Spirit without reserve', that the Father 'has entrusted everything to the Son'. John was very aware that none of those things could be said about himself. He had a profound appreciation of the uniqueness of Jesus, which is why he could say, 'he must increase, but I must decrease'. There is a sense in which we never fully appreciate the uniqueness, the specialness, of Jesus in this life. The more we see of Jesus, the more we recognise what is yet to be seen. The closer we come to him, the more we realise how deeper our relationship with him could be. There is always a sense in which we can say, with John the Baptist, 'he must increase' and 'I must decrease'. As he increases in us and we decrease, we don't cease to be ourselves. Rather, the more Jesus increases in us, the more we become our true selves, our Christ-selves, the people God is calling us to be.

### 3 May, Friday, Feast of Ss Philip and James
*John 14:6–14*

The words of Philip to Jesus in today's gospel, 'Lord, let us see the Father and we shall be satisfied', might well resonate with us. Perhaps we also sense that we will really only be satisfied when we see God, or, in other words, when we are in heaven. Yet, Jesus replies to Philip that God the Father, whom he longs to see, he already sees in Jesus: 'to have seen me is to have seen the Father'. In those words, Jesus is letting us all know that he has already begun to satisfy our deepest longings, our longing for God. Jesus has shown us the face of God in himself, in his life, death and resurrection. As we grow in our relationship with Jesus we will already begin to see the face of God, and the heaven for which we long will become a present reality, to some extent. Jesus is reminding Philip and all of us that we have already been given a great deal. What we need to do is to appreciate what we have been given, to experience the presence of God in the person of Jesus, who is with us always until the end of time; he is with us in his word, in the Sacraments, especially the Eucharist, and in each other.

### 4 May, Saturday, Second Week of Easter
*John 6:16–21*

At the end of yesterday's gospel reading, we heard that Jesus, having fed the multitude in the wilderness, withdrew to the mountain by himself. The evangelist John suggests that Jesus needed to be alone with God the Father, who had sent him into the world. While Jesus was alone, the disciples set out to cross the Sea of Galilee without

Jesus. In his absence they found themselves struggling with a strong wind and a rough sea. Even after evening had given way to night they had rowed only three to four miles. They seemed lost without Jesus. It was then that they saw Jesus coming towards them, speaking words of reassurance: 'It is I. Do not be afraid'. Almost immediately, they arrived at their destination, which they had been struggling to reach. The gospel reading is suggesting that if we are to reach our destination, we cannot do it on our own. We need the Lord's help. A little later in this same gospel, Jesus will say to his disciples, 'those who abide in me and I in them bear much fruit, because apart from me you can do nothing'. The gospel reading is suggesting to us that on our own journey, our journey of faith, we depend on the Lord to reach our destination. We depend on him especially when the wind is against us and the waters of life get stormy. Today's gospel reading assures us that the Lord comes to us in those difficult and threatening moments. If we are open to his coming and receptive to his presence we will move on through the storms that come our way and reach our destination.

## 6 May, Monday, Third Week of Easter

*John 6:22–29*

In today's gospel reading, the people come to Jesus looking for more of the bread they ate when Jesus multiplied the loaves and fish. In response, Jesus challenges them to work, not for food that cannot last but for food that endures to eternal life. Yes, Jesus fed them in the wilderness, but he has something more to give them, not just physical bread but a deeper and more enduring form of nourishment. As well as physical hungers, we also have deeper hungers within us, spiritual hungers and thirsts. In today's gospel reading Jesus identifies himself as the one who can satisfy these deeper hungers in our hearts, the hunger for God, for a love that is faithful, for a life that endures beyond this life. The Lord will go on in that same chapter of John's Gospel to speak of himself as the bread of life. If we are to experience him as the bread of life, as the one who can satisfy our deepest hungers, we must believe in him, give ourselves to him in trust and faith. When the crowds ask Jesus, 'What must we do to do the works God wants?' Jesus replies that there is only one work God wants, to believe in the one God has sent. That is our fundamental calling, to come to the Lord in faith; all else follows from that. Our presence at the Eucharist is one of the primary ways we come to the Lord in faith and open ourselves to his presence as the bread of life.

## 7 May, Tuesday, Third Week of Easter
*John 6:30–35*
Today's first reading from the Acts of the Apostles describes the martyrdom of Stephen, the first recorded Christian martyr. Luke, who wrote the Acts of the Apostles, describes the death of Stephen in a very similar way to how he had described the death of Jesus in his first volume, the Gospel. Just as Jesus prayed to God, 'Father, forgive them for they know not what they do', so Stephen prays to the risen Lord, 'Lord, do not hold this sin against them'. Just as Jesus prayed to God, 'Father, into your hands I commend my spirit', so Stephen prays to the risen Lord, 'Lord Jesus, receive my spirit'. It is as if Luke is saying that the fundamental attitudes of Jesus are to be reproduced in that of his followers.

The risen Lord wants to live out his life in and through his followers, and that includes us all. Because the Lord wants to live out his life in us, he invites us to come to him as our bread of life, in the words of today's gospel reading: 'I am the bread of life, whoever comes to me will never be hungry'.

Our coming to the Lord in faith, and our receiving nourishment from him, creates an opening for him to live out his life in us, so that, in some way, we can continue to give flesh to his fundamental outlook and attitudes, as Stephen did.

## 8 May, Wednesday, Third Week of Easter

*John 6:35–40*

In today's first reading, Philip preaches the Gospel in Samaria and the people there unite in welcoming the message he preaches. In Luke's first volume, Jesus had attempted to preach the Gospel to a Samaritan village, but they rejected him because he was heading for Jerusalem. Now the risen Lord, through Philip, preaches the Gospel to the Samaritans and this time they welcome it. The Lord continues to offer the Gospel, even to those who have rejected it. Even though we may turn from the Lord at times, he never turns from us. This is in keeping with what Jesus says in today's gospel reading: 'Whoever comes to me I shall never turn away'. Easter celebrates the faithfulness of God to his Son Jesus, and the faithfulness of Jesus to all of us. The Lord's faithfulness encourages us to keep turning back to him, to keep coming to him, even after we have turned away from him. Even when we fail to respond to his coming, he remains for us the bread of life. He continues to promise that if we come to him we will never hunger, and if we believe in him we will never thirst.

## 9 May, Thursday, Third Week of Easter

*John 6:44–51*

There are a number of similarities between the story of the Ethiopian in today's first reading, from the Acts of the Apostles, and the story of the two disciples on the road to Emmaus in Luke's first volume, his Gospel. The two disciples were journeying away from Jerusalem when the risen Lord joined them in the form of a stranger and opened the Scriptures for them. The Ethiopian eunuch was journeying away from Jerusalem when Philip, one of the missionaries of the early Church, joined him and opened up the Scriptures for him. The opening up of the Scriptures for the two disciples led them to the recognition of the Lord in the breaking of bread, the sacrament of the Eucharist. The opening up of the Scriptures for the Ethiopian led him to the sacrament of Baptism. In both cases, hearing of the word led to a deeper encounter with the Lord in the Sacrament. Afterwards, both the disciples and the Ethiopian went on their way rejoicing. That sequence of word leading to sacrament has always been central to the Church's life. It is present again in today's gospel reading. In that reading, Jesus declares that we first need 'to hear the teaching of the Father and learn from it' before we can come to him as the bread of life who gives us his flesh, his body, for the life of the world. Listening to the God's word prepares us, disposes us, to recognise and receive the Lord who comes to us in the sacraments. Today's first reading suggests that such listening to God's word will often entail a struggle to understand it. The Ethiopian was full of questions as he listened to God's word. The story of the Ethiopian shows that such questions are not an obstacle on our journey towards the Lord but can serve that journey well.

## 10 May, Friday, Third Week of Easter
*John 6:52–59*

We can often find ourselves initially resisting a request that someone makes of us, or some declaration that they make to us. We can resist for various reasons. At some level it does not make sense to us, or it appears to make too great a demand on us. In both of today's readings we have an example of such resistance. After Saul had his transforming encounter with the risen Lord on the road to Damascus, he was taken in his blind state to a house of one of the members of the Church in Damascus. Another member of the Church there, Ananias, had a vision of the Lord in which the Lord asked him to go to Saul and to heal Saul's blindness. However, Ananias resisted what the Lord asked of him because he knew Saul's reputation as a persecutor of the Church and he didn't trust him. Yet, the Lord insisted and eventually Ananias did as he was asked. In the gospel reading, the crowd resist what Jesus had just said about giving his flesh for the life of the world as bread to be eaten. Yet, in spite of this resistance, the Lord insisted all the more on the need, not only to eat his flesh, but to drink his blood. There is a clear reference here to the Eucharist as the moment when we enter into communion with the body and blood of the Lord. On this occasion Jesus did not break through the resistance of those to whom he spoke. Even some of his own disciples would walk away because of this teaching on the Eucharist. Yet, we are asked to take these words of Jesus into our own hearts, extraordinary as they are, tempted as we are to ask the question, 'How can this man give us his flesh to eat?' The Lord wants us to receive him in faith in the Eucharist, so that we can draw life from him, and become channels of his life to others.

## 11 May, Saturday, Third Week of Easter

*John 6:60–69*

In today's gospel reading there is a sharp dichotomy between how some of Jesus' followers assessed his teaching on the Eucharist and how Jesus himself assessed his own teaching. Some of his followers declared, 'This is intolerable language', whereas Jesus himself asserted, 'the words I have spoken to you are spirit and they are life'. The life-giving words of Jesus will be dismissed as intolerable language by some in every generation. Even though Jesus was aware that his teaching would lose him some of his followers, he did not dilute his teaching. Indeed, when many of his disciples left him, Jesus turned to the Twelve, his closest associates, and asked them, 'What about you, do you want to go away too?' He was prepared to risk losing his core following rather than compromise his teaching. He would be faithful to God's vision for human living regardless of the cost to himself. Those who wanted to accept his vision, and to live by the teaching it expressed, would have to make a conscious decision to do so. That is true for us who seek to be the Lord's followers today. Remaining faithful to the values of the Gospel will often mean standing our ground when many others are leaving. The response of many in the gospel reading to Jesus' teaching, 'This is intolerable language', stands over and against the response of Peter, 'You have the message of eternal life'. It is Peter's response we are invited to make our own.

## 13 May, Monday, Fourth Week of Easter
*John 10:11–18*

Today's first reading suggests that the Holy Spirit was always one step ahead of the early Church. The first Christians were Jewish, and there was a natural reluctance among them to eat food that was considered unclean in their tradition, and there was an even stronger reluctance to visit the homes of pagans. However, in that reading, Peter has a vision in which he is told to regard no food as unclean. Immediately afterwards, the Spirit prompted Peter to do something he would not have done if left to himself, namely to go to the home of a pagan so as to witness to the Lord. When Peter went to this home and preached, something happened that Peter never would have expected. The Holy Spirit came down on the members of this pagan household in the same way that the Spirit had come down upon Jesus' Jewish followers at the first Pentecost. Peter and the rest of the early Church were being led by the Holy Spirit in directions they had not expected. The Holy Spirit is one step ahead of the Church in every age. We are always trying to keep up with where the Spirit is leading us. In the gospel reading, Jesus speaks of himself as the gate and calls on us to enter through him. However, the first reading suggests that

Jesus is not a gate in any static or fixed way. Jesus, the gate, like the Spirit, is always ahead of us. We are always having to discern what it means to go through Jesus the gate. We have to keep searching for the gate that Jesus wants us to go through. It is often an unexpected gate, as Peter learned when the Spirit prompted him to go through the gate of a pagan house. We always need to be open to the Lord's guidance. He often calls on us to go through a gate that is new. We need to pray, in the words of today's responsorial psalm, 'O send forth your light and your truth; let these be my guide'.

## 14 May, Tuesday, Feast of St Matthias

*John 15:9–17*

According to today's first reading, after Judas's betrayal of Jesus and his subsequent suicide, the early Church wanted to find a replacement for Judas so as to restore the group of the Twelve to its full complement. A certain amount of human effort was put into finding such a person. First of all, Peter addressed the community of faith about the need to choose a replacement for Judas. Then the community had to discern who might be the best candidates, and two suitable candidates were put forward. However, they wanted to ensure that their final choice corresponded with the Lord's choice. As a result, they brought the fruits of their human efforts to prayer, and they asked, 'Lord, show us which of these two you have chosen to take over this ministry'. It was only after that prayerful search of the Lord's choice that they felt ready to nominate Matthias to replace Judas. The early Church recognised that the person to replace Judas had to be the Lord's choice. In today's gospel reading, Jesus says to his disciples, 'You did not choose me; no, I chose you'. 'What is the Lord's choice? What does the Lord want?' remains and important question for us today. We can easily fire ahead in a certain direction without asking that question. Asking that question inevitably brings us to prayer.

In prayer we ask the Lord to guide and direct us in our choosing; we invite him to show us his choice. Jesus himself made this kind of prayer when, in the Garden of Gethsemane, he prayed, 'Not my will but yours be done'. It is a type of prayer that he would encourage us all to enter into.

## 15 May, Wednesday, Fourth Week of Easter

*John 12:44–50*

In today's first reading, which follows on from yesterday's first reading, Barnabas and Saul are now both leading members of the Church in Antioch. In that reading, the Church of Antioch is portrayed as doing something very generous. Under the inspiration of the Holy Spirit, they release Paul and Barnabas, two of their most important members, for mission work far beyond Antioch. The Spirit moved the Church in Antioch to let go of two of its greatest assets so that the Gospel could be preached in places where it had never been preached before. The Church in Antioch was being prompted by the Spirit to empty itself, to become poorer, so that others might become spiritually rich. This was how Paul went on in one of his letters to describe the coming of Jesus among us: 'Though he was rich, for your sakes he became poor, so that by his poverty you might become rich'. According to today's gospel reading, Jesus, the light, came into a dark world so that those who believe in him need not stay in the dark any more. The Spirit will always work in our lives to reproduce in us that same pattern. The Spirit will always be moving us as individuals and as communities of faith to give of ourselves, to empty ourselves, so that other people's relationship with the Lord will be the richer.

## 16 May, Thursday, Fourth Week of Easter

*John 13:16–20*

Today's first reading gives us an insight into a Jewish liturgy of the word. Paul and his companions go to a synagogue on the Sabbath day and take their seats. A reading from the Law, the first five books of the Jewish Bible, was proclaimed, followed by a reading from one of the prophets. Then the presider of the liturgy invites Paul to preach from the readings. Our own liturgy of the word has its roots in the Jewish liturgy of the time of Jesus and Paul. In the course of his preaching, Paul makes reference to John the Baptist and quotes him as saying regarding Jesus, 'I am not fit to undo his sandals'. Taking off someone's sandals was the work of a slave. John declares that he is not worthy even to be Jesus' slave. The words of Jesus in today's gospel reading follow on from his washing the feet of his disciples, 'After he had washed the feet of his disciples, Jesus said to them … '. Washing feet was also the work of a slave. It was even more menial work than untying someone's sandals. Yet, Jesus washes the feet of his disciples, including the feet of Judas, whom Jesus refers to in the gospel reading: 'Someone who shares my table rebels against me'. In his letter to the Philippians Paul speaks of Jesus as someone who, although being in the form of God, 'emptied himself, taking the form of a slave'. Jesus became our slave, such was the extent of his self-emptying love for us. He gave not less than everything so that we may have life to the full. In today's gospel reading he makes the striking statement that 'happiness will by yours if you behave accordingly'. In other words, we don't find happiness by looking for it, but by seeking to serve each other with the same self-emptying love as the Lord has served us.

## 17 May, Friday, Fourth Week of Easter

*John 14:1–6*

In today's gospel reading, Jesus says of himself, 'I am the way, the truth and the life'. It is an extraordinary claim and one that has spoken powerfully to believers down through the ages. One way of understanding that saying is that Jesus is the way because he is the truth and the life. He is the truth in that he reveals God fully; he has shown us the full truth about God. He is the life because he is full of the life of God and he gives God's life to all who believe in him. It is because Jesus reveals God fully and is full of God's life that he is the way to God. It is through Jesus that we reach God; it is through Jesus that God reaches us. We are all trying to find our way in life. We often find ourselves asking, 'What is the right path to take in this situation?' As believers, we try to find the way, to take the path that brings us closer to God, that leads to a deepening in our relationship with God. In the gospel reading, Jesus is saying that he is the way that brings us closer to God, that leads us to a deeper relationship with God. It is in trying to take Jesus as our way that we will find our way in life, that we will take the right path in life. As followers of Jesus, we are not without a road map. He is our road map. He is our way. Every day he calls on us to take him as our way. When we take Jesus as our way, we will find God's truth and receive God's life.

## 18 May, Saturday, Fourth Week of Easter

*John 14:7–14*

Across the four Gospels several people are portrayed as approaching Jesus and asking for something, either for themselves or for others. Very often they ask for some form of healing. In today's gospel reading, one of Jesus' own disciples, Philip, asks for something quite different. He says to Jesus, 'Lord, let us see the Father and then we shall be satisfied'. He asks to see God, and he expresses his conviction that in seeing God all his deepest hungers and thirsts will be satisfied. We believe that we are destined to see God directly, face to face, in the next life, and that when we are worthy to see God in this way we will indeed finally be satisfied. Our restlessness will cease. Jesus' reply to Philip is thought-provoking. He doesn't tell Philip that he can see the Father only beyond this life. Rather, he says to him, 'to have seen me is to have seen the Father'. Jesus is saying to Philip, and to all of us, that here and now we can anticipate our final destiny in so far as we can now see Jesus, who is the revelation of God, the face of God. We cannot see Jesus in the way Philip saw him, with our physical eyes, yet we can see him with the eyes of faith. We can see him with such eyes in his word, in the sacraments, especially the Eucharist, and in each other. In so far as we see him in these ways and respond to him, we too will experience something of that satisfaction and fulfilment for which Philip longed.

## 20 May, Monday, Fifth Week of Easter

*John 14:21–26*

I often pay attention to the questions people ask in the Gospels. They can be very revealing. Sometimes it is easy to make these questions our own. We find one such question in today's gospel reading. Judas, not Judas Iscariot, asks Jesus, 'Lord, what is all this about?' It is a question that comes out of a failure to understand just what Jesus is saying. The meaning of Jesus' words is not always self-evident. We can easily find ourselves asking the same question as Judas, 'What is all this about?' It is a good question. It can set us on a search for a fuller understanding of Jesus' message. In response to Judas' question, Jesus promises to send the Advocate, the Holy Spirit, who 'will teach you everything and remind you of all I have said to you'. Jesus has been the teacher of his disciples.

Now, in the setting of the Last Supper, on the eve of his death, he promises his disciples that he will continue to teach them beyond his death in and through the Holy Spirit. That promise is made to all of us. The disciples in the upper room at the Last Supper represent us all. As we find ourselves asking, 'What is all this about?' we are not left to our own devices. The Lord is always offering us the gift of the Holy Spirit as our teacher, to help us to understand more deeply all the Lord has said and done. As Paul says in his first letter to the Corinthians, 'no one understands what is truly God's except the Spirit of God'.

## 21 May, Tuesday, Fifth Week of Easter

*John 14:27–31*

The opening words of Jesus in today's gospel reading may sound familiar to you: 'Peace I bequeath to you, my own peace I give you'. A version of those words has made its way into the text of our Mass, just before the sign of peace: 'Lord Jesus Christ who said to your Apostles: Peace I leave you, my peace I give you'. Jesus spoke those words to his disciples in the setting of the Last Supper. They had heard Jesus say to them that he was going away and that he would return. They were disturbed by his talk of going away. The full reality of what was about to happen on the following day was beginning to dawn on them. Their hearts were troubled and afraid. In that sombre setting, Jesus gives them the gift of his own peace, which he identifies as a peace the world cannot give. Jesus was at peace in this hour and he wanted his disciples to experience something of his own peace. Jesus was at peace in spite of the fact that, as he says in the gospel reading, 'the prince of the world is on his way'.

This is a likely reference to Satan and to all those who are in Satan's power. Jesus is at peace in the full knowledge that evil stalks the land. His peace is rooted in his loving relationship with God his Father. This is the peace that Jesus gives to his disciples, to all of us. It is a peace that is rooted in God's love for us through Jesus. Because it has such deep roots, it can endure even in the face of the world's hostility.

## 22 May, Wednesday, Fifth Week of Easter

*John 15:1–8*

The words of Jesus we have just heard from the Gospel of John are spoken in the course of the Last Supper. Jesus has been speaking about his imminent departure, his leaving this world and going to the Father. It is in that context of speaking about his going away from his disciples that Jesus also speaks about his presence to his disciples, the new communion between Jesus and his disciples that his departure will make possible. One image of the new quality of communion between Jesus and his disciples, between Jesus and us, is the image of the vine. Jesus says, 'I am the vine, you are the branches'. Jesus has taken the initiative to create that communion by his journey to the Father and his sending of the Spirit. We are not asked to create that communion; that has been done for us. Our calling is to preserve the communion the Lord has created, or, in the words of the gospel reading, to remain in him. We are to remain in the communion the Lord has created and is always creating. We do that by our prayerful communion with him and by our efforts to love one another as he has loved us, to be in communion with each other as he is in communion with us.

## 23 May, Thursday, Fifth Week of Easter

*John 15:9–11*

In the gospel reading two days ago, Jesus told his disciples that he was giving them the gift of his peace. On the night of the Last Supper, he was at peace, even though he knew that the hostility towards him was about to reach its climax. He was at peace in the knowledge that God his Father loved him, and that this love would lead him through death to glory. In this today's gospel reading, which is just a half chapter later, Jesus offers his disciples a share in his own joy: 'I have told you this so that my own joy may be in you and your joy be complete'. If it can be difficult to conceive of Jesus as at peace on the night of the Last Supper, it is even more difficult to think of him as joyful. Yet, his joy has the same source as his peace. As he says in today's gospel reading, 'the Father has loved me'. His Father's love for him gave him an inner joy which no one could take from him. Jesus wants his joy to be in his disciples, to be in all of us. As Jesus' joy was rooted in the Father's love for him, our joy is rooted in Jesus' love for us. In the words of Jesus in the gospel reading, 'As the Father has loved me, so I have loved you'. If we remain in his love by trying to live as he calls us to, by loving others as he has loved us, then we will experience something of Jesus' own joy. This sharing in Jesus' own joy is joy at its most complete: ' … and your joy be complete'.

## 24 May, Friday, Fifth Week of Easter
*John 15:12–17*
We all value greatly the gift of friendship. We probably all have at least one friend who means a great deal to us. Such a friend might even be a member of our family. For many of us, our closest friends are not family members. If a friendship is to happen, two people need to befriend each other; they have to choose one another. If one person chooses another but the other does nor reciprocate, the friendship won't happen. In today's gospel reading, Jesus tells his disciples, and through them, he tells all of us, 'You are my friends … I have chosen you'. Jesus declares that he has befriended us, and he declares that he has expressed his friendship of us in two ways, by laying down his life for us and by revealing to us everything he has learned from his Father. He has given his life to us and for us, and he has spoken to us out of his very depths, the depths of his relationship with God. Jesus

has befriended us. Yet, if that friendship is to come to pass, we have to befriend him as he has befriended us; we have to choose him as he has chosen us. We do that, he says, by keeping his new commandment, to love one another as he has loved us. In other words, we befriend him by befriending each other. In loving the other with his love, we respond to his gift of friendship, and our friendship with him comes to life.

## 25 May, Saturday, Fifth Week of Easter
*John 15:18–21*

There is something of a contrast between today's first reading and to-day's gospel reading. The first reading, from the Acts of the Apostles, gives us a very positive picture of Paul's ministry Phrygia, Galatia in modern-day Turkey. Luke, the author, tells us that 'the churches grew in faith, as well as growing daily in numbers'. They were growing in both quality and numbers. Paul reaches Troas, which is on the north-west coast of modern-day Turkey, and there he has a dream in which he hears the people of Macedonia in northern Greece call out to him to preach the Gospel among them. Paul immediately makes plans to cross from Turkey, which is in what we would today call Asia, to Greece, which is in Europe. This is the moment when the Gospel reaches Europe for the first time, probably less than twenty years after the death and resurrection of Jesus. Luke gives us a sense of the Holy Spirit at work guiding Paul and his companions, charting their course. It is a very encouraging picture.

However, in the gospel reading Jesus paints a somewhat bleaker picture. He tells his disciples that just as the world, the world of unbe-lief, has hated him, so it will hate them. A servant is not greater than his master. As they persecuted the master, Jesus, they will persecute the servants, his disciples. If, in the first reading, Luke depicts the work of the Spirit, the gospel reading depicts hostility to that work.

Both these realities will always be a feature of the Church's life and mission. What matters is that in the face of the hostility to the Gospel message, we never lose sight of the Spirit at work within us and among us.

## 27 May, Monday, Sixth Week of Easter

*John 15:26–16:4*

The prayer that Jesus gave his disciples to pray concludes with the petition, 'Lead us not into temptation, but deliver us from evil'. The 'temptation' Jesus had in mind was the temptation to lose faith in him, to turn away from him. Jesus was aware that his disciples would be living in a world which would not always be supportive of their faith in him, their faithful following of him. In today's gospel reading, Jesus says, 'I have told you all this that your faith may not be shaken'. This again expresses Jesus' awareness that the faith of his disciples is likely to be shaken. All Jesus says to his disciples, and to us, on the night of the Last Supper, is to help us to remain faithful to him, to enable us to resist the temptation to turn away from him. Aware of the vulnerability of the faith of his disciples, in every generation, Jesus promises to send them a helper, the Advocate, the Spirit of Truth. The Holy Spirit will witness to Jesus in the time after the death and resurrection of Jesus and will empower Jesus' disciples to witness to him. We can feel that our faith is under threat for various reasons today.

In the words of the gospel reading, we may sense that our faith is being shaken, yet we can draw encouragement from Jesus' promise to send us the Holy Spirit to keep us faithful and to give us the courage to witness to our faith. Each day, we can draw on the strength which that resource of the Spirit gives us.

## 28 May, Tuesday, Sixth Week of Easter

*John 16:5–11*

In today's gospel reading, Jesus recognises that his disciples are 'sad at heart'. It is the night of the Last Supper and he has been saying to them that he is soon to go to the one who sent him. Much of what Jesus says in this setting of the Last Supper is intended to address the sadness and distress of his disciples. His words to his disciples are addressed to us all. Jesus explains to his sad disciples that his leaving them, his return to the Father, is to their advantage. His painful leave-taking will make possible his coming to them in a new and more wonderful way, his coming to them through the Advocate, the Holy Spirit. The Holy Spirit, the Spirit of the risen Jesus, will accomplish even more than Jesus did during his earthly ministry. He will help them to see that the world of unbelief, the world that crucified Jesus, is wrong about the fundamental questions of who has sinned, who is in the right and who is judged. Those who put Jesus to death considered him a sinner and themselves to be in the right; they regarded Jesus' crucifixion as God's judgement on him. The Holy Spirit, the Spirit of Truth, will demonstrate that he was in the right and that those who crucified him were the sinners; the Spirit will show that it was those who crucified Jesus who were judged on Golgotha, not Jesus. Jesus is saying that the Holy Spirit will give a perspective on all that is happening that the disciples couldn't otherwise have. The Holy Spirit continues to give us that inspired perspective on Jesus too, and for that we can be grateful to God.

## 29 May, Wednesday, Sixth Week of Easter

*John 16:12–15*

We know from our own experience that a timely word can make all the difference. There is wisdom in knowing how much to say to someone about some important matter and when to say it. There may be a word that someone needs to hear, but that person may not be ready to hear it at a particular time. We often need to make a judgement as to when to say what we know would be helpful for someone to hear. If we get our timing wrong, the word that has the potential to be very helpful to someone can prove unhelpful. In today's gospel reading, we find Jesus making that kind of judgement. He tells his disciples on the night of the Last Supper that he has many things to say to them. However, he is aware that they would be too much for his disciples just at that time. Because of the highly-charged atmosphere of the Last Supper, the disciples simply wouldn't be able to hear all that Jesus wants to say to them. After his death and resurrection, Jesus will send the Holy Spirit, the Spirit of Truth, upon his disciples. He will continue to speak to them in and through the Holy Spirit and will tell them the many things he wants them to hear. Little by little, Jesus will lead them to the complete truth about himself and themselves and the world, in and through the Holy Spirit, the Spirit of Truth. The Lord has many things to say to us all. None of us could hear it all at one sitting. The Lord continues to speak to us throughout our lives through the Spirit of Truth, opening up for us, little by little, what he calls in the gospel reading, the 'complete truth'. What is needed from us is a listening ear, a listening heart.

## 30 May, Thursday, Sixth Week of Easter

*John 16:16–20*

Today's gospel reading gives us an insight into the confusion of the disciples on the night of the Last Supper. They cannot really grasp what Jesus is saying. 'What does he mean?' they ask. Jesus had spoken about two 'short times'. In a short time the disciples will no longer see him, and then in a short time they will see him. In the light of what subsequently happened, we understand that the first short time refers to the time between the Last Supper and Jesus' death on the cross : 'in a short time you will no longer see me', and the second short time refers to the short time between the death of Jesus and his resurrection: 'then a short time later you will see me again'. Jesus is really speaking about two different kinds of seeing here. After Jesus has been crucified, his disciples will no longer see him in the way they have seen him during the course of his earthly ministry. Yet, after he rises from the dead, they will see him in a different way, with different eyes, with the eyes of faith. That is how we see Jesus today. We see him with the eyes of faith. We recognise him in his Word, in the Eucharist, in each other, in our own hearts. The Lord who was present to his disciples on the night of the Last Supper was telling them and all of us that he would be present to them in a different way as a result of his death and resurrection and the coming of the Holy Spirit. The Lord is present to us today and it is the eyes of faith which allow us to see him, to recognise him.

## 31 May, Friday, The Visitation of the Blessed Virgin Mary
*Luke 1:39–56*

Luke's account of Mary visiting Elizabeth comes immediately after his account of the angel Gabriel visiting Mary. The Lord came to Mary through his messenger, Gabriel. Although initially perplexed by this visit of the Lord, Mary received the Lord's visit, surrendering to his will for her life. Having received the Lord's visit, Mary herself went on a visit to her older cousin in need. Having received the Lord, she brought the Lord to Elizabeth. She physically carried the Lord in her womb. Just as the Lord visited Mary through Gabriel, now the Lord visits Elizabeth through Mary. As Mary welcomed the Lord's visit through Gabriel, Elizabeth welcomed the Lord's visit through Mary, 'Blessed is the fruit of your womb'. Elizabeth also asked 'Why should I be honoured with a visit from the mother of my Lord?' Just as Mary was initially perplexed that the Lord should visit her through

Gabriel, Elizabeth is perplexed that the Lord should visit her through Mary. Both Mary and Elizabeth were humbled by the Lord's visit to them. The story of Gabriel's visit to Mary and Mary's visit to Elizabeth reveals an important truth about our own lives as the Lord's disciples. The Lord visits each of us, as he visited Mary and Elizabeth. He comes into our lives in different ways, sometimes in very ordinary ways, such as through the visit of a friend, at other times in more mystical ways, such as during a time of prayer. We are called to receive the Lord's visit with the same openness and humility that Mary and Elizabeth showed. Having received the Lord's visit, we are then called to bring the Lord to others, as Mary brought the Lord to Elizabeth. The Lord who visits us always wishes to visit others through us.

## 1 June, Saturday, Sixth Week of Easter
*John 16:23–28*
The first reading from the Acts of the Apostles gives us a very striking picture of how the members of the early Church ministered to each other. Apollos had come to Ephesus from Alexandria. He was both an eloquent and a learned man, but he needed further instruction in the faith of Jesus. This instruction was provided by a married couple, Priscilla and Aquila, who were in a position to give him the instruction he needed. Apollos then wanted to cross over from Ephesus in the Roman province of Asia to Corinth in the Roman province of Achaia. Here again, he needed help. The Church in Ephesus wrote a letter to the Church in Corinth asking that he be welcomed. It was, in effect, a letter of recommendation. Having received so much help from the Church in Ephesus, Apollos was a great help to the Church in Corinth on his arrival: 'He helped the believers considerably.' Apollos received from the gifts of other believers and gave to other believers from his own gifts. This is an image of the Church in every generation. The Holy Spirit has gifted each one of us for the service

of others in the Church. We each have something to give to others and something to receive from others. Within the Church, we are all interdependent. Even more fundamentally, we each have something to give to the Lord, present in others, and we have a great deal to receive from the Lord. It is because we have a great deal to receive from the Lord that Jesus says in the gospel reading, 'Ask and you will receive'. If we are dependent on each other, we are even more dependent on the Lord.

## 3 June, Monday, Seventh Week of Easter

*John 16:29–33*

The disciples speak with great confidence about Jesus at the beginning of today's gospel reading: 'Now we see that you know everything ... we believe that you came from God'. They speak almost as if they have finally reached their goal in their relationship with the Lord: 'we see ... we believe'. Jesus immediately punctures their self-confidence, declaring very bluntly that the time has arrived when they will abandon him, when they will be scattered, each going their own way, leaving Jesus alone. This is what happened when Jesus entered into the journey of his passion and death. The gospel reading reminds us that we can never become too complacent about our relationship with the Lord. No matter how much progress we think we have made in the faith, there is always the possibility that we will go our own way rather than the Lord's way, that we will be unfaithful to him in one way or another. When the disciples went their own way, it was not the end of the road for them. The risen Lord recommissioned them, breathing the Holy Spirit upon them, sending them out as he had been sent by his Father. When we go our own way, it is not the end of the road for us either. The same risen Lord stands ready to receive us when we turn back to him and will empower us afresh to be his followers through the gift of the Holy Spirit.

## 4 June, Tuesday, Seventh Week of Easter

*John 17:1–11*

Beginning today and for the coming few days, we hear in the gospel reading the prayer of Jesus at the last supper, as found in John's Gospel. We often reveal ourselves most fully in our prayer. How we pray can disclose what is deepest in our heart and mind. Our prayer often comes out of the depths of our being. The same is true of the prayer of Jesus. He was most himself in his prayer. His prayer in today's gospel reading reveals the heart of his relationship with God and with others. On the night of the Last Supper, he asks God in prayer to glorify him. In John's Gospel, Jesus is glorified when he is lifted up on the cross and lifted up in glory. In asking God to glorify him, Jesus is asking God to take him through death into a new and glorious life. Jesus has this difficult journey to face, and the reason he is taking it is because he wants to give glory to God and to give eternal life to all mankind, ' … so that your Son may glorify you and … let him give eternal life to all those you have entrusted to him'. Everything Jesus said and did, including his dying, was in order to give glory to God and give eternal life to all. The inner core of Jesus was shaped by these two movements towards God and towards others. They were different sides of the same movement. This two-sided movement needs to be at our core, as followers of Jesus. We are to give glory to God and give life to others. We are to acknowledge God as our Ultimate Good, and relate to others in ways that help them to take the path that leads to eternal life.

## 5 June, Wednesday, Seventh Week of Easter

*John 17:11–19*

In today's gospel reading Jesus prays for his disciples on the night before he died. This prayer really transcends that particular moment in time. It is also the prayer of the risen Lord for his disciples today, for all of us gathered here in this place. What is Jesus' prayer on our behalf? In the words of the gospel reading, he prays that we may be true to God's name and that God would protect us from the evil one. This prayer of Jesus for us reflects one of the petitions in the prayer that Jesus asked us to pray for ourselves, the prayer that has become known as the Lord's Prayer. In that prayer we pray, 'Lead us not into temptation but deliver us from evil'. This prayer must be very close to the heart of Jesus if he prays it for us and asks us to pray it for ourselves, the prayer that we be delivered from, protected from, the evil one, the prayer that we remain true or faithful to God's name, to who God is and to what God desires for us. Jesus prays this prayer in the knowledge that our faithfulness will be put to the test by what the gospel reading calls the 'world'. The gospel reading today assures us that in such testing times the Lord is praying for us, and that his prayer combined with our own prayer will ultimately keep us faithful to him and to his Father.

## 6 June, Thursday, Seventh Week of Easter

*John 17:20–26*

The section of the prayer of Jesus in today's gospel reading expresses his deepest desire for his future disciples. He wants them to be one, in the way that Jesus and his Father are one. This prayer of Jesus has become a focal text in the ecumenical movement since the Second Vatican Council. The oneness that Jesus prays for among his disciples is not just a human togetherness. It is a unity that has a vertical dimension to it. Jesus asks his Father that his future disciples would be 'one in us'. It is in and through their shared relationship with Jesus and his Father that Jesus' disciples will become one among themselves. The unity among Jesus' disciples has its roots in their communion with Jesus and his Father, 'With me in them, and you in me, may they be so completely one … '. It is the Lord who is the source of our unity. At the end of the gospel reading, Jesus expresses his hope that the love with which God the Father loved him may be in his disciples. The disciples will become one when God the Father's love for Jesus and Jesus' love for his Father finds expression in the way they relate to each other. Jesus is saying that we become one to the extent that we love one another with the very love that is God's life, that is within God. How can we love one another with God's love? The answer consists of two words, 'Holy Spirit'. The Holy Spirit is the Spirit of the love of God the Father and God the Son. It is only in and through the Holy Spirit that we can love one another with God's love and become one in the way Jesus desires and prays for.

## 7 June, Friday, Seventh Week of Easter
*John 21:15–19*

Jesus asks many questions in the course of the Gospels. The question that Jesus asks in today's gospel reading is a very personal question addressed to Peter: 'Simon, son of John, do you love me?' Peter had denied Jesus publicly three times. Now Jesus publicly asks him three times, 'Do you love me?' It is not in any way an accusing question. Rather, it is an inviting question. It is a question that gives Peter the opportunity to make a new beginning in his relationship with Jesus. It is a question that holds out the promise of a renewed friendship between Jesus and Peter. Peter may have denied Jesus, but Jesus now affirms Peter with the question, 'Do you love me?' When Peter answers Jesus' question with the declaration, 'You know I love you', Jesus entrusts Peter with the pastoral care of Jesus' own disciples: 'Feed my sheep'. The flock, the Church, does not belong to Peter. It belongs to Jesus, 'my sheep', but Jesus is entrusting his disciples to Peter's pastoral care, in spite of Peter's past failures. Whenever we fail the Lord, he asks us the same inviting question he asked Peter: 'Do you love me?' In our case as in Peter's, it is a question that holds out the promise of a new beginning. If we can answer that question in the way Peter did, the Lord will entrust us also with some pastoral care of others in the community. The Lord has work for us all to do, but first he needs us to receive the gift of his faithful love and to pledge him our faithful love in return.

## 8 June, Saturday, Seventh Week of Easter
*John 21:20–25*

I have always been struck by the concluding sentence of today's gospel reading. It is actually the concluding sentence of the fourth Gospel. The evangelist declares that there were many other things Jesus did that are not mentioned in his Gospel. He goes on to declare that the world itself could not contain all the books that would have to be written if everything Jesus said and did were written down. The evangelist may be indulging in some hyperbole here, but he is nevertheless expressing his conviction that the full mystery of Jesus' identity cannot be fully expressed in any one piece of literature, not even in a Gospel that is rooted in eyewitness tradition, like his own. Even the four Gospels taken together do not exhaust the mystery of Jesus. There is more to Jesus than all four evangelists together have managed to express. Each evangelist gives us an inspired portrait of Jesus. We are fortunate to have these four portraits of Jesus, even if no one of them and not even all four together, fully capture the mystery of Jesus, who was the fullest revelation of God possible in human form. Yet, the Gospels reveal all we need to know about Jesus for our lives of faith. They give us the portrait of Jesus that the Holy Spirit wants us to have. The Holy Spirit, working through various human agents, has given us this wonderful gift of the four Gospels. Today's gospel reading speaks of the beloved disciple as the one who wrote down, or caused to be written down, what we now know as the fourth Gospel or the Gospel of John. We give thanks to God today for all four evangelists and for the priceless legacy they have left us, under the guidance and direction of the Holy Spirit, whose feast we celebrate this Sunday.

## 10 June, Memorial of the Blessed Virgin Mary, Mother of the Church

This newly introduced memorial of our Lady is to be celebrated on the Monday after the Feast of Pentecost. The first reading gives us the picture of Jesus' disciples gathered with certain women, including Mary, the Mother of Jesus, as well as with Jesus' brothers. They were constantly devoting themselves to prayer in preparation for the gift of the Holy Spirit that the risen Lord had promised. Although Mary is described as the 'Mother of Jesus', it is easy to imagine her maternal role embracing Jesus' disciples, whom he had earlier addressed in the Gospel as his brothers and sisters. The community of disciples down the ages, the Church, has continued to look to Mary as their mother. Her prayerful communion with Jesus' disciples in that first reading finds an echo in the prayer that has come to be associated with Mary, the 'Hail Mary', in which we ask Mary to pray for us, sinful disciples of Jesus, now and at the hour of our death. Luke's portrait of a community of believers at prayer with Mary at its heart is complemented by John's portrait in the gospel reading of a community of believers at the foot of the cross with Mary at its heart. Mary is there with three other women and the male disciple who is referred to only as the disciple Jesus loved. In the fourth Gospel, this nameless disciple represents all disciples. We are each invited to give him our own name. In saying to this disciple from the cross, 'This is your mother', Jesus is addressing disciples of every generation. When Jesus says to Mary, 'This is your son', she is being called to relate to this disciple and all he those he represents as she has related to Jesus. The disciple Jesus loves becomes the brother of Jesus, and all those disciples whom he represents become Jesus' brothers and sisters. At the foot of the cross, a new community is being formed who can look to Jesus as a brother, to his Father as their Father and to his mother as their mother. As the beloved disciple took Mary into his home, we are all invited to take Mary into our lives as mother and friend. On this memorial, we give thanks to the Lord for sharing with us this precious gift of his mother.

## 11 June, Tuesday, Feast of St Barnabas

*Matthew 10:7–13*

Barnabas was known in the early Church as the 'son of encourage-ment', according to the Acts of the Apostles. As nicknames go, it is one of the nicer ones. It was clearly a term that reflected the nature of the man. He had that marvelous ability to recognise the good qual-ities in people and to draw them out so that they could be placed at the service of the Church. We find two examples of this in today's first reading. The first community of believers comprised only Jewish people, but in Antioch there emerged a community of believers made up of Jewish and non-Jewish people. When Barnabas was sent from Jerusalem to investigate this new development, he was delighted with what he saw and 'he urged them all to remain faithful to the Lord with heartfelt devotion'. Then, some time later, Barnabas recognised that Saul, the former persecutor of the Church, could make a wonderful contribution to this mixed Church in Antioch. He travelled all the way to Tarsus to find Paul and bring him to Antioch. Paul went on to become a leading member of the Church in Antioch. Recognising the gifts of others and creating openings for those gifts to flourish – this was the strength of Barnabas. We all have it in us to be a Barnabas within the Church and within the wider community. We may not have the gift for a particular task, but we can have the ability to recognise that gift in others and to create a space for their gift to flourish. This is one of the ways that we can all respond to the Lord's call in today's gospel reading to go out and proclaim that the kingdom of God is close at hand.

## 12 June, Wednesday, Tenth Week in Ordinary Time

*Matthew 5:17–19*

We are familiar with the proverbs, 'you cannot judge a book by its cover', and 'all that glitters is not gold'. Like all proverbs, they express a truth about human reality that has been gleaned from people's experience over a long period of time. People have learned, sometimes from all too bitter experience, that what you see is not always what you get when it comes to other people. Jesus makes the same observation in today's gospel reading when he speaks of those who 'come to you disguised as sheep but underneath are ravenous wolves'. There is a sharp contrast between a sheep and a wolf, the latter being a dangerous enemy of the former. In John's Gospel, Jesus makes reference to the hired hand, as distinct from the shepherd, who 'sees the wolf coming and leaves the sheep and runs away'. Jesus declares in today's gospel reading that we judge a person's character not by how they appear to us but by what he calls 'their fruits'. Today's gospel reading is part of the conclusion of the Sermon on the Mount. By 'fruits' Jesus means the fundamental attitudes and values, along with the actions or 'good works' that flow from them, which he has been portraying throughout the sermon, beginning with the Beatitudes. This is not far removed from what Paul, in his letter to the Galatians, calls the fruit of the Spirit: 'love, joy, peace, patience, kindness, generosity, faithfulness, gentleness and self-control'. It is Paul who reminds us that if Jesus' Gospel message is to bear the appropriate fruit in our lives, we will need to open our lives to the Holy Spirit who, as Paul declares in his letter to the Romans, 'helps us in our weakness'.

## 13 June, Thursday, Tenth Week in Ordinary Time

*Matthew 5:20–26*

In today's first reading, Paul declares that 'where the Spirit of the Lord is, there is freedom'. He is declaring that those who are open to the Holy Spirit's influence and guidance are free to live in the way the Lord desires us to live. They have the freedom to do God's will as Jesus has revealed it to us. Most of us don't have that freedom, most of the time. We struggle to live according to the Lord's desire and will for our lives because we are no yet fully open to the working of the Holy Spirit within us. In the gospel reading, Jesus identifies one dimension of how God wants us to live. It is one example of the deeper virtue Jesus mentions at the beginning of the gospel reading, which only the Holy Spirit can give us the freedom to live by. Very few would dispute the commandment in the Jewish Law, 'do not kill'. Jesus goes beyond that commandment; he goes deeper, focusing on the underlying attitude that can lead to murder. We are not to harbour the kind of anger that can have such deadly consequences; we are not to use the kind of disrespectful language, such as 'Fool', that can so easily spill over into disrespectful and deadly actions. Jesus is speaking about the freedom to be at a very deep level the kind of person God desires us to be and has created us to be. It is only the Spirit who can give us this quality of freedom, the freedom to be virtuous in heart so as to be virtuous in action.

## 14 June, Friday, Tenth Week in Ordinary Time

*Matthew 5:27–32*

We often speak about the importance of getting to the heart of the matter. Jesus had an uncanny ability to do just that. When it came to human behaviour, he looked beyond the external behaviour to the heart from which it sprang. In today's gospel reading, he looks beyond the act of adultery to the lust residing in the heart from which it springs. Jesus insists that the problem begins with a man's fundamental attitude towards a woman. Going beyond the area of sexual behaviour, Jesus invites us to reflect on how we perceive others, not just with our eyes but with our heart. We know from the history of the twentieth century that regimes that view some groups as less than human treat them accordingly. In Nazi propaganda films, Jewish people were portrayed as rodents. On a more personal level, if someone is perceived primarily as an object for one's sexual satisfaction, then that person will be treated inhumanely. The extreme advice that Jesus goes on to give in the Gospel – 'if your right eye should cause you to sin, tear it out and throw it away' – is intended to bring home to us the urgency of taking radical action to change our perception of others, to change our hearts. Paul would remind us that such a change of heart is not just down to us. It is ultimately God's work with which we need to cooperate. As he says in today's first reading, 'such an overwhelming power comes from God and not from us'.

## 15 June, Saturday, Tenth Week in Ordinary Time
*Matthew 5:33–37*

In the gospel reading today, Jesus seems to envisage a world in which there is no need for anyone to take an oath to show they are speaking the truth. Rather, it can be taken for granted that when people speak they are speaking truly and honestly. When they say 'yes' they mean 'yes' and when they say 'no' they mean 'no'. They don't say 'yes' and 'no' at the same time. In other words, we can trust what people say because we know it corresponds to reality or will correspond to reality. As elsewhere in the Sermon on the Mount, Jesus seems to place the bar very high. At least within the community of his disciples, he holds that there should be no need for the taking of an oath because it is to be assumed that people's word will always be reliable and trustworthy. It could be said of Jesus that he was as good as his word. He did what he said. His word could be trusted. It doesn't need an oath to uphold it. It stands on its own. It is an authoritative word that can be relied upon. We are reading these days from the second letter of Paul to the Corinthians. Towards the beginning of that letter Paul declares that 'Jesus Christ, the Son of God … was not "Yes" and "No", but in him it is always "Yes". For in him every one of God's promises is a "Yes".' Jesus is the 'Yes' to all God's promises in the Jewish Scriptures. He reveals God's word to be a faithful word that can be trusted. In the gospel reading, Jesus is calling on us his disciples to speak in a way that is faithful and trustworthy, that reflects the trustworthiness of God's word.

## 17 June, Monday, Eleventh Week in Ordinary Time

*Matthew 5:38–42*

In the gospel reading Jesus calls on his disciples not to repay evil with evil, but to respond to evil with goodness. Paul says something similar in his letter to the Romans: 'Do not be overcome by evil, but overcome evil with good'. The worst instinct in human nature is to overcome good with evil, which is what brought Jesus to a Roman cross. The best instinct of human nature is to overcome evil with good. This in fact could be termed the divine instinct, God's instinct. It was the way of Jesus. He lived and died to overcome evil with good. It is not easy to remain good in the face of evil, to be loving in the face of hatred, to be faithful in the face of unfaithfulness, to remain just in the face of injustice done to us, to be peacemakers in the face of violence done to us. We cannot live in this way drawing on our own strength and resources alone. We need God's strength, God's resources, God's Spirit, because such a way of life is the fruit of God's Spirit at work within us.

## 18 June, Tuesday, Eleventh Week in Ordinary Time

*Matthew 5:43–48*

The Sermon on the Mount puts some very challenging teaching before us, and nowhere more so than the section we have just heard in today's gospel reading. Jesus calls on us to love our enemies and to pray for those who persecute us. The second part of that call makes the first part more concrete. We love our enemies by praying for them. Praying for others is always an act of love, whether we are praying for our friends, members of our family, those who are in need or, in the case of the gospel reading today, our enemies, those who wish us ill. Of the four evangelists, it is Luke who presents Jesus as doing just that. As he hung from the cross, Jesus prayed, 'Father, forgive them for they know not what they are doing'. That prayer of Jesus – and all prayers in the spirit of Jesus' prayer – displays an extraordinary generosity of spirit. Jesus calls on us to pray for those who persecute us because that is the kind of person that he is, and, more fundamentally, that is who God is like. God's love does not discriminate between the morally good and the morally bad; he makes the sun to shine and the rain to fall on honest and dishonest alike. God's love is the same for all; what differs is the response of people to that love. In so far as our love for others is not dependent on how people respond to it, we will be as perfect as God is perfect.

## 19 June, Wednesday, Eleventh Week in Ordinary Time

*Matthew 6:1–6, 16–18*

The gospel reading reminds us that there is always a danger that our good deeds can end up being quite self-serving, whether it is the good deed of almsgiving, praying or fasting. Jesus calls on us not to do our good deeds to attract the attention of others. Our focus in doing what we do is not so much other people and how they see us, but God. Three times the gospel reading refers to the Father who sees all that is done in secret. We live our lives in the conscious awareness of the presence of God with whom we have an intimate relationship through faith and Baptism. The Father who sees in secret is not to be understood as a kind of Big Brother watching us and waiting for us to fall. Rather, Jesus, God-with-us, has promised to be with us to the end of time out of love for us. Our good deeds are our loving response to God's love for us through Jesus. In all we say and do our focus is to be on the Lord who is always present to us, rather than on ourselves. In this way we give expression in our lives to the beatitude that declares, 'Blessed are the pure in heart, for they shall see God'.

## 20 June, Thursday, Eleventh Week in Ordinary Time
*Matthew 6:7–15*

Jesus' giving of what has come to be known as the Lord's Prayer is to be found in two gospels, those of Matthew and Luke. In Matthew's Gospel Jesus prefaces the giving of the prayer by calling on his disciples, when praying to God, not to use too many words, not to babble as the pagans do. Jesus is referring to the pagan practice of bombarding the gods with various formulae, with the intention of forcing the gods to behave in a way that is favourable to humankind. However, the disciples of Jesus are not to relate to their heavenly Father in that way. God is not there to be manipulated by our many words. Rather, as the opening petitions of the Lord's Prayer suggests, we begin by surrendering to whatever God may want, to God's purpose for our world and our lives. What matters is God's name, God's kingdom, God's will. We don't try to force God to do what we want; we surrender to what God wants. After doing that, as the prayer indicates, we acknowledge our dependence on God for our basic needs – for food for the day, for forgiveness, for strength when our faith is put to the test. The Lord's Prayer is powerful in its simplicity. It is not simply one prayer among many; it is a teaching on how to pray always.

## 21 June, Friday, Eleventh Week in Ordinary Time

*Matthew 6:19–23*

In today's first reading Paul boasts of experiences that most people would consider great misfortunes that should only be mentioned in hushed tones. He speaks of beatings, imprisonment, flogging, stoning, shipwreck and much more. Yet, he is prepared to boast of all these negative experiences because he endured them in the service of the Gospel. It was because of his devotion to Christ and his Gospel that all this suffering and misfortune came his way. They demonstrate where his true treasure lies, in the language of the gospel reading. His true treasure is the person of Christ, as he says in his letter to the Philippians: 'I regard everything as loss because of the surpassing value of knowing Christ Jesus my Lord'. When Jesus calls on us to store up for ourselves true treasures in heaven, he is calling on us to take him as our true treasure. In the language of one of the parables of Matthew's Gospel, Jesus is the pearl of great price. The Eucharist gives us an opportunity to treasure the surpassing value of this priceless pearl.

## 22 June, Saturday, Eleventh Week in Ordinary Time

*Matthew 6:24–34*

We all spend a certain amount of our lives trying to figure out what our priorities should be. People often find that there can be a tension between the demands of work and the demands of home, for example. Where should the priority lie at any particular time? Sometimes we just have to live with the tension of competing priorities and try to order them as best we can. We will probably never get the perfect solution to competing priorities. However, we can get our most basic priorities right, those fundamental priorities that shape all the decisions we make as to what is the best thing to do in the here and now. It is those basic priorities that Jesus is talking about in the gospel reading. When he says that you cannot be the slave both of God and of money he is declaring that money should never be our ultimate priority. When he says do not worry about what you are to eat or about your clothing, but set your hearts on God's kingdom first, and his righteousness, he is declaring that doing God's will, living in accordance with the values of God's kingdom, is a higher priority than food or clothing. He states this as one who elsewhere demands that we feed the hungry and clothe the naked. Jesus is talking in the gospel reading about that fundamental priority, that decision for God and his kingdom, which is to shape everything else that we do in life. He seems to be saying that we must get that right first, and then all else will follow.

## 24 June, Monday, The Nativity of John the Baptist

*Luke 1:57–66, 80*

It is probably true to say that children are called by a much greater variety of names today than would have been the case in the past. Until relatively recently, a newborn child might have been called after someone in the family. However, many of the names that children are given today would not have featured in their family tree. In the time of Jesus there was a very traditional approach to naming children. They were named after a family member or a member of the wider clan. When Elizabeth declared that her son was to be named John, everybody objected, 'But no one in your family has that name'. When the child's father, Zechariah, confirmed in writing, 'His name is John', he regained the power of speech he had lost when he doubted the angel Gabriel's announcement that his wife would bear him a son. Here was a real break with a family tradition; a new name emerged than no one in the family had ever been given. God was about to do something new, and the son of Elizabeth and Zechariah would, as an adult, announce this new initiative of God. He would speak of the one coming after him who would baptise people with the

Holy Spirit and fire. The question of the neighbours on the occasion of John's naming and circumcision was a valid one, 'What will this child turn out to be?' He turned out to be the one who prepared a way in people's lives for the coming of God's Son. Here, indeed, was a new moment in God's dealings with humanity. God was doing a new thing. God continues to do a new thing in all our lives. God, through his Son, the risen Lord, is always at work within us, opening up new ways for Jesus, the Lord, to enter more fully into our lives. Our calling is to cooperate with God's ongoing work of renewal in our lives. John the Baptist's parents and John the Baptist himself were open to God's surprising new work, even when others objected. They have something to teach us as we strive to do the same.

## 25 June, Tuesday, Twelfth Week in Ordinary Time
*Matthew 7:6, 12–14*

In the gospel reading Jesus reduces all of the Jewish Law and the prophets to a very short maxim: 'always treat others as you would like them to treat you'. Jesus invites us to imagine how we would like people to treat us, to ask ourselves the question, 'What is it I really want from another person?' Most of us would answer that question along similar lines. We want from others respect, tolerance, loyalty, understanding, compassion and justice. Having engaged in that exercise of imagining how we would like others to treat us, Jesus then declares that we should act towards others in a way that reflects those very same qualities.

The following verse in the gospel reading, 'enter by the narrow gate', implies that following this rule of treating others as we would want them to treat us will not always be easy. Narrow gates require an effort to get through. The narrow gate Jesus speaks about leads to what he calls a hard road. Jesus' teaching requires a daily dying to self, putting the good of the other before our own good. The way of life that he sets before us is a difficult and challenging way, yet he declares that it is the way that leads to life. It is a life-giving path for us in the course of our earthly life, and it will lead us to eternal life, a sharing in the Lord's own risen life.

## 26 June, Wednesday, Twelfth Week in Ordinary Time

*Matthew 7:15–20*

In today's gospel reading, Jesus draws attention to the separation that can often exist between appearance and reality. Just as there can be more to some people than meets the eye, so there can be less to some people than meets the eye. It is that second situation that Jesus highlights in the gospel reading. He speaks of those who look like harmless sheep but underneath are ravenous wolves. Projecting a false image, living a lie, is an ongoing part of the human experience. Where our hearts lie does not always correspond to how we appear. Jesus declares that the real test of what is in our hearts is the kind of fruit that our lives bear. 'You will be able to tell them by their fruits'. Paul used that same language of 'fruit' when he wrote about the 'fruit of the Spirit', which he describes as 'love, joy, peace, kindness, generosity, faithfulness, gentleness and self-control'. Paul doesn't speak of 'fruits', but of 'fruit'. There is one fruit of the Spirit, which can be described in all these different ways. If our lives bear that kind of good fruit, our heart belongs to God, regardless of how we may appear at times. We need to keep opening our hearts to the Spirit whom we have been given, so that the good fruit of the Spirit will be more abundant in our lives.

## 27 June, Thursday, Twelfth Week in Ordinary Time

*Matthew 7:21–29*

In today's gospel reading, which is the conclusion of the Sermon on the Mount, Jesus lays emphasis on the importance of 'doing the will of my Father in heaven'. This takes priority over powerful works done in Jesus' name or declaring him publicly to be 'Lord'. Earlier in the Sermon on the Mount, Jesus had declared, 'Set your hearts on his kingdom first and on his righteousness'. By 'righteousness', Jesus means the doing of God's will. In the middle of the Sermon on the Mount, the prayer that Jesus gave his disciples begins, 'Your kingdom come, your will be done, on earth as in heaven'. It is clear that, for Jesus, becoming his follower can be summarised as doing the will of his Father in heaven. Throughout the Sermon on the Mount and throughout the whole Gospel of Matthew, Jesus reveals what doing the will of his Father in heaven involves. It means, above all, loving others as God loves us, including our enemy; it entails recognising and serving Jesus in those who are broken in body, mind or spirit, in those who are weak and vulnerable, like children. In so far as we live in this way, the kingdom of God will come into our world in and through our lives. Then our lives will be firmly rooted, like a house built on rock. We will be revealing something of the enduring quality of God's love for all in Jesus.

## 28 June, Friday, Feast of the Most Sacred Heart of Jesus
*Matthew 11:25–30*
One of the shortest and yet most profound statements about God is to be found in today's second reading, 'God is love'. Much has been spoken and written about God since that statement was made nearly two thousand years ago, yet everything that could be said or written about God only serves to open up the depths of that statement, 'God is love'. That reading further states that God was revealed as Love by God's sending of his Son into the world so that we could have life through him, a sharing in God's own life. It is the sending of God's Son into the world, the life, death and resurrection of Jesus, which reveals God to be Love. In the gospel reading, Jesus declares that no

one knows the Son except the Father, and no one know the Father except the Son. It is only Jesus who knows God, which is why, as Jesus says in the gospel reading, he can reveal God to those whom he chooses. It is Jesus who reveals God to be Love.

The heart of Jesus is the heart of God, which is a heart of love. In celebrating the feast of the Sacred Heart of Jesus, we are celebrating Jesus as the one who reveals God's heart, God's core, to be Love. The invitation that Jesus issues in today's gospel reading comes straight from his heart, straight from the loving heart of God: 'Come to me, all you who labour and are overburdened and I will give you rest'. It is an invitation that has brought consolation to believers down the centuries. It is God's loving heart in Jesus calling out to our hearts to come. Before Jesus asks us to do anything, he first invites us to come to him. If we respond to his invitation, we will experience what he calls his rest, or his peace, a peace the world cannot give, and we will discover that whatever burdens we carry are not as heavy as they once seemed.

## 29 June, Saturday, Ss Peter and Paul

*Matthew 16:13–19*

The two saints whose feast we celebrate today were key members of the early Church. Peter was the leader of the Twelve. According to the gospel reading, it was to Peter that Jesus gave the keys of the kingdom of heaven, a symbol of Peter's authoritative role in the early Church. Paul never met Jesus before Jesus' death. Whereas Jesus called Peter by the Sea of Galilee, it was the risen Lord who called Paul on his way into the city of Damascus. Whereas Jesus called Peter to be the authoritative rock on which he would build his Church, the focal point of the Church's unity, the risen Lord called Paul to be the apostle to the pagans. Each of these great disciples had very different experiences of Jesus and each received a very different mission from

Jesus. Yet, it is clear from today's first reading and second reading that both Peter and Paul had one thing in common: They both suffered in the exercise of their mission. The first reading tells us that King Herod Agrippa imprisoned Peter, and in the second reading Paul writes from prison to Timothy in the awareness that his life is coming to an end. Indeed, both men were executed because of their preaching of the Gospel. Today the two basilicas of St Peter and St Paul in Rome stand over their tombs and are places of pilgrimage. The particular way the Lord calls us to follow him will be unique to each one of us, yet what we can all have in common is a dedication to the Lord's way, even though it may mean the way of the cross.

When Peter and Paul took this way, they both discovered that the Lord was supporting and sustaining them. Peter says in the first reading, 'The Lord has saved me from Herod', and Paul declares in the second reading, 'The Lord stood by me and gave me power'. When we try to be faithful to the Lord's way, we will make the same discovery of the Lord's sustaining presence in our lives.

## 1 July, Monday, Thirteenth Week in Ordinary Time
*Matthew 8:18–22*

When people show enthusiasm for some project we are involved in, we would normally welcome their enthusiasm and give them every encouragement. This would be especially true if there was a general lack of enthusiasm for what we were doing, or even a great deal of opposition towards it. In the gospel reading today, Jesus encounters a man who shows great enthusiasm towards Jesus and all he stands for. He comes up to Jesus and says to him, 'I will follow you wherever you go'. Yet, rather than respond to this man's enthusiasm with an equal display of enthusiasm, Jesus almost seems to pour cold water on his enthusiasm. He reminds this potential disciple that the person he is so enthusiastic to follow will often find himself with nowhere to lay his head. If that is true of Jesus, it will also be true of anyone who would follow him. Jesus is suggesting that the man's enthusiasm needs to be tempered with a good dose of reality. As disciples of the Lord today, we need both something of this man's enthusiasm and something of Jesus' realism. We may be fortunate to have a place to lay our head but following Jesus remains a challenging path. Taking the way that Jesus calls us to take will involve a readiness to deny ourselves in the service of the Lord and his people, a willingness to empty ourselves so that others can be filled. Our enthusiasm for the Lord and our recognition that following him will not be easy are two contrasting poles that we need to keep holding in tension.

## 2 July, Tuesday, Thirteenth Week in Ordinary Time

*Matthew 8:23–27*

As we know our weather can change suddenly. The gospel reading suggests that the onset of this particular storm on the Sea of Galilee was sudden: 'without warning a storm broke over the lake'. We know from our own life experience that our own personal circumstances can change without warning. We can suddenly find ourselves in the midst of some raging personal storm. One day all is well; the next day we are in crisis. To that extent the gospel reading today speaks to our own personal experience. Matthew's way of telling the story of the storm at sea links it much more closely to the experience of the people who made up the Church than Mark's way of telling the same story. The cry of the disciples in Matthew's account, 'Save us, Lord, we are going down', is very much the cry of those believers for whom Matthew was writing his Gospel. It is the cry of us all at some time in our lives. Matthew seeks to reassure us that the Lord will respond to such a cry; our prayer for help in vulnerable times will not go unanswered. The Lord is stronger than the storm that threatens, and, in turning towards the Lord, we will draw from his strength.

## 3 July, Wednesday, St Thomas, Apostle

*John 20:24–29*

We may find it easy to identify with Thomas in today's gospel reading. When the other disciples approached him with the good news of Easter, 'We have seen the Lord', their message did not resonate with him in any way. The darkness of Good Friday was still too real for him and prevented his being moved by their Easter proclamation. His own reasoning did not allow him to believe that life had triumphed over death, that the crucified Jesus was now the risen Lord. Thomas stood in the light of Easter, yet that light did not dispel his darkness. If his fellow disciples were full of Easter faith, he was full of doubt. They claimed to have seen the risen Lord; Thomas declared that he would not believe until he not only saw the Lord but touched his wounds. Many believers can be troubled by their sense that the light of Easter does not seem to have penetrated their lives sufficiently. We can be distressed at the degree of doubt that we experience within ourselves, troubled that such doubts may even become more pronounced as we get older. Like Thomas, we can struggle to identify fully with those whose faith seems so much more assured than ours. The prayer of one of the more minor Gospel characters, 'Lord, I believe, help my unbelief', may find a ready place our heart. Today's gospel reading assures us that the Lord understands a doubting, questioning faith. When the Lord appeared to Thomas, he did not rebuke him. His first words to him were, 'Peace be with you'. He invited Thomas to touch his wounds as he had requested, and then called on him to 'doubt no longer but believe'. Seeing the risen Lord was enough to dispel his doubt. Then, out of the mouth of the great sceptic, came one of the most complete professions of faith in the four Gospels, 'My Lord and my God'. We are being reminded that serious doubt and great faith can reside in one and the same person.

## 4 July, Thursday, Thirteenth Week in Ordinary Time

*Matthew 9:1–8*

I have often been struck by the image in today's gospel reading of people carrying a paralysed man to Jesus on a stretcher. He couldn't make his own way to Jesus in search of healing, so they carried him. It was an act of love, of care and compassion. There are times in all our lives when, like the paralysed man, we need to be carried, even if not physically, by others. There comes a time when we need the support of others to take us places we cannot reach ourselves. There are other times when we might find ourselves in the role of the people who carried the paralytic. We find ourselves in a position of being able to support someone who needs our support at that time. We help carry them until they can find their own feet. This is the human story at its best. It is also, of course, the Christian story. It is said in today's gospel reading that when people brought the paralytic to Jesus, he saw their faith: 'seeing their faith'. Underpinning this act of love was a deep faith. Paul in one of his letters speaks about faith working through love, or faith expressing itself in love. Genuine faith will always find expression in acts of loving service. Nothing is said of the faith of the paralytic. Seeing the faith of the people who carried the paralytic, Jesus then addresses himself to the man himself. It was the faith of others that brought this man to Jesus. There is an image here of the Church. As people of faith, we are called to bring each other to the Lord. When our own faith is weak, we need the faith of others to bring us to the Lord, to open us up to the Lord's presence.

## 5 July, Friday, Thirteenth Week in Ordinary Time

*Matthew 9:9–13*

When people do something out of the ordinary, we often ask the question 'Why?' It sparks our curiosity and we want to know what it is that drives this person to do something so unconventional. The

Pharisees regarded Jesus as someone who took seriously the will of God for our lives, just as they did. However, he did things which to their eyes were very unconventional. The Pharisees would have separated themselves from those they regarded as 'sinners', so as not to be contaminated by them in some way. Jesus, in contrast, shared table with tax collectors and sinners, those who habitually broke the Jewish Law as the Pharisees interpreted it. Jesus knew that he would not be any the worse for engaging with such people. Rather, they would be the better for his entering into communion with them. Goodness flowed from him to others; lack of goodness or sin did not flow from others to him. He saw himself as the heavenly physician sent to heal broken humanity. All would be the healthier in every sense for being around him, even those who thought of themselves as already virtuous in God's eyes.

We all come before the Lord in our brokenness, in our various forms of dis-ease. We come before him present to us in his word, in the sacraments, above all in the Eucharist. As we do so, we will encounter what Jesus in the gospel reading calls 'mercy'. We will be received by the Lord's merciful presence, and if we are truly open to that presence, we will come away from it more alive, more whole, more complete.

## 6 July, Saturday, Thirteenth Week in Ordinary Time
*Matthew 9:14–17*
We often find ourselves wondering if the time is right. I am not thinking so much of the time our watches, clocks and mobile phones show us but of time in the more general sense. Is this the right time to say this or to take that course of action? We may be aware that something needs to be said or done, but it is the question of timing that is the issue. It is not so much 'if' but 'when'. It is this question of timing that is being discussed by Jesus and the disciples of John the Baptist

in today's gospel reading. They want to know why Jesus' disciples are not fasting in the way the disciples of John the Baptist fast. In reply, Jesus declares that the time is not right. The time of Jesus' ministry is a celebratory time. He is like the bridegroom at a wedding feast and his disciples are his attendants. It is time to rejoice, to celebrate the presence of God's gracious love.

Jesus will soon be taken away from his disciples in death, and then the time will be appropriate to fast. Fasting is timely for Jesus' disciples after his death and resurrection, in the period of the Church, but it is not timely during the period of Jesus' public ministry. It takes wisdom to know the right time for something. As the Book of Ecclesiastes declares, 'there is a time for everything under heaven'. We can all get our timing wrong every so often and, it is to be hoped that we can learn from the experience. The wisdom that allows us to discern the right time for something is ultimately a gift of the Holy Spirit. This gift is one expression of the 'new wine' Jesus speaks about in today's gospel reading. It is given to all who know their need of it and ask for it with persevering faith.

## 8 July, Monday, Fourteenth Week in Ordinary Time

*Matthew 9:18–26*

There is nothing sadder than the funeral of a child. When a child dies everyone is rendered speechless. What words could be adequate to address the loss and grief experienced by the child's parents? The prayer of the grieving father to Jesus in today's gospel reading would surely find an echo in the heart of every grieving parent, 'My daughter has just died, but come and lay your hand on her and her life will be saved'. It is a prayer that acknowledges the dark reality of the death of a child – 'my daughter has just died' – but also expresses hope that somehow this death will not have the last word – 'lay your hands on her and her life will be saved'. Jesus went on to raise this man's daughter to life. There must have been many children who died in the time and place of Jesus whom Jesus did not restore to life. However, his raising of the official's daughter to life served as a sign for all grieving parents. God's power in Jesus will always work to bring new life out of every death. Jesus' own experience of death has not abolished death, but his resurrection from the dead reveals that death does not have the last word.

Our relationship with God and God's relationship with us will endure beyond the moment of physical death, just as Jesus' death was not the end of his relationship with God or of God's relationship with him. If our relationship with God does not end with death, neither will our various human relationships end, because they are all contained within our relationship with God. In coming closer to God, we come closer to each other.

## 9 July, Tuesday, Fourteenth Week in Ordinary Time
*Matthew 9:32–38*

There is a very striking contrast in  today's gospel reading between the way the people respond to the healing ministry of Jesus and the way the religious leaders respond. The people were amazed and said, 'Nothing like this has ever been seen in Israel'. The religious leaders said, 'It is through the prince of devils that he casts out devils'. Both saw Jesus perform the same deeds, yet both interpreted what they saw in very different ways. One group saw the presence of God and the other group saw the presence of evil. One group was open to the truth of who Jesus really was; the other was blinded by prejudice. These were two very different ways of seeing. The people's way of seeing Jesus was like Jesus' way of seeing people. He saw the goodness in people, just as the people saw the presence of God in Jesus. The gospel reading calls on us to be alert to the signs of goodness in others, to the signs of God's presence all around us, especially in those who cross our path in life. We need the generous vision of the people, and especially of Jesus, rather than the jaundiced vision of the religious leaders, if we are to see the many ways that the Lord is present and active among us..

## 10 July, Wednesday, Fourteenth Week in Ordinary Time
*Matthew 10:1–7*

Famine is a stark reality in many parts of eastern Africa today. Various aid agencies are looking to us to support their work in meeting the needs of the huge numbers affected by famine. The phenomenon of famine is very present in today's first reading. When famine struck in the countries of the Near East in the ancient world, people looked to Egypt for food. Egypt was a kind of bread basket. Even when the rains ceased, crops could grow along the Nile and in the Nile Delta. When the sons of Jacob left Canaan for Egypt in search of food, they met the official in charge of distributing grain. Without their realising it, he was their brother Joseph, the brother they had sold into slavery many years earlier. The brother they had rejected was now in a position to be their life-saver. Although Joseph's brothers did not recognise Joseph, he recognised them. They went to Egypt like lost sheep in search of pasture. In Joseph, they encountered someone who could be their shepherd. The stone that the builders rejected had become the corner stone. Joseph went on to be their shepherd; he fed those who had rejected him. In the gospel reading, Jesus sends out the Twelve like shepherds for the lost sheep of the house of Israel. They are to share in Jesus' own shepherding role. He sought out the lost, regardless of their past behaviour. He died for the lost, including those who rejected and crucified him. We are all called to be shepherds to each other, even to those who have no claim on our care because of how they may have treated us in the past.

## 11 July, Thursday, St Benedict, Abbot, Patron of Europe
*Matthew 19:27–29*

Today's gospel reading for the feast of St Benedict begins with a question from Peter: 'What about us? We have left everything and followed you'. Peter and the other members of the Twelve had given up a great deal to become followers of Jesus. They may have been wondering if it was really worth it all. We, too, have responded to the Lord's call, although not in the same very radical way that those intimate associates of Jesus or men like Benedict answered it, leaving livelihood and family for a very uncertain future. Perhaps on our off days we might be tempted to ask a similar question to that of Peter: 'Is it worth the effort, this following of Jesus, this struggle to live by the values of the Gospel day in and day out'.

The answer of Jesus to Peter and to us all is that, 'yes, it is worth the effort'. Jesus promises us in that gospel reading that when we respond to his call, when we give of ourselves for his sake, we will receive far more than we will give. In particular, he says that we will gain a new experience of family, far beyond the confines of our blood family, the family of believers. We will find ourselves co-travellers with others who are trying to take the same path as ourselves; we will experience the richness of the Church, the community of the Lord's followers. That community that journeys with us embraces not only those still on their pilgrim way, but all who have passed beyond this life, including the saints, like St Benedict, what the letter to the Hebrew calls that 'great cloud of witnesses'.

## 12 July, Friday, Fourteenth Week in Ordinary Time
*Matthew 10:16–23*

The words of Jesus to his disciples in today's gospel reading reflects the experience of the early Church. Those first generations of believers were indeed handed over to the Jewish sanhedrins and scourged in synagogues; they were dragged before pagan kings and governors and asked to give an account of their beliefs. Within the same family, there were those who professed faith in Jesus and those who did not, and, so, sibling did betray sibling to death, parents betrayed their children and children their parents. The kind of experience Jesus describes may seem somewhat remote from us, yet it is not far removed from the experience of many Christians today who live in a culture dominated by religious fundamentalism and intolerance. Even the secular culture, for all its espousal of liberalism and tolerance, can be very hostile to the public expression of religious belief, including the religious values of the Gospel. Towards the end of that gospel reading, Jesus speaks of the need to 'stand firm to the end'. He was very aware of the temptation to hide or deny our faith in him, when not to do so might entail exposing ourselves to opposition and ridicule, or worse. That is why Jesus promises us a share in God's own Spirit to empower us to stand firm to the end: 'The Spirit of your Father will be speaking in you'. We all need to keep asking for and opening our hearts to the gift of this Spirit, if we are to stand firm to the end, in our own time and place.

## 13 July, Saturday, Fourteenth Week in Ordinary Time
*Matthew 10:24–34*

Three times in the course of today's gospel reading, Jesus says to his disciples, 'Do not be afraid'. They are not to fear those who will treat Jesus' disciples as they have treated Jesus himself, who can kill the body of the disciples as they killed Jesus' body. The disciples are to fear God, who can destroy body and soul in hell. However, Jesus immediately qualifies this God, whom the disciples are to fear, as a heavenly Father who is so lovingly involved in their lives that he knows the number of hairs on their heads. As believers in Jesus, we enjoy a familial relationship with God, which is a sharing in Jesus' own relationship with God as Son.

We are valued and watched over by God, just as Jesus was. This sense of God's loving care for us gives an assurance and a confidence to proclaim our relationship with Jesus our brother, and God, the Father of Jesus and our Father. We are to proclaim this graced relationship from the housetops, not as a self-congratulatory boast, but as good news for all to hear, because all are called into this same relationship. We are to declare ourselves for the Lord in the presence of others, knowing that the Lord will declare himself for us in God's presence. The grace and privilege of being taken up into Jesus' own relationship with God is at the same time an empowering call to witness publicly to who we are and what we have received.

## 15 July, Monday, Fifteenth Week in Ordinary Time
*Matthew 10:34–11:1*

Jesus declares in the gospel reading that whoever gives a cup of cold water to someone thirsty will most certainly not lose his or her reward. The reward Jesus refers to is an eternal reward. At one level, the giving of a cup of cold water to someone can seem like a very small act of kindness, yet Jesus declares that such an act has eternal significance. There is more going on there than meets the eye. Small acts of kindness and generosity, like the giving of a cup of cold water, can reveal a bigness of heart and spirit, the heart of Jesus. The Lord's love is often revealed in our lives in little ways, by attention to the little details that make people feel at home. It is such acts of kindness towards others, no matter how small, that create openings for the coming of God's kingdom on earth.

Through our acts of kindness, the Lord of life comes to others. Also, such acts of kindness and hospitality lead us to encounter the Lord in those we serve. Earlier in today's gospel reading, Jesus had said to his disciples, 'anyone who welcomes you, welcomes me, and those who welcome me welcome not me but the one who sent me'. When we welcome another in need, no matter in how small a way, not only are we helping to make the Lord present, but we are meeting the Lord and God, his Father and our Father, in those we serve. Wherever there is kindness, care and hospitality shown, there the Lord is present in various ways. Such encounters have a real sacramental quality to them. They help to make the Lord present in the world.

## 16 July, Tuesday, Fifteenth Week in Ordinary Time
*Matthew 11:20–24*

We are all very aware of how, from time to time, we can fail to respond to certain situations in the most appropriate way. We might realise very shortly afterwards that our response left a lot to be desired. It is to be hoped that we can learn from such experiences. The Lord speaks to us through our failings as much as through our virtue. Both of today's readings put before us examples of an inappropriate response to situations.

In the first reading, Moses saw an Egyptian strike a Hebrew, one of his countrymen. He responded by killing the Egyptian and burying his body in the sand. As a result, he had to flee to a different country, leaving what was familiar to him for the unknown.

In the gospel reading, Jesus complains about three towns in Galilee who responded with indifference to the mighty works that he performed among them. One of those towns, Capernaum, is known to us from the Gospels as a focal point for Jesus' teaching and deeds. Moses' response was one of violence to an act of violence. The response of these towns was one of indifference to many life-giving acts on behalf of others. The Lord calls out to us from every situation in life, both those that proclaim death and those that proclaim life. In each and every situation, we need to 'seek the Lord' in the words of the response to today's psalm. With the help of the Holy Spirit, we try to discern what the Lord is saying to me in and through this situation and how he is calling on me to respond.

## 17 July, Wednesday, Fifteenth Week in Ordinary Time
*Matthew 11:25–27*

In the gospel reading, Jesus draws a sharp distinction between what he calls 'the learned and the clever' and 'mere children'. The term 'children', or 'little ones', is probably a reference to Jesus' disciples who would not have been considered learned and clever at the time. The learned and the clever were the experts in the Jewish Law, those who considered themselves to have a clear understanding of God and God's will. Many of Jesus' disciples were anything but experts in the Jewish Law but would have been considered 'sinners', breakers of the law, by the religious experts. Yet, it was these people who were open to Jesus' revelation of God, whereas the learned and clever rejected Jesus' revelation of God. When it comes to matters of faith, we need to keep acknowledging how little we know, and how far we have yet to travel in coming to know God with our mind and our heart. This is what Jesus refers to elsewhere in Matthew's Gospel as poverty of spirit. It is to the poor in spirit that the kingdom of God belongs. It is the awareness of our own poverty of spirit, mind and heart, that disposes us to receive God's gift of his Son. Jesus assures us in the gospel reading that when we receive the Lord out of our poverty, we will be enriched, because we will be taken up into Jesus' own intimate relationship with God his Father.

## 18 July, Thursday, Fifteenth Week in Ordinary Time
*Matthew 11:28–30*

When Jesus declares in today's gospel reading, 'my yoke is easy and my burden light', he is saying that his teaching, his understanding of God's will, is not something burdensome. Rather, his teaching is liberating and life-enhancing. If his teaching is received and lived, it lightens the burden of oppression; it brings joy. That is not to say that Jesus' teaching is not demanding. We only have to listen to the Sermon on the Mount to realise that Jesus' teaching is in many ways more demanding than the teaching of the Jewish Law. If the Law prohibits murder, Jesus prohibits the kind of anger that can lead to murder. If the Law says, 'an eye for an eye', Jesus says, 'love your enemy'. His teaching is demanding but not burdensome. That is because Jesus does not ask us to live his teaching out of our own strength alone. He empowers us to live out his teaching. In today's gospel reading, Jesus does not say, 'Come to my teaching', but 'Come to me'. He does not say, 'learn my teaching', but 'learn from me'. He calls us into a personal relationship with himself. It is in coming to him that we receive his Spirit, the Holy Spirit, and so are empowered to live his teaching and, thereby, to become fully alive as human beings. Jesus promises that here and now we will experience something of that rest that awaits us in eternity if we come to him and allow him to empower us to live his teaching in our daily lives.

## 19 July, Friday, Fifteenth Week in Ordinary Time
*Matthew 12:1–8*

In the gospel reading, Jesus accuses his critics among the Pharisees of condemning the blameless. They condemned Jesus' disciples for plucking corn on the Sabbath to satisfy their hunger. They would have regarded such 'work' as a form of reaping, which was forbidden on the Sabbath. However, Jesus in his response to their criticism, reminds them that if they were as attuned to their own religious tradition as they claim to be they would not have condemned the 'blameless'. He reminds them that the overriding value in the Jewish tradition is 'mercy', and points out that are precedents in the Jewish Scriptures for what his disciples are doing. The Sabbath rest was an important value. However, 'mercy' is a greater value in God's eyes. The actions of others need to be viewed with the eyes of mercy, eyes that seek to understand why people are doing what they are doing, eyes that recognise that basic human needs take priority over the keeping of religious law. The failure to look upon others with eyes of mercy often results in the condemnation of the blameless. The temptation to condemn the blameless is always with us. It is a temptation we can resist to the extent that something of God's merciful vision has taken flesh in our lives.

## 20 July, Saturday, Fifteenth Week in Ordinary Time
*Matthew 12:14–21*

There is a striking contrast in today's gospel reading between those who plot against Jesus in order to destroy him and Jesus himself, who has not come to destroy but to cure and to heal. From early on in his ministry, many were out to bring death to Jesus, whereas Jesus himself was always in the business of bringing life to others, a share in God's own life. This is why Matthew the evangelist applies to Jesus a text about God's servant in the Book of Isaiah which says, 'he will not break the bruised reed, nor put out the smouldering wick'. The bruised reed and the smouldering wick refer to those who are broken in body and depressed in spirit. It is very easy to break a bruised reed and put out a smouldering wick. Those who are broken in body or depressed in spirit tend to be very vulnerable. The gospel reading presents Jesus as one who is sensitive to those who are vulnerable. He can recreate the bruised reed and fan into a living flame the smouldering wick. There are times when we need to come before the Lord in our brokenness and vulnerability and ask him to renew and strengthen us. That prayer to the Lord could take the form of the wonderful prayer to the Holy Spirit we say on Pentecost Sunday, 'Come thou Father of the poor … Heal our wounds, our strength renew, on our dryness pour thy dew'. When we are touched by the power of the life-giver we, in turn, can become life-givers for others.

## 22 July, Monday, Feast of St Mary Magdalene
*John 20:1–2, 11–18*

One of the titles of Mary Magdalene in the early Church is 'apostle to the apostles'. That title is based on the gospel reading we have just heard. In the Gospel of John, Mary Magdalene is the person to whom the risen Lord appears and the first person to proclaim the Gospel of Easter, and she does so to the disciples of Jesus. Today's gospel reading suggests that before she made that outer, geographical, journey of bringing the Gospel to others, she first had to undergo an inner journey. She begins still in the darkness of Good Friday. Not only has Jesus died but his body appears to have been stolen. Mary's dismay and grief find expression in her tears. Gradually she is led out of this darkness of spirit by the risen Lord. When Jesus came to her, she did not recognise him initially. However, when he spoke her name, her eyes were opened and she saw. Even then, she still had an inner journey to travel. She held on to him as if Jesus had returned to the life he once lived, yet Jesus had been transformed through his resurrection from the dead, and his relationship with Mary and his other disciples had been transformed. He would now relate to them through the Holy Spirit, who he would send from God the Father, his Father and our Father. It was only when Mary could let go of the relationship she and other disciples once had with Jesus and was open to this new kind of relationship with him that she could be sent out to proclaim the Easter Gospel to the disciples. There is always some inner journey we need to undergo before we can go out to others in the Lord's name. The Lord keeps calling us by name, inviting us to turn towards him more fully, and calling on us not to cling to whatever may be coming between us and him. This inner journey is the journey of a lifetime.

We cannot wait for it to be complete before going out to witness to the Lord, because it isn't complete this side of eternity. All the Lord asks is that we remain faithful to this inner journey of growing in our relationship with him as we go out in his name.

## 23 July, Tuesday, Feast of St Bridget of Sweden

*John 15:1–8*

Bridget was born in the year 1303, the daughter of a wealthy governor in Sweden. She married a well-to-do man and they had eight children. She went on to serve as the principal lady-in-waiting to the queen of Sweden. She had a reputation as a woman of great prayer. After her husband died she became a member of the third order of St Francis. She then founded a monastery for sixty nuns and twenty-five monks who lived in separate enclosures but shared the same church. She journeyed to Rome in 1349 to obtain papal approval for her order, and spent the rest of her life in Italy or on various pilgrimages, including one to the Holy Land. She impressed with her simplicity of life and her devotion to pilgrims, to the poor and the sick. She experienced visions of various kinds; some of them were of the passion of Christ. She died in Rome in 1373. She was canonised not for her visions but for her virtue. The gospel reading for her feast is Jesus' wonderful image of the vine and branches, 'I am the vine, you are the branches'. It is very difficult to distinguish between the vine and its branches. Where does the vine end and the branches begin? Surely the branches are themselves the vine? There is certainly a very close relationship between the vine and its branches. The image Jesus uses of the vine and the branches expresses the very intimate relationship that he desires between himself and ourselves, his disciples. The Lord is intimately involved with his Church. He is in communion with us. That is a given. What Jesus calls for in the gospel reading is that we be in communion with him, that we make our home in him. The image of the vine and the branches Jesus uses also expresses our dependence on him. We need to be in a deeply personal communion with Jesus so as to live off the sap that reaches us from him. We need to live in close contact with Jesus, if we, the Church, are to be fruitful in the way he wants us to be. It is only in and through our communion with Jesus that we as Church can bear his fruit, the fruit of the Spirit. The primary fruit of the Spirit is love, a love that brings life to others, just as Jesus's love has brought life to us all.

## 24 July, Wednesday, Sixteenth Week in Ordinary Time
*Matthew 13:1–9*

When Jesus saw the farmer going out to sow seeds, it reminded him of the way God was at work in his ministry. Jesus noticed that the farmer scattered the seed with abandon, almost recklessly, not knowing what kind of soil it would fall on. Inevitably, a great deal of the seed that was scattered was lost; it never germinated. Yet, some of the seed fell on good soil and produced an extraordinary harvest. In what way would this scene have spoken to Jesus about his ministry? God was scattering the seed of his life-giving word through Jesus' ministry. Through Jesus, God wanted to touch the lives of everyone, regardless of how they were perceived by others or even by themselves. God gave the most unlikely places the opportunity of receiving the life-giving seed of his word. There was nothing selective about Jesus' company. Jesus once spoke of God as making his sun to rise on the evil and on the good. This was the God that Jesus revealed in his own ministry. As with the farmer in the parable, much of what Jesus scattered was lost; it met with little or no response. Indeed, his gracious word often met with hostility. Yet, Jesus knew that some people were receiving the seed of his word, and that would be enough to bring about the harvest of God's kingdom. Jesus may have been speaking a word of encouragement to his disciples, saying to them, 'Despite all the setbacks, and hostility, God is at work and that work will lead to something wonderful'. In other words, 'the seed is good and powerful. Whatever the odds against us, we must keep sowing'.

## 25 July, Thursday, Feast of St James, Apostle
*Matthew 20:20–28*

According to the Gospels, Jesus called two sets of brothers who were fishermen, Peter and Andrew and James and John. Today we celebrate the feast of St James, the brother of John and the son of Zebedee. James's father, Zebedee, seems to have had a flourishing fishing business by the shore of the Sea of Galilee. According to Mark's Gospel, he had 'hired men' working for him. In today's gospel reading, it is the mother of James and John who is to the fore. Like any mother, she wants what is best for her sons. If they are going to leave a flourishing fishing business to follow this carpenter from Nazareth, he had better have something just as good in store for them. Hearing Jesus proclaim the coming of a kingdom, she wants her sons to have the places of honour in that kingdom, one at Jesus' right hand and the other at his left. Her request, well-meaning as it is, is one that Jesus cannot grant in the way she imagines. If the mother of James and John wants something from Jesus for her sons, Jesus wants something very different from them: 'Can you drink the cup that I am going to drink?' At the Last Supper, Jesus would hand them the cup he drank from. He needed them to be ready to share his cup of suffering, to follow him even if it would cost them not less than everything. On this occasion the two sons display a willingness to drink Jesus' cup: 'We can'. Yet, when the hour of Jesus' passion arrived, they would abandon him with the other disciples. However, we know from the Acts of the Apostles that James did indeed drink Jesus' cup beyond the time of Jesus' death and resurrection. He was put to death by Herod Agrippa, about the year AD44, and was the first of the apostles to die for Christ.

Every time we gather to celebrate the Eucharist, the Lord asks us, 'Can you drink the cup that I am going to drink?' In coming to the Eucharist, we are dedicating ourselves to following in the Lord's way, even though it may cost us a great deal. If we strive to follow in the Lord's way and to live by his truth, we can be confident that, in the words of Paul in today's first reading, 'he who raised the Lord Jesus to life will raise us with Jesus in our turn'.

## 26 July, Friday, Sixteenth Week in Ordinary Time
*Matthew 13:18–23*

The ten commandments in the first reading present the values by which God wants us to live. The first four commandments concern our relationship with God. The last six concern our relationship with others. When Jesus was asked on one occasion what the two greatest commandments were, he responded that the first and most important commandment is to love God with all our heart, mind, strength and soul, and the second commandment is to love our neighbour as ourselves. The ten commandments spell out those two commandments in more detail, with the first four showing what loving God with all our being entails, and the last six articulating the minimum that love of neighbour demands. Jesus has shown us by his life, death and resurrection, what love of God and love of neighbour looks like. It is by following Jesus, by living according to his word, that we come to live the ten commandments and the two great commandments which condense these ten. In the gospel reading, Jesus outlines some of the ways we can be prevented from living according to his word. We may not allow the Lord's word to take sufficiently deep root in our lives. We may allow the worries of life and the pleasures of the world to choke his word. Jesus was aware that there are many obstacles to our following him, to our allowing his word to shape our lives. That is why he taught us to pray, 'Lead us not into temptation but deliver us from evil'. Such obstacles need not have the last word, because the Lord is always at work in our lives, helping us to withstand these temptations, and when we fail, he remains faithful to us.

## 27 July, Saturday, Sixteenth Week in Ordinary Time

*Matthew 13:24–30*

In today's parable Jesus was warning us against a premature separation of wheat from weed, of good from bad. He was saying that this kind of separation is really God's work, not our work, and that it will happen at the end of time rather than in the course of time. Just as the servants in the parable would have been unable to distinguish the wheat from the weeds if they had been let loose, we do not always have the necessary insight to distinguish who is good and who is evil. We can get it terribly wrong; we only have to think of those innocent people who have been wrongly imprisoned. How often in our own lives have we judged someone harshly, only to discover in time that we were very wide of the mark. The Church itself has not always heeded the warning of Jesus about the dangers of premature separation. The Inquisition was not in the spirit of the parable that Jesus speaks in today's gospel reading. Too great a zeal to purify the wheat field risks doing more harm than good. A weed-free garden may be highly desirable, but the gospel today suggests that we may have to learn to live with weeds. We need to be patient with imperfection, in ourselves and in others. As we know only too well, life is not tidy. It is not like a well-manicured garden, in which order and harmony prevail. Each of us is a mixture of wheat and weed; we are each tainted by sin and yet touched by grace. Our calling is to grow in grace before God and others, as Jesus did. We look to him to help us to keep on turning from sin and growing in grace.

## 29 July, Monday, Feast of St Martha

*Luke 10:38–42*

The Gospels give the impression that Jesus was very close to the family of Martha, Mary and Lazarus. He often found a welcome in their home. They were among his friends. We can forget that because Jesus was fully human he had the same need for human friendship as every other human being. There is an intimacy to the scene in today's gospel reading that we associate with a gathering of friends. Jesus is welcomed by Martha into her home. She gives expression to her friendship of Jesus by preparing a meal for him. She is evidently a good and generous host. Mary, Martha's sister, expresses her friendship for Jesus in a different way. She sits at Jesus' feet and listens to him speaking. Hospitality and friendship can take more than one form. We can be very active on friends' behalf, such as by preparing a fine meal for them, or we can simply be present to them and listen to them. The gospel reading suggests that Martha did not appreciate the way that Mary was giving expression to her friendship of Jesus. She wanted Jesus to put pressure on Mary to help her in preparing the meal. It is an example of the tensions that can emerge in all close relationships. Jesus shows his love for Martha by addressing her twice by her own name – 'Martha, Martha'. However, he does not comply with Martha's request but declares that on this occasion Mary has chosen the better part. Jesus seems to have wanted someone to listen to him more than someone to feed him. The Book of Qoheleth declares that there is a time for everything under the sun. In the light of today's gospel reading, we might say that 'there is a time to be still and a time to be busy'. When Jesus entered their home, it was Mary who recognised that it was a time to be still. There are times in our lives when all the Lord wants from us is that we be still in his presence and listen to his word.

## 30 July, Tuesday, Seventeenth Week in Ordinary Time

*Matthew 13:36–43*

Today's gospel reading speaks of Jesus as the 'sower of good seed' who sows good seed throughout the world. Those who allow that good seed to take root in their hearts are 'the subjects of the kingdom'; they already belong to God's kingdom on earth. Whenever people respond to the Lord's call, they form what we might call a 'beachhead' of the kingdom of God on earth. This is what the Lord desires for us all. The community of his disciples, the Church, is to be that beachhead of the kingdom of God on earth; it is to be the earthly expression of the goodness of the kingdom of heaven. Yet, the gospel reading also acknowledges another reality that is to be found in our world, what it terms 'darnel', or 'weeds', which are sown by the devil. The Lord's good work in the world is opposed by evil forces. The Gospels suggest that Jesus took the reality of evil in the world very seriously. He was also aware that it could infect his followers, the community of those who believed in him, which is why he taught us to pray, 'Lead us not into temptation, but deliver us from evil'. We shouldn't need much convincing about the reality and power of evil in our world and, indeed, in the Church and in our own lives. However, the gospel reading declares that evil will not have the last word. God will eradicate evil fully but only at the end of time, when God's kingdom fully comes. In the meantime, the Lord wishes to work in and through each of us to confront evil in all its forms, so that something of that final triumph of good over evil can become a reality in the here and now.

## 31 July, Wednesday, Seventeenth Week in Ordinary Time

*Matthew 13:44–46*

I sometimes watch *The Antiques Roadshow* on BBC 1. I love watching people's faces when they discover that some object they have had on a sideboard or wherever for years is worth thousands of pounds. On one such programme, a man was interviewed who had been digging in his garden. He had found a ring which turned out to be a medieval love ring with a ruby stone in the centre that was worth about £20,000. Sometimes people can hit upon something of great value, a true treasure, purely by accident. I was reminded of that by the first parable in today's gospel reading. The scene is that of a poor labourer working in someone's field; out of the blue he hits upon this great treasure. It comes his way as a gift. Shrewd man that he is, he scrapes together his few possessions and buys the field from the man he was working for, to hold on to this unexpected grace.

When Jesus says the kingdom of heaven is like this man's experience, he may be saying that a great deal of value in life comes to us as a gift, without our having to work for it. So much in life has come to us as a gift, such as the relationships we value and the beauty of God's creation. The Lord himself comes to us as a gift. Our faith in him is a gift. Most of us were brought to the Lord without our having to look for him. The treasure of the Lord and his Gospel has been put into our laps. We have been greatly graced by the Lord. As the first chapter of John's Gospel declares, 'from his fullness we have all received, grace upon grace'. The appropriate response to being graced is to give thanks, which is why Paul, in one of his letters, says simply, 'Give thanks in all circumstances'.

## 1 August, Thursday, Seventeenth Week in Ordinary Time
*Matthew 13:47–53*

Much of Jesus' ministry was around the shores of the Sea of Galilee. The sight of fishermen casting a large dragnet into the sea would have been an everyday occurrence. All kinds of fish – clean and unclean from a Jewish point of view – would have been caught in such a net. Jesus declares in today's gospel reading that the kingdom of heaven is like this everyday reality. Because Jesus announced that the kingdom of God was present in his own ministry, he is really saying that his own ministry has something of the quality of the casting of the dragnet. There was nothing selective about Jesus' ministry. He cast a very wide net which embraced those considered clean and unclean according to the Jewish Law. Jesus revealed and continues to reveal a gracious God who has no favourites. If God present in Jesus has favourites it is those regarded by others as 'sinners', just as a doctor favours the sick over the healthy. Jesus is saying that you don't have to be 'good' to be grasped by God's reign present in his ministry. The parable also declares that just as the fishermen sit down by the shore of the sea, to separate the good fish from the bad, so at the end of time there will be a separation of the good and the bad. God's grace embraces us all, but we need to respond to that grace. Jesus reveals a God who loves us before we love God. He assures us that we stand within God's love; we are God's beloved. Yet, he also calls on us to keep on receiving that love so that we can love others as God has loved us. We are to allow God's goodness towards us to make us good, or at least to keep us on the path towards personal goodness, so that, in the words of Paul, we 'may be blameless before our God and Father, at the coming of our Lord Jesus with all his saints'.

## 2 August, Friday, Seventeenth Week in Ordinary Time

*Matthew 13:54–58*

We are all familiar with the saying, 'familiarity breeds contempt'. Like all proverbs, this one expresses a partial truth. Sometimes familiarity can breed contempt. It is also true that the more familiar some people become to each other, the closer they grow together and the more they want to share each other's lives. Familiarity can breed love as well as contempt. Today's gospel reading seems to be a case of familiarity breeding contempt. The people of Nazareth regarded Jesus as someone very familiar to them. He was one of their own, the son of the carpenter. They knew his mother, Mary, and his brothers and sisters. They didn't think of Jesus as being in any way different from themselves. Their comments suggest that, at one level, Jesus wasn't any different from the other people of Nazareth, yet there was so much more to Jesus than they realised while he was living among them. It was only when he moved away that his difference from them became evident. It was only then that they began to get reports of his teaching, his 'wisdom' and his 'miraculous powers'. They couldn't reconcile Jesus being one of them with his being so different from them. This remains the mystery of Jesus for us today. He was fully human, yet he had a special relationship with God as Son of the Father. He was like us in all things but sin. His humanity revealed God in a way that was unique among human beings. We need not be scandalised at this, as the people of Nazareth were. Rather, we can rejoice that God has been revealed to us in such a human way, in a way that makes God so accessible to us. Jesus has given God a human face. God has drawn close to us in Jesus so that we can draw close to God through Jesus. The Lord humbled himself to share in our humanity so that we might share in his divinity.

## 3 August, Saturday, Seventeenth Week in Ordinary Time
*Matthew 14:1–12*

Herod Antipas, the tetrarch of Galilee, had married the wife of his brother Philip. John the Baptist confronted Herod Antipas for marrying in contravention of the Jewish Law, much to the annoyance of Herod and to the even greater annoyance of his wife, Herodias. For his faithful proclamation of the Jewish Law, even to the mighty and powerful, John the Baptist was imprisoned and eventually beheaded on Herod's orders, as we hear in today's gospel reading. At the end of the gospel reading we are told that when the disciples of John the Baptist had buried their master, they went off to tell Jesus. When Jesus heard this news, he must have had a premonition of his own fate. Jesus proclaimed an even more radical version of God's will than had John the Baptist. He was already in the process of making enemies among the powerful in the land. As John the Baptist was executed in Galilee by a client king of Rome, Herod Antipas, Jesus would be executed in Jerusalem by the governor of Rome, Pontius Pilate. The Gospel story as a whole and today's gospel reading especially indicate that the proclamation of God's word is not always well received, especially when it challenges our self-centredness, our desire to protect ourselves and all we are attached to. It is in the nature of the Lord's word that it will both comfort us and unsettle us. It will both build up and tear down. We need to keep holding ourselves open to both sides of the Lord's word.

## 5 August, Monday, Eighteenth Week in Ordinary Time
*Matthew 14:13–21*

Many of the prayers in the Jewish Scriptures may strike us as very daring. There is a large number of psalms where the person praying complains bitterly to God and seems to hold God to account. This kind of prayer of complaint, or lament, is often punctuated with questions addressed to God: 'Why?' 'How long?' 'Where?' We have a very good example of such a prayer on the lips of Moses in today's first reading: 'Why do you treat your servant so badly? Why have I not found favour with you?' ... 'Where am I to find meat to give to all this people?' Within the Jewish tradition, this was considered a perfectly acceptable way of addressing God. It was a valid form of prayer. People trusted God sufficiently to address him honestly from the heart. They didn't think they had to tiptoe around God, talking politely to him so as not to anger him. The exchanges between believers and God very often had quite an edge to it in the Scriptures. The exchange between Jesus and his disciples in today's gospel reading has an edge to it. The disciples call on Jesus to send the people away so that they can buy themselves some food. Jesus replies that there is no need for them to go and that the disciples should give them something to eat. The disciples reply that all they have at their disposal is five loaves and two fish, as much as to say, 'How can you be serious?' Yet, somehow, Jesus went on to feed the crowd with these few resources. The crowd didn't have to buy anything, as the disciples suggested. Jesus would feed them abundantly, without charge. The early Church understood this scene as pointing ahead to the Last Supper and to the gift of the Eucharist. At the Eucharist, the risen Lord continues to feed us freely and abundantly with the gift of himself, his body and blood. It is above all in the Eucharist that the Lord gives, without charge. Having received without charge, we are sent from the Eucharist to give as we have received.

## 6 August, Tuesday, The Transfiguration of the Lord
*Mark 9:2–10*

Peter's comment in today's gospel reading, 'Master, it is wonderful for us to be here', can find an echo in our own lives. It can remind us of those moments in our lives when we too felt it was wonderful to be somewhere. Each of us is likely to have at least one experience when we could have said with Peter, 'Lord, it is wonderful for us to be here'. The experience that moved Peter to say this was the vision of Jesus transfigured on the mountain. The gospel reading says that Peter and the other two disciples saw Jesus' glory. They sensed God's presence in Jesus in a way they had never sensed it before. It could be said that this was an experience of heaven, of Jesus' heavenly glory. Those who get a taste of heaven in this life do not want to let it go. Peter, too, wanted to preserve this experience: 'Let us make three tents. … '. This vision needed to be preserved, Peter felt. However, it could not be preserved. Jesus, along with his three disciples, had to come down the mountain. He had to face into what the gospel reading calls 'his passing which he was to accomplish in Jerusalem', his passing over from this world, his death. His disciples had to face into it too. This was just a momentary grace given to sustain them. Such graces are given to us all, if we are open to receive them. Every so often the Lord will give us too a wonderful sense of his presence in our lives so as to sustain us on our life journey.

## 7 August, Wednesday, Eighteenth Week in Ordinary Time
*Matthew 15:21–28*

Today's gospel reading strikes many of us as surprising. Jesus' attitude towards the pagan woman seems harsh and unfeeling. When she approaches him to heal her sick daughter, she is first met with stony silence. When she continues to shout after Jesus and his disciples, Jesus informs her that he was sent only to the lost sheep of the house of Israel. When she comes closer to Jesus and kneels at his feet, pleading with great simplicity, 'Help me', Jesus responded with what sounds to our ears like a harsh parable,: 'It is not fair to take the children's food and throw it to the house-dogs'. The 'children' here are the children of Israel, the 'house-dogs' are the pagans. Yet, this woman won't take 'no' for an answer. She takes Jesus' parable and, with great wit, turns it to her advantage, declaring that even house-dogs often get to eat the scraps that fall from the children's plates at table. In that way, the children and the house-dogs eat at the same time. The gospel reading suggests that Jesus was not ready to begin his ministry to the pagans; that would come later. His work of renewing Israel came first. Yet, this woman's love for her daughter would change Jesus' timetable. He could not remain unmoved by her great faith. Her daughter would be healed. The woman encourages us to keep on seeking, to keep on knocking, to keep on asking, even when the Lord seems silent and unresponsive. Jesus once spoke of a faith that moves mountains. The woman's faith moved Jesus; it was a faith that created an unexpected space for him to work in a life-giving way. That is the kind of faith that is needed more than ever today, from all of us.

## 8 August, Thursday, Eighteenth Week in Ordinary Time

*Matthew 16:13–23*

The first question that Jesus asks of his disciples, 'Who do people say the Son of Man is?', is a relatively easy one. Even today we probably all feel we could say something about how other people see Jesus. Jesus' second question is a more difficult one, because it is much more personal. 'Who do you say I am?' The question invites us to give our own personal confession of faith in Jesus. 'Who is Jesus for me?' We might struggle a little more to answer that question. We don't always find it easy to articulate our own personal faith in the Lord. In the gospel reading, Peter comes forward to give his own personal answer to Jesus' question, 'You are the Christ, the Son of the living God'. It is a great answer, really, and Jesus declares Peter blessed because of his God-given insight into the identity of Jesus. Because of his answer Jesus sees in Peter the rock on which he can build his Church. Peter can be the firm foundation on which the community of believers relies. He can be entrusted with the keys of the kingdom of heaven, which allow him to bind and loose. The image of 'keys' suggests authority. The language of binding and loosing specifies that authority as a teaching authority. Peter is being given a very important role in Jesus' Church. Yet, almost immediately, Peter, the rock, because a stumbling stone for Jesus. When Jesus explains the kind of Christ or Messiah he will be, one who is to suffer grievously and be put to death, Peter rebukes Jesus and tries to deflect him from this path. The one whom Jesus declared blessed is now identified by Jesus as Satan. Jesus did not take back the role in his Church he had given Peter, but he was reminding Peter in no uncertain terms that he had a lot to learn. We all have a lot to learn when it comes to Jesus. We are constantly having to surrender to who Jesus is in all his mysterious reality, rather than trying to shape him in accordance with our own wishes.

## 9 August, Friday, St Teresa Benedicta of the Cross

*Matthew 25:1–13*

St Teresa Benedict of the Cross, also known as Edith Stein, was born a Jew in 1891 in Poland. She had abandoned her Jewish faith by the time that she was thirteen and declared herself an atheist. A brilliant student, she gained her doctorate in philosophy at the age of twenty-three. In the wake of the awful slaughter of the First World War Edith began to feel a growing interest in religion. In 1921 she came upon the autobiography of St Teresa of Avila, the sixteenth-century Carmelite nun. Fascinated, she read through the night and by morning concluded, 'This is the truth'. She was baptised a Catholic the following New Year's Day in 1922. Edith felt that by accepting Christ she had been reunited with her Jewish roots. She went on to obtain an academic post in the University of Münster in Germany in 1932. However, with the rise of Nazism she was dismissed from her post because she was considered a Jew. The loss of her job enabled her to pursue her growing attraction to the religious life. She applied to enter the Carmelite convent in Cologne and was formally clothed with the Carmelite habit on 15 April 1934. She took the name Sister Teresa Benedicta of the Cross. Believing that her presence in the convent endangered her sisters, she allowed herself to be smuggled out of the country to a Carmelite convent in Holland. In 1940 the Nazis occupied Holland. She was captured and sent to Auschwitz where she died in the gas chamber on 9 August 1942. In 1998 she was canonised as a confessor and martyr of the Church by Pope John Paul II. In the parable Jesus tells in today's gospel reading, only some of the bridesmaids had their lamps lit when the bridegroom arrived. When a child is baptised, the priest says to the parents, 'keep the flame of faith alive in his/her heart'. The parable calls on us to keep that flame of faith alive in our hearts, in good times and in bad. The dark experiences of life can sometimes cause the flame of our faith to flicker or even go out. St Teresa Benedicta kept the flame of her faith burning brightly in the most difficult of human situations, and she is an inspiration for us to do the same. There was a time in her life when the flame of her faith did go out. It was the reading of a saint's life that fanned her faith into a living flame again. Her experience reminds us that when the flame of our own faith grows weak or is even extinguished, the Lord can relight that flame once more. He can touch our hearts through some human experience, such as the reading of a saint's life. The Lord is always working to find a way through to us.

## 10 August, Saturday, St Lawrence, Deacon and Martyr

*John 12:24–26*

Lawrence was a deacon in the Church of Rome in the early part of the third century. He worked closely with Pope Sixtus II. Both of them were martyred in the year AD258 during the persecution started by the Roman emperor Valerian. There is a basilica in Rome dedicated to him, St Lawrence outside the Walls, which is built over what is believed to be his tomb. Few historical details of his life are known, apart from his reputation for almsgiving, which was part of his work as a deacon. Both readings chosen by the Church for his feast contain the image of the seed. The gospel speaks of the seed which falls into the ground and dies and in dying yields a rich harvest. It was above all Jesus who was the seed that fell into the ground and died, and in dying yielded a rich harvest for himself and all who believe in him. He is the servant who emptied himself so that others may have life and have it to the full. In the gospel reading, Jesus calls on his servants, his disciples, to follow him, to be ready to lose their lives in the service of others. In becoming the seed that falls to the ground and dies, we, too, will reap a rich harvest. In the first reading, Paul declares that those who sow seed generously will reap generously. In that reading Paul calls on the Church in Corinth not only to give generously but to give cheerfully, for God loves a cheerful giver. Paul was calling on his Gentile Christian Church in Corinth to be generous in their support for the collection he was taking up for the Jewish Christian Church in Jerusalem. Giving generously and cheerfully is the way of the Lord; it is the Gospel way. Both the first reading and the gospel reading assure us that if we follow that way, as Lawrence did, we will reap a rich harvest, as will others; we will receive from the Lord more than we have given.

## 12 August, Monday, Nineteenth Week in Ordinary Time
*Matthew 17:22–27*
Today's gospel reading makes reference to the half-shekel tax. This was not a tax imposed by the Romans but a Jewish tax. Devout Jews paid the half-shekel tax to the Temple in Jerusalem every year to defray the costs of the sacrifices that were offered in the Temple. Peter is asked by the collectors of this tax whether his master, Jesus, paid it or not. They were testing Jesus' credentials as a devout and orthodox Jew. Peter did not hesitate to say that Jesus did pay this annual tax. In the conversation that Jesus subsequently has with Peter, Jesus suggests that neither he nor his disciples are bound to pay this tax. This seems to be the meaning of his statement that 'the sons are exempt'. Jesus, of course, was the supreme Son of God, but his disciples were called to share in his relationship with God as Son, and to that extent were sons and daughters of God. Even though 'the sons are exempt', Jesus instructs Peter to pay the tax for both of them, so as not to give offence to the collectors of the half-shekel tax. Jesus suggests that just because we are free in relation to some matter does not mean it is

always a good thing to exercise that freedom. Jesus implies that freedom is an important value but it is not an absolute value. There are
other values that take precedence over the value of freedom, such as
consideration for the sensitivities of others, the value of self-emptying love of others. For Jesus and for the Christian tradition that flows
from him, love, the primary fruit of the Holy Spirit, is a higher value
than freedom. Such love of the other shapes how we give expression
to our freedom. As Paul puts it so succinctly, 'where the Spirit of the
Lord is, there is freedom'.

## 13 August, Tuesday, Nineteenth Week in Ordinary Time
*Matthew 18:1–5, 10, 12–14*

The Gospels are full of questions. Some of the questions are asked
by Jesus; others are asked by his opponents and some are asked by
his disciples. In today's gospel reading a question is asked by one of
Jesus' disciples, 'Who is the greatest in the kingdom of heaven?' It is
a question that reveals something about our human nature, an interest in status and position and prestige. Perhaps behind that question
of the disciples stood another question: 'How do we get to become
the greatest in the kingdom of heaven?' Jesus' answer to his disciples' question gave them, and us, much to ponder. Jesus speaks about
something more basic than becoming the greatest in the kingdom.
He says that in order just to *enter* the kingdom, his disciples have to
change and become like little children. Children in those days had no
rights; they had no status in law. They were completely dependent on
others, especially their parents, for everything. Jesus is recommend-
ing a childlike trust in a loving Father, a trust that waits for everything
from God and grabs at nothing. Jesus is making a sharp challenge to
the will for power and status that exists in every human community,
including the community of disciples. Rather than seeking to exalt
ourselves, we entrust ourselves to God who exalts the humble.

## 14 August, Wednesday, Nineteenth Week in Ordinary Time

*Matthew 18:15–20*

Jesus' message in today's gospel reading takes it for granted that within the community of his disciples, people will invariably take a wrong path. He was very aware that the Church he was forming would not be a community of the perfect.

It would always be a community of sinners who are striving to be better. As a result, Jesus suggests a procedure for helping others who do wrong to come back to the right path again. The one to whom the wrong is done is to have it out with the person responsible for the wrong. If that doesn't work, one or two others are to be brought along to address the person in the wrong. If that doesn't work, the whole community of believers is to get involved. Jesus' suggested procedure may not be valid in every situation for every age. Yet, the underlying principle holds true. Jesus is declaring that we have some responsibility for each other's well-being, not just physical well-being, but moral well-being.

He looks to us to help each other towards goodness. We have a role to play in helping one another to be more loving in the way Jesus was loving. It is not that some of us are the moral superiors of others. We are all sinners and we each need other members of the believing community to help us on our way towards God. Being human, being Christ-like, being loving, is a complicated business.

We all make mistakes in the process of learning to do it right, and we need to find a way of standing together in that process. When we stand together in this vital work of helping each other become all that God wants us to be, Jesus promises us in today's gospel reading that he will be with us. We are not on our own. 'Where two or three meet in my name, I shall be there with them'.

## 15 August, Thursday, The Assumption of the Blessed Virgin Mary
*Luke 1:39–56*

Today we celebrate what the Gospel calls the great things that the Almighty has done for Mary, in bringing her to share in a unique way in the risen life of Jesus. Mary had a unique relationship with Jesus throughout her earthly life. She carried Jesus in her womb for nine months. Having given birth to Jesus, she cared for and looked after him in the way that any mother cares for her child. She lived under the same roof as him for the first thirty years of his life. She was there throughout his public ministry, even if in the background. She was there at the foot of the cross. She was there with the disciples when the Holy Spirit came down upon them all at the first Pentecost. Just as Mary had a unique relationship with Jesus during her earthly life, the church believes that she now has a unique relationship with the risen Lord in heaven. She has come to share fully in his risen life. Mary's unique relationship with Jesus in her earthly life does not leave her remote from us. Yes, she was the mother of Jesus, but she was also a disciple of Jesus, and we are all called to be the Lord's disciples. Her life shows us what it means to be the Lord's disciple. Today's gospel reading is Luke's account of Mary's visit to Elizabeth. Just before this gospel reading, we have Luke's account of the annunciation to Mary. The angel Gabriel declared to Mary that God had chosen her to be the mother of his Son. After struggling to come to terms with what was being asked of her, Mary eventually declared, 'Here I am, the servant of the Lord; let it be with me according to your word'. Luke portrays Mary here as a woman of faith, who surrenders to God's purpose for her life. It is this faith which Elizabeth recognises in today's gospel reading. 'Blessed is she who believed that the promise made her by the Lord would be fulfilled'. Mary believed and surrendered to God's word as spoken to her by Gabriel. She allowed God's word to shape her whole life. Later in Luke's Gospel, Jesus will say, 'my mother and brothers are those who hear the word of God and do it'. Mary was above all a woman who heard God's word and did it. This is the essence of faith. Through Baptism, we are all called to such faith,

The faith that Mary displayed at the Annunciation immediately found expression in love. She made the long journey from Nazareth in Galilee to the hill country of Judah to be with her relative Elizabeth, who was also with child. This is one of the ways our faith finds expression today. We journey to others in love. When we journey towards others in faith and love, we too bring the Lord to them. The Lord wants to visit others through us. Today's gospel shows that Mary's faith not only found expression in love, but also in prayer. In response to Elizabeth's greeting, Mary immediately praised and gave thanks to God. God was the horizon within which Mary moved. God was at the heart of all her human relationships of love. One of the ways our love of God finds expression is through prayer.

If Mary exemplifies a life of faith that finds expression in love and prayer, she also shows where such a life ultimately leads. Those who follow this path, in the words of Paul in today's second reading, 'will be brought to life in Christ'. Mary shows us that all who live lives of prayerful and loving faith will be brought to life in Christ beyond this earthly life.

## 16 August, Friday, Nineteenth Week in Ordinary Time
*Matthew 19:3–12*
In the gospel reading, Jesus upholds both the value of lifelong fidelity in marriage, and the value of celibacy for the sake of the kingdom of heaven. The Jewish tradition did not place great value on celibacy, and divorce was quite common and acceptable. The Pharisees quote from the Book of Deuteronomy, which was the basis of the Jewish divorce law. The law in the time of Jesus was very heavily weighted in favour of the male. Men could divorce their wives but wives could

not divorce their husbands. One school of thought within the Jewish tradition held that husbands could divorce their wives on any pre-text whatever. A second school held that husbands could divorce their wives only on certain pretexts. That is why the Pharisees ask Jesus the question, 'Is it against the law for a husband to divorce his wife on any pretext whatever?' Their question took divorce for granted; they simply wanted to know which of the two schools of thought Jesus favoured. In his answer, Jesus went back beyond the Book of Deuteronomy to the Book of Genesis, to what Jesus considered God's original intention: 'a man must leave his father and mother and cling to his wife, and the two become one body'. In highlighting the value of lifelong fidelity in marriage, Jesus could be understood as protect-ing women in marriage from being cast aside at the whim of their husbands. Jesus proclaims the value of a love between a man and a woman that is constant and faithful unto death. We are all aware that marriages break down. There will always be a tension between the ideal and the real, between the goal and what is reached. Jesus wants us to live with that tension and not to collapse it. He keeps holding before us the value of a human love that is a reflection of God's faith-ful love, whether such love finds expression within marriage or in the single life.

## 17 August, Saturday, Nineteenth Week in Ordinary Time

*Matthew 19:13–15*

Very often in the gospels we find Jesus and his disciples at odds with each other. We have a good example of that in today's gospel reading. Children were brought to Jesus, presumably by their parents, for Jesus to lay his hands on them in blessing. The disciples turned them away and Jesus has to rebuke them, calling on them not to stop children from coming to him. Why the disciples would try to stop parents bringing their children to Jesus is not clear. What is clear is Jesus' insistence that children have complete access to him. He is upholding the dignity of children and declaring that they are to have a central place in the community's life and worship. Whenever parents or grandparents or teachers bring children to Jesus in any way, they are doing something that the risen Lord delights in and strongly desires. As a community of faith, we have a calling from the Lord to open up the treasures of the Gospel to our children and our young people. We have to keep searching for new and creative ways of doing this. Jesus goes on to declare that not only are children to have a central place in the community's life, but that as adults we have something to learn from them. It is to such children, Jesus says, that the kingdom of God belongs. He is suggesting that, if we are to enter the kingdom of God, we need something of that trusting, open, response to the gift of the Gospel that comes naturally to children.

## 19 August, Monday, Twentieth Week in Ordinary Time
*Matthew 19:16–22*

The gospel reading today presents us with an idealistic young man. He wants to be sure of possessing eternal life, and he asks Jesus regarding the one good deed he must do to ensure his entering into eternal life. He is clearly a young man who takes his religion seriously. He tells Jesus that he has kept the commandments that Jesus quotes to him. Jesus declares that this is sufficient to enter into life. The conversation could have ended there. Yet, this young man ensures that the conversation does not end by pressing Jesus further. 'What more do I need to do?' He senses in himself that he is capable of even more than what he is already doing. Jesus respects his desire for 'more' and there and then calls on him to sell what he owns, give it to the poor and become one of that group who follow Jesus in a very close and personal way. If he wanted 'more', Jesus would give it to him. However, the young man couldn't live with Jesus' answer to his second question. He was too attached to his possessions to be free to do what Jesus invited him to do, and a great sadness came over him. We can probably all find within ourselves the same longing to be better, to do more, that was so evident in the life of this young man. After all, our hearts are restless until they rest in God. Yet, like this young man, we too often find within ourselves obstacles to the Lord's call to grow towards that more we so desire. We discover that we are not as free as we need to be. Attachments of various kinds hold us back. We don't yet have the glorious freedom of the children of God, in the words of Paul. We need to keep praying to grow in the freedom to fully become the person the Lord is calling us to be.

## 20 August, Tuesday, Twentieth Week in Ordinary Time
*Matthew 19:23–30*
Jesus spoke the words in today's gospel reading immediately after the scene where the rich man refused the call of Jesus to follow him because of his riches. Jesus goes on to say that attachment to wealth can hinder us from entering the kingdom of heaven. When possessions become our god, we no longer need to rely on the true God, the Father of Jesus. Jesus was aware that over-reliance on our possessions can get in the way of our reliance on God. God can become superfluous, unnecessary. Yet, if we are to reach our ultimate goal of life in God's kingdom, we desperately need God. That is very clear from the little exchange between Jesus and Peter in today's gospel reading. In response to Peter's question, 'Who can be saved?' Jesus answers, 'for men this is impossible, for God everything is possible'. It is only with God's help that we can reach the goal God desires for us. In this matter, we are not self-sufficient; we rely on God throughout the whole course of our lives. We cannot afford to entrust ourselves to, put our reliance upon, anything less than God.

## 21 August, Wednesday, Twentieth Week in Ordinary Time

*Matthew 20:1–16*

Today's gospel reading contains one of those parables of Jesus that leave us feeling a little uneasy. The complaint of those who worked for the whole day in the vineyard seems very reasonable to us: 'you have treated those who only worked one hour the same as us'. This certainly doesn't correspond to modern employment practice. It would be unheard of for two people doing the same work to be paid the same wage if one worked all day and the other worked for one hour. Such a practice would have been just as unacceptable in the time and place of Jesus. Jesus must have known that his parable would leave people feeling uncomfortable. This is not the way the world works. Perhaps that is the very point of the parable. Life within God's kingdom does not work as the world does. The parable ends with the vineyard owner's question, 'Why be envious because I am generous?' It is a question that goes to the heart of the parable's meaning. Jesus is declaring that God is generous in a way that goes way beyond the norms of human justice. God's way of relating to us is not based on human merit. Jesus reveals God to be someone whose boundless mercy and generosity can appear scandalous to many, including those who thought of themselves as religious. This is the God revealed by the father in the parable of the prodigal son. The son did not deserve the welcome he received, no more than those who worked an hour deserved a day's wages. Jesus declares that God does not treat us on the basis of what we deserve. God's favour is freely bestowed on those who are unworthy of it. It is an unmerited free gift. We are called to receive this gift in all humility and to allow this grace to shape our lives. We are to give freely to others as we have freely received from the Lord.

## 22 August, Thursday, Queenship of Mary

*Luke 1:26–28*

This memorial of Mary is relatively recent in the history of the Church. Pope Pius XII prescribed this feast for the universal Church at the close of the Marian Year in 1954. It is placed on this date, 22 August, exactly a week after the feast of the Assumption, to stress the connection of Mary's queenship with the Assumption. Even though the official declaration of the Queenship of Mary as a memorial is relatively recent, the appreciation of Mary as queen of heaven has a very long tradition in the Church. I am reminded of some of the wonderful and very ancient mosaics in the apse of some churches in Rome depicting Jesus as king and Mary as queen seated beside each other. The beautiful mosaic in the apse of the Basilica of St Mary Major in Rome comes to mind. Depicting Mary as queen, alongside her son as king, was a way of showing honour to Mary for the person she had been in her earthly life. The gospel reading today depicts her as saying 'yes' to God's desire for her to be the mother of his Son. Out of all women, she was chosen to give birth to a son who would also be the Son of God, who, in the words of today's first reading would be a 'great light' in the darkness, a Wonder Counsellor, a Mighty God, a Prince of Peace. The Church came to appreciate from its earliest days just how significant Mary's 'yes' to God's purpose for her life was for all of humanity. It was because Mary surrendered to God's purpose for her life that God's purpose for all our lives could come to pass. It was Mary's faithful response to God's word spoken by Gabriel that made it possible for us all to become people of faith. Her 'yes' created the opening for God's Son to be given to us all and for us to respond in faith to this wonderful gift. Mary was pivotal in God's saving purpose, so the Church believed from earliest times that she must have a special place in heaven, alongside her Son. Today, we honour Mary as Queen of heaven. We are also reminded that our own 'yes' to the

Lord's call, just like Mary's, can have important consequences for good in the lives of others. Even if in a lesser way than was the case with Mary, the faith of each one of us is instrumental in helping others come to faith and in nurturing the faith of others.

## 23 August, Friday, Twentieth Week in Ordinary Time
*Matthew 22:34–40*

The Pharisee who questioned Jesus in today's gospel reading claimed to be looking for the most important commandment out of the hundreds that were set out in the Jewish Law. However, Jesus responded to his question by giving him not one commandment, but two, what he called the greatest or first commandment, and a second commandment that 'resembles it'. It seems that Jesus did something very original here. He took two commandments that were in different books of the Jewish Scriptures, the first commandment that you love the Lord your God with all your heart, soul, mind and strength, which is in the Book of Deuteronomy, and the second commandment that 'you must love your neighbour as yourself', which is in the Book of Leviticus. Jesus brought these commandments together in a way that was unique to him. What is common to both commandments is that little word 'love'. It is as if Jesus is saying, 'if you really want to get to the heart of God's Law, what God wills for our lives is love'. Love is the centre of the Jewish Law. It is also, of course, the centre of Jesus' message. If these two commandments to love are the most important of all the commandments in the Jewish Law, Jesus insists that one of these commandments to love is more important than the other. The first and most important of the two is to love God with all our hearts, all our souls and all our minds. In that first commandment, we are being asked to give God first place in our lives. God alone is to be loved with all our being. This involves acknowledging our dependence on God, recognising how much we receive from God and then offering all that back to God in love. Jesus implies that this love of God is the inspiration and foundation for our love of others, a love that is to have something of the quality of God's own love for humanity.

## 24 August, Saturday, Feast of St Bartholomew
*John 1:45–51*

Bartholomew is listed as one of the twelve apostles. He is traditionally identified with the figure of Nathanael, who features in today's gospel reading. When Philip shared with Nathanael his emerging faith in Jesus of Nazareth, Nathanael dismissed it with the remark, 'Can anything good come from Nazareth?' Yet, this dismissive, sceptical attitude would not go on to define Nathanael. There was some little openness in him, because when Philip went on to say to him, 'Come and see', Nathanael did come and he saw for himself. When Jesus saw Nathanael, he drew attention not to his initial dismissive attitude but to his openness: 'an Israelite who deserves the name, incapable of deceit'. Jesus admired his honesty; there was no pretence in him. As a result of his meeting with Jesus, Nathanael goes on to make his confession of faith in Jesus of Nazareth: 'You are the Son of God, you are the King of Israel'. Nathanael had moved from scepticism to faith, yet Jesus assures him that he is still only at the beginning of his journey; he has only begun to see. Jesus promises him, 'You will see greater things … you will see heaven laid open and, above the Son of Man, the angels of God ascending and descending'. Nathanael will come to recognise Jesus as the meeting point of heaven and earth, as God in human form. Like Nathanael, we are all on a journey. The Lord invites us to 'come and see', no matter where we are on that journey, and, if we do manage to see something of the Lord, he promises us that one day we will see greater things than what we now see.

## 26 August, Monday, Twenty-First Week in Ordinary Time

*Matthew 23:13–22*

The gospel reading is a series of accusations that Jesus brings against the religious leaders of the time. The first one seems the most serious. Jesus accuses them of shutting up the kingdom of heaven in people's faces, neither going in themselves nor allowing others to go in who want to. Jesus is claiming that not only do some of the religious leaders reject his proclamation of the nearness of God's kingdom, but they put pressure on others to reject Jesus' message and ministry as well. They are a stumbling block to others coming to faith in Jesus. Elsewhere in the Gospels, Jesus warns his own disciples of the danger of becoming a stumbling block to others who already believe in him. Indeed, on one occasion he accused Peter, the leader of the Twelve, of becoming a stumbling block to himself: 'Get behind me, Satan! You are a stumbling block to me'. The opposite of a stumbling block, which trips us up, is a stepping stone, which helps us to walk across difficult terrain. We are all called to be stepping stones rather than stumbling blocks, to help each other towards the Lord rather than hindering each other from receiving the Lord. In the first reading, Paul sees the young Church in the Greek city of Thessalonica as a stepping stone. He declares, 'it was from you that the word of the Lord has started to spread ... for the news of your faith in God has spread everywhere'. Paul suggests that other young Churches are being greatly encouraged and built up by the faith of the Thessalonians. In every age, we need to help each other towards the Lord by the lived witness of our faith. As Paul goes on to say later in his first letter to the Thessalonians, our earliest Christian document, 'encourage one another and build up each other'.

## 27 August, Tuesday, Twenty-First Week in Ordinary Time
*Matthew 23:23–26*

There were many religious laws and regulations in Jesus' time. In the gospel reading Jesus criticises those who give too much attention to the less important laws and regulations and too little attention to what was really important, what Jesus calls the weightier matter of the Law. He names the less important aspects of the Law as the regulations relating to the tithing of various herbs, and the more important aspects of the Law as justice, mercy and faith. When it comes to our relationship with God, Jesus wants us to put our energy into getting the basics right. It would be difficult to come up with anything more basic than the 'justice, mercy and faith' that Jesus refers to in the gospel reading. Justice and mercy have to do with how we relate to others. We are to be just and merciful in our dealings with each other. Faith has to do with how we relate to God. We are to be faithful to God, which means being faithful to Jesus and to all he stands for, even though that may cost us a great deal at times. There is clearly a close link between faith, on the one hand, and justice and mercy, on the other. Faithfulness to Jesus entails showing justice and mercy to others, as he did. When we find ourselves getting very worked up about something in the religious sphere, it can be good to step back and ask ourselves just how basic, how fundamental, the issue in question really is.

## 28 August, Wednesday, Twenty-First Week in Ordinary Time
*Matthew 23:27–32*

Today's responsorial psalm is, perhaps, one of the most striking of the psalms in the Book of Psalms. In that psalm, the person praying celebrates the presence of the Lord throughout the whole universe. The psalmist declares that the Lord is present even at the heart of darkness. There is that lovely line, 'even darkness is not dark for you and the night is as clear as the day'. The Lord penetrates the darkness. He is there at the heart of our darkest experiences; the darkness of life can never extinguish the light of his presence. In the words of Paul in today's first reading, this is 'God's message and not some human thinking, and it is still a living power among you who believe it'. The Lord's message, the Lord's word, is a living power; it continues to speak to us today. This psalm remains a living word for us today, especially for those who may find themselves in some kind of darkness at this time, reminding us that even darkness is not dark for the Lord. The more challenging side of the Lord's message, which we hear in today's gospel reading, is also a living word among us. There, Jesus accuses the religious leaders of hypocrisy. How they appear to others does not correspond to the reality of their lives. There is a disconnect between the outside and the inside. Jesus always places the emphasis on what is within, on what is in our hearts, what it is that drives us and motivates us. Going back to the psalm, the Lord who is present throughout the universe wishes to reside in our hearts above all. That is why we are encouraged to pray, 'Come Holy Spirit, fill my heart; kindle in me the fire of your love'. The Lord wants his love to reside in our hearts so that we can each be mediators of his presence in our world.

## 29 August, Thursday, The Passion of St John the Baptist

*Mark 6:17–29*

Towards the beginning of the summer on 24 June, we celebrated the birth of John the Baptist. Now, as the summer draws to a close, we celebrate his passion and death. We have just read from Mark's account of the beheading of John the Baptist. It is a very dark story. It comes in a section of Mark's Gospel where Jesus has been doing God's work. Just prior to this rather grisly story, Jesus sends out the Twelve on mission, empowering them to heal the sick and broken.

Just after this story, Jesus feeds the multitude in the wilderness, firstly with his word, his teaching, and secondly with an abundance of bread and fish. Jesus gave life to others in various ways and empowered his followers to do the same. Yet, in the midst of all that life-giving work of Jesus, we have this murderous act, the taking of a good man's life by a combination of a weak king, a vindictive mother and a compliant daughter, a kind of unholy trinity. Indeed, this banquet of death where the head of the saintly John the Baptist is served up on a dish is the antithesis of the banquet of life in the wilderness that immediately follows in Mark's Gospel. In the midst of so much light and life, great darkness leading to death is to be found; in the midst of divine goodness there stands satanic evil. The Gospels rejoice in proclaiming the goodness of God made present in Jesus, but they do not shy away from depicting the dark and disturbing side of human nature. In our world today, great goodness and disturbing evil are often found side by side. The energy for good, the energy of the risen Lord's Spirit, comes up against the powers that deal in death. Our calling is to align ourselves with God's good work of bringing life in all its forms to the world, in the same generous and courageous way that John the Baptist did. Yes, darkness and evil stalk the land, but we have the Lord's word that such forces will not win out in the end. We must not allow ourselves to become discouraged or disheartened by them, because God's good work begun in Jesus is continuing all around us and deep within us, in and through the Spirit of the risen Lord.

## 30 August, Friday, Twenty-First Week in Ordinary Time
*Matthew 25:1–13*
Behind today's gospel reading is a marriage custom that we cannot be fully sure of today. The custom may have been for a group of young unmarried women to go to the family home of the bride on her wedding day and to wait with her for the bridegroom to arrive. When the

bridegroom arrives, these women would go meet him with blazing torches. They would then accompany the bride and bridegroom to the bridegroom's house for the celebratory meal, all the while holding their blazing torches aloft. In the story, five of the ten members of the welcoming group of women discovered too late that they did not bring enough oil to keep their lamps burning for the important role they were expected to play. By the time they had bought the necessary oil, the welcoming procession was over, the meal had started and the heavy door of the banqueting room had been shut. In that culture, this would have been a very shameful experience for these women. It would have taken a while for them to live it down. The message of the parable is clear. We need to be ready to meet the Lord, the bridegroom, when he comes, whether that is at the end of time or at the end of our lives or, indeed, in the course of our daily lives. We need to keep the light of our faith burning. Earlier in Matthew's Gospel, Jesus called upon his disciples to let their light shine, the light of their faith, so that people could see their good works and give glory to the Father in heaven. We let the light of our faith shine when our faith expresses itself in good works, in works of loving service of others. In one of his letters Paul speaks about faith expressing itself in love. This is the faith that burns brightly, and the parable assures us that such faith will leave us ready for the Lord's coming, whatever form that might take and whenever it occurs.

## 31 August, Saturday, Twenty-First Week in Ordinary Time
*Matthew 25:14–30*

When we hear the word 'talent' today, we think in terms of natural abilities or gifts that people have. In Jesus' day, a talent was a very large sum of money and that is the meaning of the word in today's parable. A wealthy person entrusts sums of money to three servants in accordance with their ability. The person who received two talents and made two more was just as successful as the one who received five talents and made five more. Each performed very well according to what they were given. The servant to whom the master gave one talent was obviously capable of making one more talent and ending up with two. However, out of fear of his master he did nothing with the one talent he was given.

His image of his master as a demanding person, reaping where he hadn't sown and gathering where he hadn't scattered, may not have been true to the master's nature. The rest of the parable suggests that the master was a generous man who was willing to entrust his servants with great responsibility.

The third servant's image of his master left him paralysed by fear and incapable of taking any action at all. If he had trusted his master to the extent that his master had trusted him, then he would have been free to do the little he was capable of doing. Perhaps one of the messages of the parable is that the Lord has entrusted us with gifts out of his love for us. He wants us to love him in return by placing what he has given us at the service of others.

The first letter of John in the New Testament declares that perfect love casts out fear. Our recognition of the Lord's love for us gives us the freedom to make use of what he has given us, without being held back by the fear of failure or the fear of our own inadequacies. As Mother Teresa, now a saint, once said, the Lord does not ask us to be successful, but only to be faithful. We do our best with what the Lord has given us, knowing that the Lord looks lovingly on our efforts and will work powerfully through them, even when they seem to us to be a failure.

## 2 September, Monday, Twenty-Second Week in Ordinary Time

*Luke 4:16–30*

We have been reading from the Gospel of Matthew on weekdays for some months now. From today until the end of the liturgical year, the feast of Christ the King, the weekday gospel reading will be taken from Luke. In today's gospel reading, Luke presents Jesus at the beginning of his ministry as setting out the priorities of his ministry in the synagogue of his home town of Nazareth. He finds those priorities already contained within a passage from the prophet Isaiah, which he finds and reads aloud. Jesus declares that, like Isaiah, his priority is to proclaim good news to the poor, the captives, the blind and the downtrodden. His mission is to show God's favour, especially to all who were out of favour in that time and culture. Furthermore, he declares that his mission is not just to those out of favour in Israel. Like the prophets Elijah and Elisha before him, his mission will embrace struggling humanity beyond Israel as well. It was this aspect of Jesus' mission which aroused the anger of the people of Nazareth. Jesus proclaimed a God whose favour towards those who struggled crossed all boundaries, including the boundary between Israel and the pagans. This was indeed good news, but it wasn't heard as good news by everyone. Jesus' message of a God whose love seeks out the struggling and the lost wherever they are remains good news for us today. We are invited to open our hearts to this healing and all-embracing love of God that Jesus reveals, and we are then called to reflect something of this love in our own lives.

## 3 September, Tuesday, Twenty-Second Week in Ordinary Time

*Luke 4:31–37*

In today's gospel reading, Jesus encounters great hostility from a man who is described as being 'possessed by the spirit of an unclean devil'. The hostility takes the form of shouting at Jesus, asking him an aggressive question, 'What do you want with us, Jesus of Nazareth?' When we encounter aggressive hostility in others we tend either to respond in kind, showing our own aggression, or to retreat from what we perceive as a danger. Jesus did not respond in either way. He initially sought to quieten the man's agitation: 'Be quiet!', and then he delivered the man of the cause of his aggression and hostility: 'Come out of him!' The gospel reading suggests that the Lord does not respond to us in the way we tend to respond to one another. Rather than taking flight from us or relating to us as we relate to him, he works to bring us whatever is lacking in our lives. The man in the gospel reading lacked peace; he was not at peace with himself or with others. We can come to the Lord as we are, in the assurance that we will always find a compassionate and healing presence. This is the life-giving and liberating authority which so impressed the onlookers in today's gospel reading. We can experience the Lord's life-giving authority for ourselves, and as we do so we can become channels of it to others.

## 4 September, Wednesday, Twenty–Second Week in Ordinary Time
*Luke 4:38–44*

At the beginning of the gospel reading, several people are engaged in the work of bringing Jesus to people or bringing people to Jesus. Some people approach Jesus and ask him to do something for the mother-in-law of Simon who was in bed with a high fever. They bring Jesus to someone who is sick and, as a result, Jesus cures her of her fever. Early the following day, some people bring the sick to Jesus, and, as a result, he lays his hands on them and cures them. Some brought Jesus to the sick and others brought the sick to Jesus. In each case, people mediated between Jesus and those in need. This is something we can continue to do today. We can bring Jesus to the sick. We do this by bringing ourselves to the sick and allowing Jesus to touch their lives through us.

The Lord wishes to continue his healing and life-giving work through each of us. We can also bring the sick to Jesus. One of the ways we do this is by praying for them. This is the prayer of intercession. When we pray for those who are sick, we bring them before the Lord and call on him to touch their lives and heal their brokenness. Both of these ways of mediating between the sick and the Lord are important. At different times in our lives, one or other of these ways will sit more comfortably with us. We may not always have the energy to visit the sick, but we can pray for them. At other times, visiting the sick in person will be a priority for us. Either way, we will be exercising our priestly role of mediating between the Lord and others.

## 5 September, Thursday, Twenty-Second Week in Ordinary Time
*Luke 5:1–11*

The words of Simon Peter in today's gospel reading, 'We worked hard all night long and caught nothing', would find an echo in many people's hearts. We can all have the experience of investing a lot of time and energy in something or someone and discovering that there is very little to show for all our investment. We live in a very result oriented world. Targets and outcomes are all important and if they are not reached we can be judged a failure by others. The gospel reading today suggests that the Lord does not relate to us on that basis. The Lord spoke a word into Simon Peter's situation of failure, 'Put out into deep water and pay out your nets for a catch'. The Lord saw life in abundance in the deep where Simon and others had only experienced absence. When Simon and his companions responded to the Lord's word, the night of failure gave way to the day of abundance. The Lord's way of seeing is always more hopeful than ours. The Lord's word is always directing us to the presence of new life in places we have come to experience as having little to offer. After the abundant catch of fish, Simon Peter came to see himself as having little to offer: 'Leave me, Lord; I am a sinful man'. Yet, Jesus saw Simon with the same hopeful eyes as he had seen the Sea of Galilee. 'Do not be afraid, from now on it is people you will catch'. The Lord invites us to see as he sees, to see our situation, to see ourselves and others with his hopeful, expectant and generous eyes.

## 6 September, Friday, Twenty-Second Week in Ordinary Time
*Luke 5:33–39*

Jesus was very observant of people and of life. At the end of today's gospel reading, he imagines a person who has come to appreciate wines that have matured over many years, 'old wine'. Such a person has no interest in wines that have been made recently. He says, 'the old is good'. Jesus was aware that this mindset, which says 'the old is good', can be found in areas other than that of wine drinking. He found himself up against this mindset on the part of the religious leaders of the time.

There was a newness to Jesus' teaching and behaviour which, while it excited the people, disturbed and troubled the religious experts of the day. Jesus uses the image in the gospel reading of 'new wine' for his ministry. This new wine simply could not be contained by the old wineskins that the religious leaders and experts were keen to preserve. There is always a newness to the Lord's work among us. He is always prompting us to change, to be renewed, to be open to the new thing he is always doing among us. We can look for security in the old way of doing things, especially in matters of faith, but the Lord asks us to find our security in him. He asks us to entrust ourselves to his purpose for our lives, a purpose that will always keep us pilgrims, and prevent us becoming too settled in our ways of relating to him. The author of the letter to the Hebrews puts it well when he calls upon us to 'run with perseverance the race that is set before us, looking to Jesus, the pioneer and perfecter of our faith'.

## 7 September, Saturday, Twenty-Second Week in Ordinary Time
*Luke 6:1–5*

In today's first reading, Paul calls on the Church in Colossae to stand firm on the solid basis of the faith and not to allow themselves to drift away from the hope promised by the good news that was preached to them. Paul makes a very close association there between faith and hope. Our faith in the Lord is always a hopeful faith. Our faith relationship with the Lord always leaves us hopeful. We respond in faith to the Lord's working in our lives and we look forward in hope to the Lord bringing his work in our lives to completion. We hope because we believe that our faith relationship with the Lord has a future which extends beyond this earthly life.

A hopeful faith is a joyful faith. One of the prayers of the Mass speaks about waiting in joyful hope. Our joy is rooted in our present relationship with the Lord and also in the promise which that relationship holds out to us. In today's gospel reading there is an almost joyful quality to the disciples plucking and eating ears of corn as they walk through a cornfield. They were hungry and here was nature's answer to their hunger. The criticism levelled at the disciples by the Pharisees for doing this seems almost joyless.

They could not join in this little celebration, but held it up as a breach of God's Sabbath Law. Jesus comes to the defence of his disciples, declaring himself to be Lord of the Sabbath and announcing that his disciples' behaviour was not in breach of God's Law. There is always a place for healthy criticism within the community of disciples, the Church, but some forms of criticism can risk undermining the joyful and hopeful dimension of our faith. The Lord who stands among us is always calling us to an ever more hopeful and joyful faith.

## 9 September, Monday, Twenty-Third Week in Ordinary Time
*Luke 6:6–11*

In today's first reading, Paul gives us one of his many summaries of the Gospel. He refers to the mystery of the Gospel that God has revealed to all as 'Christ among you, your hope of glory'. There is a present and a future dimension to that summary of the Gospel. Christ is among us now. The Lord is present deep within each believer through the power of the Holy Spirit, and he is present in a special way in and through the community of believers, the Church. Today's gospel reading suggests that the Lord's presence among us is always a life-giving presence. Jesus' immediate response to the presence of the man with the withered hand was to heal him, even though he knew that performing such a healing work on the Sabbath would infuriate the scribes and Pharisees. During his public ministry, the Lord was always at work, healing what was withered in people, regardless of the consequences for himself. That is also the nature of his presence as risen Lord among us and within us today. The Lord works to restore what is withered in us and to heal our brokenness. We can come before the Lord in our weakness in prayer and in the sacraments, knowing that he will touch our lives in a life-giving way. The Lord's life-giving presence among us points to the future dimension of the gospel in Paul's summary. The Lord is our hope of glory. His life-giving work among us now gives us hope that he will bring that life-giving work to completion in eternity, where we are destined to share fully in the Lord's glorious and risen life.

## 10 September, Tuesday, Twenty-Third Week in Ordinary Time
*Luke 6:12–19*

In today's first reading, Paul calls on the members of the Church of Colossae to be 'rooted in him (Christ)' and to be 'built on him'. Paul uses two metaphors here, one drawn from a rural setting and the other from an urban setting. Being rooted in Christ suggests the image of a tree or a plant rooted in good soil; being built on Christ suggests the image of a building that is built on very solid foundations. Paul invites us to root our lives in Christ and to build our lives on him. Both images suggest the central place that Jesus is to have in our lives as his disciples. Paul goes on to state why the Lord is worthy of such a central place in our lives. In him, according to Paul, 'lives the fullness of divinity and in him you too find your own fulfilment'. Jesus is the fullness of God; God is fully revealed and fully present in Jesus, and, for that reason, we find our own fullness, our own fulfilment, in Jesus. As the fullness of God, he is the one who alone can fulfil our deepest longings and hopes. He is the best soil in which we can root our lives and the firmest foundation on which we can build our lives. The gospel reading speaks of a large crowd of people from Judea and beyond coming to Jesus to listen to him and be cured by him. They sensed God's presence in Jesus and they recognised that he could respond to their deepest needs. We are all invited to be part of that great throng who recognise Jesus for who he really is and who respond to his presence in a wholehearted way.

## 11 September, Wednesday, Twenty-Third Week in Ordinary Time
*Luke 6:20–26*

The Beatitudes as we find them in Luke's Gospel are not the Beatitudes with which we we are familiar, which are to be found in Matthew's Gospel: 'Blessed are the poor in spirit … '. The Beatitudes in Luke seem especially strange to our ears. Jesus seems to consider blessed or happy or fortunate those we would normally consider unfortunate – the poor, the hungry, the sad, the rejected. On the other hand, he seems to consider unfortunate those who would generally be regarded as fortunate by the standards of the world – the rich, the well-fed, the happy, the highly regarded. Jesus certainly does not consider poverty, hunger, sadness or rejection as blessings in themselves. In the course of his public ministry, he called for the poor to be cared for, he fed the hungry, he brought joy to the grieving, he showed hospitality to the rejected. Jesus is declaring that the poor, the hungry, the sad and the rejected are happy or blessed because he is assuring them that God is working on their behalf in and through his ministry. They may feel abandoned by others, but God has not abandoned them. God is working to create a better future for them, not just in eternity but in the here and now of Jesus' ministry and that of his followers. This word of Jesus is both a reassuring and challenging one for us today. We are being reassured that when we are at our most vulnerable, whatever form that might take, the Lord is especially close to us, even if we feel abandoned by others. We are also being called to make present and tangible in the here and now the Lord's loving commitment to those who are most vulnerable among us.

## 12 September, Thursday, Twenty-Third Week in Ordinary Time
*Luke 6:27–38*

There is an extraordinary wealth in both of today's readings. It is very difficult to know where to focus. Any line from either of the two readings would give food for thought for the day. What both read-ings have in common is that they call us to live in a certain way. In essence, both Paul and Jesus call us to live loving lives, lives which reflect the loving life of Jesus. Paul calls on us to put on love as a kind of outer garment that covers the other garments of compassion, kind-ness, gentleness, patience and readiness to forgive. Jesus takes the call to love to a new level by insisting that we love even our enemies and that we do good even to those who hate us.

This is the call of the Gospel. Yet, in both the first reading and the gospel reading, there is something that comes prior to the call of the Gospel and that is the Gospel itself. Paul expresses that Gospel very simply in the opening line of the first reading, 'God loves you'. It is because God loves us in all our frailty that we are to be clothed in love so as to love others. In a similar way, Paul goes on to say, 'The Lord has forgiven you; now you must do the same'. It is because the Lord has forgiven us that we are to forgive one another. Likewise, in the gospel reading, Jesus' call to love, the call of the Gospel, is rooted in the Gospel itself.

We are to be compassionate as God our Father is compassionate towards us. We are to love our enemies because we are sons and daughters of the Most High who is kind to the ungrateful and the wicked, which is the Gospel itself. Both readings suggest that we need to hear the Gospel as addressed to each of us personally, the Gospel of God's unconditional, undeserved and all-forgiving love for us all, before we can rise to the call of the Gospel.

## 13 September, Friday, Twenty-Third Week in Ordinary Time
*Luke 6:39–42*

In the gospel reading, Jesus reminds us how easy it is to notice the faults of others while being blind to our own failings. We may notice a minor fault in someone, a 'splinter', and, at the same time, not notice a major fault, a 'plank', in ourselves. We judge others to be blind, having a splinter in their eye, while being unaware of our own greater blindness, a 'plank' in our eye. We are blind and yet we claim to be able to lead the blind. We can easily think of ourselves as better than others and set ourselves up as the judge of others, criticising their faults in our own minds and even to others. Jesus is suggesting that a healthy awareness of our own failings and weaknesses can make us hesitate to address the failings of others. We are all sinners, without exception. We are loved sinners but we are sinners nonetheless. Our sin prevents us seeing as the Lord sees, with eyes of love and compassion. In that sense, we are all blind. We do not see clearly, in the clear light of God's love. We can so easily get it wrong when it comes to others, because, as the Scriptures tell us, we look at appearances and it is only God who looks at the heart. We may all be blind but we are not isolated in our own blindness or sin because the Lord looks upon each of us with love and hope. If we but recognise our own failings, the 'plank' in our eye, then the Lord will renew us in his love.

## 14 September, Saturday, The Exaltation of the Holy Cross
*John 3:13–17*

The expression 'exaltation of the cross' would have made very little sense in the time of Jesus. 'Exaltation' suggested glory, honour and status, whereas death by crucifixion was the most shameful death imaginable. It was the complete absence of glory, honour and status. Why did the early Christians begin to speak of the death by crucifixion of Jesus as exaltation? They could only do so in the light of Jesus' resurrection. In today's second reading, Paul says that because Jesus 'was humbler yet, even to accepting death, death on a cross', God raised him high, or highly exalted him. In that sense, Jesus' exaltation by God followed his death on the cross. Yet, the early Church understood that Jesus was already being exalted by God as he hung from the cross. When people were doing their worst to Jesus, God was standing over his Son vindicating him, confirming all that his Son lived by and stood for. It was because Jesus was totally faithful to the work God gave him to do that he was crucified. What was that work that God gave Jesus to do? Jesus' work was to reveal God's love for the world. As St John says in today's gospel reading, 'God loved the world so much that he gave his only Son'. On one occasion in John's Gospel Jesus said, 'my food is to do the will of the one who sent me and to finish his work'. According to that same Gospel Jesus' last words before he died were 'it is finished'. Jesus' work of revealing God's love for the world, for Jews, Samaritans and pagans, was experienced as threatening by many, especially those in power. They crucified him to put a stop to his work. Yet, in killing Jesus, they enabled Jesus to finish the work God gave him to do. If his life proclaimed God's love for the world, his death proclaimed that love even more powerfully. His death revealed a divine love, a love that endured in the face of all the very worst that evil and sin could inflict on him. That is why we can speak of the exaltation of the cross. When we look upon the cross, we believe we are looking upon an explosion of love, the glorious revelation of God's love, a love that is stronger than sin and death, a love that embraced the world and embraces each of us in a very personal way. We can each say, with Paul in his letter to the Galatians, 'I live by faith in the Son of God who loved me and gave himself for me'.

## 16 September, Monday, Twenty-Fourth Week in Ordinary Time
*Luke 7:1–10*

In today's first reading, Paul gives us a very generous vision of God. He declares that God wants everyone to be saved and reach full knowledge of the truth. God desires all of humanity to hear the truth of the Gospel. Paul articulates that Gospel truth in a very succinct way in the reading: 'There is only one God, and there is only one me-diator between God and mankind', Christ Jesus who sacrificed him-self for our sins, who gave himself through his life and especially his death so that we might be reconciled to God. This truth of the Gospel is so rich that no one of us will ever fully exhaust its meaning in this life. In today's gospel reading, God's generous vision for humanity meets with a very generous response from a non-Jew, a pagan centu-rion. This pagan had a deep appreciation of the Jewish faith. Accord-ing to the gospel reading, he paid for the building of the synagogue in Capernaum, the foundations of which can still be seen today. He clearly had a tremendous faith in one particular Jew, Jesus from Nazareth. He trusted Jesus to heal his servant at a distance by means of his word. He did not consider himself worthy that someone as close to God as Jesus should enter his pagan home. Jesus was deeply impressed by his trusting faith and his humility. 'Not even in Israel have I found faith like this'. Indeed, a version of this centurion's words has made its way into the text of our Mass. At every Mass, we are invited to make the words of this centurion our own, and to make our own the trusting faith and humility that lie behind them. If we can do that, then God's generous vision for our lives will begin to come to pass.

## 17 September, Tuesday, Twenty-Fourth Week in Ordinary Time
*Luke 7:11–17*

It is said of Jesus in today's gospel reading that when he saw the widow accompanying the body of her son for burial, he had compassion on her. He saw and had compassion. Jesus once told a parable in which it is said of one of the characters that 'he saw and had compassion'. It was the Samaritan who saw the broken Jewish person by the roadside and had compassion. The Samaritan in the story behaves in the way that Jesus behaves in real life. In that story, the broken traveller did not make any request of those who were passing by and in today's gospel reading the widow did not make any request of Jesus. It wasn't the heartfelt cry of the broken traveller or the widow that made the difference, rather it was the particular way that the Samaritan and Jesus saw those who were in need. The Lord sees us with eyes of compassion. He is aware of our need before we articulate that need in prayer. In other words, he is present to us before we are present to him. The Lord sees us, before we see him with the eyes of faith. The Lord is not watching us in some kind of inquisitorial way; he is seeing us with eyes of compassion. The Lord's way of seeing us encourages us to come before him in our need. His way of seeing us also calls on us to see others with his compassionate eyes.

## 18 September, Wednesday, Twenty-Fourth Week in Ordinary Time

*Luke 7:31–35*

Music is something we all appreciate. We may have different tastes in music, but we are all drawn to some kind of music. I was recently reading a book entitled *Life after Life*. It is the prison memoirs of Paddy Armstrong, one of the four wrongly convicted for the bombings in Guildford, Surrey, in the mid-1970s. I was struck by how, in his darkest days in prison, music lifted his heart and his spirits, the music of bands like Pink Floyd.

Listening through his headphones in a prison cell momentarily brought him into another world. In today's gospel reading, Jesus uses the language of music to speak of his own ministry and the ministry of John the Baptist. He compares the Baptist's ministry to children in the market place singing dirges, playing at funerals, and he compares his own ministry to children in the market place playing pipes, as at a wedding or some other celebratory event.

There was a sombre character to the ministry of John the Baptist which was absent from Jesus' ministry, and there was a joyful, celebratory character to Jesus' ministry which was absent from the Baptist's. Jesus declares that neither the sombre music of John's ministry nor the joyful music of his own ministry moved many of his contemporaries. They dismissed John as possessed and Jesus as a glutton and drunkard. Jesus played the music of God in a way no one else has ever done.

The risen Lord continues to play the music of God through the Holy Spirit today. We try to become more and more attuned to that music of the Spirit, so that its melody feeds our spirit and its rhythm shapes how we live.

## 19 September, Thursday, Twenty-Fourth Week in Ordinary Time

*Luke 7:36–50*

The story that we have just heard in today's gospel reading puts before us a study in contrast. Jesus is at table as the guest of a Pharisee, but his host neglects to show him the normal signs of hospitality in that culture. Although the Pharisee has invited Jesus to his table, his way of receiving Jesus shows great reserve. In contrast, a woman, who had a reputation as a sinner, gate-crashes the meal and showers hospitality on Jesus in the most extravagant way imaginable. The one who would have been expected to show hospitality to Jesus doesn't really show it. The outsider who would have been written off by people more than makes up for the hospitality Jesus was denied. How can we explain the difference? Jesus gives his own explanation. The woman had experienced through Jesus the gift of God's forgiveness; her gestures were an outpouring of gratitude for that gift. The Pharisee had no sense of his need to receive God's forgiveness from Jesus. He had no sense that he owed Jesus anything. The story invites us to ask ourselves, 'Who do we stand with, the Pharisee or the woman?' When we know ourselves to be forgiven sinners we are more likely to respond to Jesus in the way the woman did. At the source of our lives as followers of Jesus is the experience of God's forgiveness in Jesus, God's unconditional love through Jesus. Our lives then become a grateful, spontaneous response to that grace we have received. Like the woman, we give generously to the Lord, not out of duty but out of loving gratitude for all we have received. In the words of Paul in today's first reading, 'you have in you a spiritual gift which was given to you'.

## 20 September, Friday, Twenty-Fourth Week in Ordinary Time

*Luke 8:1–3*

From the beginning of his public ministry, Jesus has been gathering a community of disciples about himself. Today's short gospel makes it clear that this community embraced not only men, but women, with three being mentioned by name, including one from the best society. Joanna was the wife of an administrator at the court of Herod Antipas. In the context of that culture, this was a highly unusual community to be forming, one which would invariably encounter strong resistance. This group of Galilean women will be mentioned again by Luke as standing at a distance from Golgotha, watching all that took place around the death of Jesus, as seeing Jesus' tomb and how his body was laid and then as coming to the tomb on the first day of the week after Jesus' death, with Mary Magdalene and Joanna mentioned by name. It is said of the women in today's gospel reading that they had experienced Jesus' healing power. Mary Magdalene (not to be confused with the sinful woman of the previous episode) had been in particular need of healing. In gratitude for what they had received from Jesus, they now devote themselves to his service and the service of the disciples, providing hospitality out of their means. They model for us both the openness to receive from Jesus and the willingness to give generously from what has been received. We too have been greatly graced and we are called to give from what we have received. In giving from what we have received, Jesus assures us that we will receive even more, 'give, and it will be given to you'.

## 21 September, Saturday, St Matthew, Apostle and Evangelist

*Matthew 9:9–13*

I have a framed print of the call of Matthew by the artist Caravaggio. It is a painting that appeals to me very much. Jesus is depicted on the right side of the painting pointing towards Matthew. Matthew is seated at his tax booth with one hand on his money and the other pointing towards himself, as if to ask, 'Are you calling me?' Tax collectors were considered sinners in the time of Jesus. Apart from being in the pay of the Romans, it was presumed that they were taking more than their share of people's money. The professionally religious people of the time were aghast at Jesus, a religious teacher, calling such a person and, then, to compound matters further, going on to share table with Matthew and his associates, more tax collectors and sinners. Yet, Jesus was celebrating the mercy of God with those who desperately needed to be assured that God loved them and forgave them their sins. Jesus did not come to stand in judgement on people; he came to invite them to celebrate the gift of God's unconditional love and mercy. He was the Physician who came for those in need of healing, which is everyone, including those who had no awareness of their need for healing, for God's mercy. Later in the Gospel of Matthew, Matthew, the tax collector, will be called by Jesus to become one of the Twelve. The foundation pillars of the Church included those who by reason of their profession were considered outcasts and 'sinners'. Every Eucharist shares something of the quality of the meal in today's gospel reading; it is a celebration of God's forgiveness. The Church is a community of forgiven sinners who are aware of their need for forgiveness and healing. Having celebrated the Lord's mercy at the Eucharist, we are sent out from the Eucharist as instruments of God's mercy to others.

## 23 September, Monday, Twenty-Fifth Week in Ordinary Time
*Luke 8:16–18*
Today's first reading depicts a wonderful moment in the story of the people of Israel, their return from exile in Babylon. Cyrus, the emperor of Persia, whose armies had brought about the collapse of the Babylonian Empire, had a much more benign attitude towards his subject

peoples. He allowed them to practise their faith in their own land, as long as they remembered that Persia was now their overlord. In the wake of Cyrus's edict, many of the exiles left Babylon and returned to their native land and to the city of Jerusalem and began to rebuild their destroyed city and Temple. The responsorial psalm reflects this moment of national restoration: 'When the Lord delivered Zion from bondage, it seemed like a dream ... What marvels the Lord worked for us'. In exile, the people had come to appreciate that their dire situation was somehow linked to their failure to be faithful to the Lord, to hear his word and live by it. Yet, they came to understand that the Lord remained faithful to them and brought them back home from exile. In the gospel reading, Jesus calls on his disciples: 'Take care how you hear; for anyone who has will be given more; from anyone who has not, even what he thinks he has will be taken away'. Jesus is saying there that if we truly listen to him and allow his word to shape our lives, then we will receive more and more from him. If we refuse to listen to him, we will lose even what he has already given to us. The Lord's call in today's gospel reading, 'Take care, how you hear', is one that we need to take to heart every day of our lives. We strive to listen to his word more attentively and to live by it.

## 24 September, Tuesday, Twenty-Fifth Week in Ordinary Time
*Luke 8:19–21*

The first reading describes the rebuilding of the Temple in Jerusalem after the people of Israel returned from exile in Babylon towards the end of the sixth century BC. Shortly afterwards, they celebrated the feast of Passover in the Temple. The return of the Temple and its worship was a cause of great joy for the people. That same sense of joy is reflected in the responsorial psalm. The pilgrim to Jerusalem declares, 'I rejoiced when I heard them say, "Let us go to God's house".' Jerusalem and its Temple was a place that Jews were always trying to get to, whether they lived in Judah or much further afield. Jesus once said of himself in the Gospels, 'there is something greater than the Temple here'. God was understood to be present in the Temple in a special way. Jesus was implying that God's presence is to be found uniquely in himself. As people flocked to the Temple, so in the Gospels people flock to Jesus. In today's gospel reading, it is Jesus' family, his mother and brothers, who set out to look for him, yet they cannot get to him because a large crowd of people has already arrived and they are all around him. What those people hear Jesus say is that they can become members of his family, his mother, brothers and sisters, if they hear the word of God and put it into practice. The prophet Isaiah provides an image of people going up to the Temple in Jerusalem because, as he says, 'Out of Zion shall go forth instruction, and the word of the Lord from Jerusalem'. In the Gospels, it is from Jesus that the word of God goes forth. In the gospel reading he promises that those who hear God's word as he proclaims it and lives by it will have the most intimate of relationships with him; they will become his family.

## 25 September, Wednesday, Twenty-Fifth Week in Ordinary Time
*Luke 9:1–6*

Today's first reading is the prayer of Ezra, the priest, on behalf of the people of Israel. In that prayer, he recognises that God's people have sinned, have rebelled against him. As a result, they found themselves in slavery to a foreign power. Yet, Ezra declares that God did not forget his people in their slavery. Working through the kings of Persia, God brought his people out of exile, back to their land, and enabled them to rebuild their city and Temple. This is a prayer that proclaims the faithfulness of God to his sinful people. It comes very close to the message of Jesus in the Gospels. Jesus revealed the faithfulness of God to all humanity. Jesus' death proclaims God's faithfulness even to those who put Jesus to death. This is the Gospel, or good news, that

Jesus sends out the disciples to proclaim in today's gospel reading. They are to proclaim this Gospel not just in word, but in action, by their healing the broken. There was such an urgency to the proclaiming of this good news that the disciples were to travel as lightly as possible. Nothing was to hold them back from making this announcement, and if they got any kind of a welcome at all they were to stay put, because this was their opportunity to proclaim the good news of God's faithful love for all. This is the same Gospel message that we need to hear over and over again today. Yes, we are sinners; we have failed. Yet, the Lord remains faithful to us. As Paul says in his letter to the Romans, Christ Jesus has lived and died for us and is now living to intercede for us.

## 26 September, Thursday, Twenty-Fifth Week in Ordinary Time
*Luke 9:7–9*

In the Gospels curiosity can sometimes be the first step on the path to faith. The person of Nicodemus in John's Gospel comes to mind. He came to Jesus by night, under cover of darkness, because he was curious about him. At the end of John's Gospel, he is found alongside Joseph of Arimathea, arranging a dignified burial for Jesus. Curiosity and the questions that arise from it can open us up to faith, or to a deeper faith if we are already people of faith. In today's short gospel reading, Herod, the tetrarch of Galilee, is curious about Jesus. He is full of questions about this man Jesus on the basis of the reports he has heard about him. 'Who is this I hear such reports about?' Luke tells us in the gospel reading that Herod was anxious to see Jesus. It is only in Luke's Gospel that Herod does get to see Jesus. During the passion of Jesus, Pilate decided to send Jesus to Herod for an opinion, because Jesus was from Galilee, Herod's territory. Herod got his wish to see Jesus. However, Luke tells us that Herod and his soldiers treated Jesus with contempt and mocked him before sending him back to

Pilate. In Herod's case, curiosity did not lead to faith. The questions generated by our reason, on their own, do not bring us to faith. Faith is ultimately a gift from God. It is given to all but to receive this gift we need to become like little children, as Jesus said. We need to acknowledge our poverty before the Lord and entrust ourselves to the gift he is offering us, which is none other than the gift of himself. As Jesus states in the first Beatitude, 'Blessed are the poor in spirit, for theirs is the kingdom of heaven'.

## 27 September, Friday, Twenty-Fifth Week in Ordinary Time

*Luke 9:18–22*

Luke, more than the other evangelists, portrays Jesus as regularly at prayer. In today's gospel reading from Luke, it is when Jesus is praying that he asks his disciples the two questions, 'Who do the crowds say I am?' and 'Who do you say I am?' Luke suggests that these questions came out of his prayer. They were important questions. The first question was a general question; the second question was a much more personal one. We can hear both questions as addressed to all of us but it is the second question that is the more demanding one because it asks us to say who Jesus is for us, for me personally. It is easier to say what Jesus means to people in general; it takes a little more out of us to say what he means to me personally. Yet, it is the answer to that second question that Jesus is more interested in. He wants us to give expression to our own personal faith in him. We are each being asked, 'What do you believe?' Paul in his letters answered that question in a number of different ways. In his letter to the Galatians he said, 'I live by faith in the Son of God who loved me and gave himself for me'. It is as if Paul is answering Jesus' question by saying, 'You are the Son of God who loves me and gave yourself for me'. The gospel reading today invites us to reflect on the answer we would give, as individuals, to that question of Jesus, 'Who do you say I am?'

## 28 September, Saturday, Twenty-Fifth Week in Ordinary Time

*Luke 9:43–45*

There is much in life we do not fully understand. The experience of suffering is one of those mysteries of life that we struggle to fathom. Illness, including fatal illness, can strike anyone at any time, regardless of their age. On a regular basis we are made aware of tragedies in which innocent people are killed. We are speechless before it all. Our faith can help us deal with our own suffering or the suffering of a loved one, but the mystery of it all remains. In today's gospel reading, at the very moment when people were full of admiration for Jesus, he announced to his disciples that he was going to be handed over into the power of men, who would put him to death. The gospel reading says that the disciples did not understand him when he said this, and they were afraid to ask him about what he said. They could not grasp how this messenger of God, who was so admired by so many, could suffer at the hands of others. They did not understand the mystery of his destiny, which entailed suffering and death. How could someone so good, so innocent, fall into the power of people who wanted him dead? It was only after Jesus' resurrection that the disciples understood why Jesus had to die in the way he did. His death was the consequence of his loving fidelity to his mission. Perhaps, for us too, it is only beyond the resurrection, from the perspective of eternity, that we will understand the mystery of suffering in our own lives and in the lives of others. In the meantime, the first reading assures us that the Lord has come to dwell in the middle of us and is all around us like a wall of fire. In our own Calvary experience, the Lord is with us, just as God was with Jesus on the cross. Even when we seem to be at our most vulnerable, he is protecting us, like a wall of fire around us.

## 30 September, Monday, Twenty-Sixth Week in Ordinary Time

*Luke 9:46–50*

The Gospels suggest that Jesus had many an argument with the religious leaders of the day who understood God very differently to how Jesus understood God. Jesus needed to argue his case on these occasions; he needed to challenge those whose image of God was too narrow. He had a more intimate relationship with God than his opponents; he knew God better than they did. He needed to try and enlighten them. These were necessary arguments. Sometimes we all have to engage in necessary arguments. There can also be arguments which are misplaced and unnecessary. We have an example of that in today's gospel reading. The disciples were arguing about which of them was the greatest. From Jesus' perspective, this was the wrong argument to be having. It showed that the priorities of his disciples were wrong. Jesus challenged their preoccupation about which of them was the greatest by placing a child before them, a symbol of weakness, vulnerability. In that culture a child lacked status and position, lacked 'greatness'. Jesus must have astonished his disciples by identifying himself and the one who sent him, God his Father, with this child. Jesus was suggesting to his disciples that this child was great in a way that they were not. In other words, greatness in God's kingdom is not what the world considers greatness. Jesus was trying to show them how misplaced their argument was. Because we can all get caught up into the wrong kind of argument with others, we need to keep turning to Jesus, his life and his message, to learn what is really worth arguing over and what is not worth arguing over.

## 1 October, Tuesday, Twenty-Sixth Week in Ordinary Time

*Luke 9:51–56*

Both readings today are linked by the theme of the journey to Jerusalem. The first reading envisages a joyful journey to Jerusalem. Not just the people of Israel but nations of every language want to go to Jerusalem because they have learned that God is present there in the Temple. They go to entreat the Lord and to seek his favour. There is an excitement to their journey. If you have had the opportunity and the privilege of going to the Holy Land, something of that same excitement takes hold of you. We are on a pilgrimage to a place that has somehow been touched by God. As followers of the Lord, we believe that we are all on a pilgrimage, a life-long pilgrimage, towards the heavenly Jerusalem where we will see the Lord face to face. In the gospel reading, Jesus sets out for the city of Jerusalem. However, this will not be a joyful journey towards an encounter with God. Jesus has to take the road to Jerusalem resolutely. He has to steel himself for this journey, because, as he will say later in this Gospel of Luke, Jerusalem is a city that has a reputation for killing prophets. Jesus knows that at the end of this journey, he will fall into the hands of sinful men. The rejection he immediately receives from a Samaritan village is a foretaste of the bloodier rejection he will encounter in Jerusalem. There are times in all our lives when we have to steel ourselves for some journey. At one level we do not want to make the journey, but at a deeper level we know we have to take it if we are to be true to our deepest calling. It is at such times that we can call upon the same resource that Jesus called upon, just before he set out on his journey to Jerusalem. He went up the Mount of Transfiguration to pray. We too can draw on the strength that the Lord gives us in prayer when we have to face into some difficult journey.

## 2 October, Wednesday, The Guardian Angels

*Matthew 18:1–5, 10*

There is a reference to angels in each of today's readings. In the first reading, the role of God's angel is to guard God's people and bring them safely to their destination. This angel reveals God's protective and guiding presence in the lives of God's people. This role of the angel is very much in keeping with today's feast of the guardian angels. It is a feast that reminds us that God is present to us, guarding us and leading us to our final destination, which we understand as eternal life. This guarding and guiding role of God in our lives was fully revealed in the person of Jesus. He is with us to the end of time, guarding and guiding us. In the gospel reading, it is not God's angel who is with his people, but rather it is the angels of the 'little ones' who are with God. The 'little ones' are not just children but the Lord's disciples whom the world considers lowly and insignificant. Their angels are in God's presence, working on their behalf. This role of the angels was also fully revealed in the person of Jesus. Paul declares, in his letter to the Romans, that the risen Lord is at the right hand of God interceding for us. The angels remind us of the role of the Lord in our lives. He is with us in this life to guard and guide us and he is with God in heaven, interceding for us, working on our behalf. The angels, and to a much greater extent, Jesus, reveal that 'God is for us'. Today's feast is a good opportunity to ask, with Paul, in his letter to the Romans, 'If God is for us, who is against us?'

## 3 October, Thursday, Twenty-Sixth Week in Ordinary Time

*Luke 10:1–12*

There is a wonderful depiction of a Jewish liturgy of the word in today's first reading. Ezra the priest stands at a wooden stand, just like our ambo, to proclaim the word of the Lord, the law of the Lord. The people stood up to listen, as we stand for the gospel. Before he began reading, Ezra blessed the Lord and the people answered, 'Amen', just as we bless the Lord before we read the gospel: 'Glory to you, O Lord'. Ezra not only read from the Law but explained it as he went along so that people could understand it, just as in our liturgy the celebrant might give a homily. The people were deeply touched by the proclamation of the word of God. Indeed, they were in tears, mindful perhaps of their lack of response to that word in the past. Likewise, God's word can touch our hearts in different ways when it is proclaimed. Today's first reading reminds us just how much our own liturgy is rooted in the Jewish liturgy. In the gospel reading, Jesus sends out his disciples to proclaim the word of God, the same word that Jesus has been proclaiming: 'The kingdom of God is very near to you'. Jesus sends out seventy-two to make this proclamation. A much wider group than the Twelve is entrusted with the task of proclaiming the good news of God's powerful presence in and through the person and ministry of Jesus. This is the Gospel that has been proclaimed to each of us and to which we are doing our best to respond. We are called to allow this Gospel to sink deep into our hearts, so that it shapes our lives. Then we can become proclaimers of the Lord's Gospel, not just with our words but with the way we live.

## 4 October, Friday, Twenty-Sixth Week in Ordinary Time
*Luke 10:13–16*

In today's gospel reading Jesus identifies himself very closely with his disciples: 'Anyone who listens to you listens to me; anyone who rejects you rejects me'. The risen Lord continues to identify himself with his disciples today, with each one of us. Each of us is called to be a living sign of the Lord's presence. The Lord wants to be present in our world through each one of us. We have each received the extraordinary calling to be the Lord's ambassador in our world, to reveal his presence to others. We are all aware of our capacity to hide the Lord as well as reveal him. We can relate to others in ways that are not of the Lord. In the words of today's first reading, 'we have not listened to the voice of the Lord our God'. Yet that does not stop the Lord from continuing to call us to be his presence to others. He continues to want to live in us, to speak and act through us. We are the members of his body. As he was present in Galilee and Judea in and through his physical body, he wishes to be present in our world today in and through his body, the Church, and in and through each individual member of that body. He needs all of us if he is to be fully present, because each of us can reveal a different facet of the Lord. As Paul says in his first letter to the Corinthians, every member of the body of the Church has a vital role to play in ensuring that Christ's body is fully alive.

## 5 October, Saturday, Twenty-Sixth Week in Ordinary Time
*Luke 10:17–24*

When we do a job well we are generally quite pleased with ourselves and we are happy to talk about it with others. In today's gospel reading, the disciples were very pleased after a successful period of mission and they couldn't wait to share their success with Jesus. Full of joy, they said to Jesus, 'even the devils submit to us when we use your name'. Yet, Jesus immediately deflected their focus from the success of their mission to something even more important. They should really be rejoicing not so much in the success of their mission but in the fact that their names are written in heaven. It is their relationship with God and the future it promises that is the real source of joy. That is true for all of us. There will come a time when we won't have the energy or the health to achieve a great deal. Our labours and the fruits of our labours can diminish at any stage of our lives. However, what remains constant is God's relationship with us through Jesus, and all it promises. We can always rejoice in that wonderful gift, even when all else fails. Jesus says to us what he says to his disciples in today's gospel reading, 'Happy the eyes that see what you see'. The Son has chosen to reveal his Father to us, and to draw us into his own relationship with God the Father. That is something to rejoice in, not only for what it gives us in the present, but also for what it promised beyond this earthly life.

## 7 October, Monday, Our Lady of the Rosary

*Luke 1:26–38*

October has been traditionally the month of the rosary. When I visited one of the First Holy Communion classes during the week, the teacher invited the children to show me the rosary rings that they had made. This is a little ring with ten beads on it, made out of various materials, representing one decade of the Rosary. The two readings for today's Mass reflect two of the fifteen traditional mysteries of the Rosary. The first reading is linked to the third glorious mystery, the coming of the Holy Spirit at Pentecost. The eleven disciples were gathered in prayer, along with several women, including Mary, the mother of Jesus, and other members of Jesus' family. It was in that context of prayer that the Holy Spirit came down upon them all. The gospel reading is the first joyful mystery, the annunciation to Mary of the birth of Jesus, her son and God's Son. Mary is told by the angel Gabriel that the Holy Spirit would come upon her, and, as a result, her child will be called Son of God. Through the coming of the Holy Spirit on Mary, Jesus was conceived and born. Through the coming of the Holy Spirit on the disciples, including Mary, at Pentecost, the Church was born.

Through the working of the Holy Spirit in our own lives, we are continually reborn as sons and daughters of God, and brothers and sisters of Jesus. Paul, in his letter to the Romans, tells us that the Spirit is given to us to help us in our weakness, because we do not know how to pray as we ought. We need the Spirit to pray as God desires us to pray. Whether we pray the Rosary or pray in some other form, our opening prayer needs to be, 'Come Holy Spirit, help me in my weakness; empower me to pray as God desires me to pray'.

## 8 October, Tuesday, Twenty-Seventh Week in Ordinary Time
*Luke 10:38–42*

In today's first reading, Jonah finally goes to the Assyrian capital of Nineveh in response to God's call, having tried unsuccessfully to run from that call. Jonah initially had no desire to preach God's word in the capital city of Israel's enemies. When he did so, the people of Nineveh, from the king down, responded wholeheartedly to Jonah's preaching. The Jewish author of the story that we know as the Book of Jonah may have been challenging the narrow outlook of his con-temporaries, who saw those beyond Israel as beyond God's reach. The author was making the point that not only were they not beyond God's reach but they were capable of responding more generously to God's word than God's own people, Israel. Jonah was among the traditional enemies of Israel when he was in Nineveh. In the gospel reading, Jesus is among friends in the home of Mary and Martha. He, too, came to their home to proclaim God's word, and, on this occasion, it was Mary who sat at Jesus' feet to listen to his word. Martha was distracted by all the serving she had taken upon herself. Jesus gently rebukes Martha when she rebukes her sister. Martha has allowed excessive anxiety about what was not so important to prevent her attending to what was truly important, God's word as proclaimed by Jesus. We can all go the way of Martha. With the best of intentions, we can all allow ourselves to become distracted by non-essentials to the neglect of what really matters. When that happens, we have something to learn from Mary, Martha's sister and, even, from the Ninevites.

## 9 October, Wednesday, Twenty-Seventh Week in Ordinary Time

*Luke 11:1–4*

Both of today's readings are linked by the theme of prayer. There is a great honesty about Jonah's prayer at the beginning of the first reading. He is outraged that the people of Nineveh, Israel's great enemies, have come to experience the loving mercy of God. He is angry because God does not share his enmity towards the people of Nineveh. He couldn't live with this God who was full of tenderness and compassion and rich in graciousness, even towards Israel's enemies. Jonah was so upset by this gracious God that he asked God to take away his life. If God couldn't be made in Jonah's image, then Jonah might as well be dead. Jonah's prayer is an honest prayer, but there is a great deal of self in it. It is not a prayer that reflects the heart of God. In the gospel reading, Jesus teaches his disciples a very different kind of prayer. In this prayer, we who pray it are invited to surrender to what God wants, rather than trying to impose what we want on God. The prayer begins, 'may your name be held holy, your kingdom come'. It is a prayer which invites us to let God be God. We declare before God that we want what God wants. Jonah, in contrast, really wanted God to want what he wanted. In the prayer Jesus taught, having acknowledged the priority of what God wants, the coming of God's kingdom, we go on to acknowledge our dependence on God for daily sustenance, for forgiveness and for protection from evil. We are being encouraged in this second part of the prayer to ask God to give us what God wants to give us. Here, indeed, is a prayer that reflects the heart of God.

## 10 October, Thursday, Twenty-Seventh Week in Ordinary Time

*Luke 11:5–13*

Luke's Gospel, from which we are reading these days, has preserved much more of Jesus' teaching on prayer than the other Gospels. In today's gospel reading, Jesus encourages us to pray the prayer of petition, to petition God: 'Ask, and it will be given to you; search and you will find; knock and the door will be opened to you', literally, 'Keep on asking ... keep on searching ... keep on knocking'. Any father will give only good things to his children even if they ask for something harmful to them. Jesus concludes on the basis of this human experience that our heavenly Father will certainly give good things to us when we petition God in prayer. Jesus seems to be suggesting that the prayer of petition opens us up to the good things that God wants to give us. What does God want to give us? At the end of the gospel reading, Jesus identifies the good that God wants to give us with the Holy Spirit. 'How much more will the heavenly Father give the Holy Spirit to those who ask him?' Even if our prayer of petition is not answered in the way we would like, such prayer will always upon us up to God's gift of the Holy Spirit and this is a greater gift than anything else we could ask for. Pentecost is not just a once-off event at the beginning of the Church's life. It is a daily event for those who persevere with the prayer of petition, those who come before God in their need and open their hearts to God's gift.

## 11 October, Friday, Twenty-Seventh Week in Ordinary Time
*Luke 11:15–26*

In the Gospels Jesus calls on people not to judge others. Using a humorous image, he declares that we cannot expect to see the splinter in another's eye while all the time having a plank in our own. In other words, we are all blind to some degree and cannot see others sufficiently clearly to make a sound judgement. In today's gospel reading, it is Jesus who is being judged by some of the people. He has been engaged in the work of healing the broken; he had just healed a person who had been unable to speak. Some have made the judgement that the power that is at work in the ministry of Jesus is the power of Satan. They do not dispute that powerful things are happening in Jesus' ministry, but they judge the source of that power to be Satan, not God. Their judgement of Jesus could not be further from the truth. As Jesus says in reply, it is God, the finger of God, not Satan, that is at work in and through him. It is the kingdom of God that has overtaken them, not the kingdom of Satan. To see good and to judge it to be evil is surely the most extreme form of blindness imaginable. The portrayal of Jesus' opponents in this gospel reading brings home to us the potential we all have of getting it terribly wrong. Today's responsorial psalm declares that the Lord judges the world with justice. We do not always judge others justly. This is why Paul says to the Church in Corinth, 'do not pronounce judgement before the Lord comes, who will bring to light the things now hidden in darkness and will disclose the purposes of the heart'. Paul implies that we remain to some extent in darkness with regard to others and we need the humility to keep acknowledging our blindness.

## 12 October, Saturday, Twenty-Seventh Week in Ordinary Time

*Luke 11:27–28*

In today's very short gospel reading, two women feature. A nameless woman in the crowd pronounces a beatitude over another woman, Mary, the mother of Jesus: 'Happy the womb that bore you and the breasts that you sucked!' The woman is so impressed by Jesus that she declares his mother blessed. We honour Mary for the same reason. We venerate her as the mother of Jesus, the one through whom God visited his people and all humankind in a unique way. Jesus replies to this woman's beatitude with a beatitude of his own: 'Still happier those who hear the word of God and keep it'. In this Gospel of Luke, Mary is portrayed as the one who truly heard the word of God and kept it. She surrendered to God's word proclaimed to her by the angel Gabriel: 'Let it be with me according to your word'. She allowed herself to be shaped by God's word spoken by Gabriel, not just in a physical sense, but in the sense of her whole life being shaped by God's word. Jesus' response to the woman's beatitude could be understood as saying, 'Yes, my mother is blessed, but she is blessed primarily because she heard the word of God and kept it'. None of us can be embraced by the woman's beatitude, because Jesus had only one physical mother. However, we can all be embraced by Jesus' beatitude, because, like Mary, we can all hear the word of God and keep it. When we ask Mary in the Hail Mary to pray for us sinners now, we are asking her to help us to open our hearts to the creative power of God's word as generously as she did. In Luke's Gospel, the seed that fell on good soil is compared to 'the ones who, when they hear the word, hold it fast in an honest and good heart, and bear fruit with patient endurance'. This corresponds exactly to Luke's portrait of Mary in his Gospel. It is a portrait we are all called to grow into.

## 14 October, Monday, Twenty-Eighth Week in Ordinary Time
*Luke 11:29–32*

The Jewish Scriptures are full of memorable and striking figures. In today's gospel reading, Jesus mentions two such figures from the Jewish Scriptures, a king and a prophet, Solomon and Jonah. People responded to their presence and their message. Jesus highlights in the gospel reading that even people from outside of Israel responded to their message, the people of Nineveh in the case of Jonah and the Queen of Sheba in the case of Solomon. Yet, as Jesus bewails, some of his own Jewish contemporaries were not responding to him, even though he was so much greater than Solomon and Jonah. It seems that not everyone appreciated the significance of this carpenter's son from Nazareth. In a sense, we have an advantage over Jesus' contemporaries. They were in the middle of Jesus' story, or even at the beginning of it. We, however, can look back over the whole story of Jesus from his birth to his death, and we can do so in the light of his resurrection and with the guidance of the Holy Spirit. Strange as it may seem, we are in some ways even more privileged than Jesus' contemporaries. We can more easily appreciate the extent to which Jesus is indeed greater than Solomon and greater than Jonah, indeed greater than all the kings and prophets of Israel. We know that Jesus' life, death and resurrection is good news for all of humankind. Our lifelong calling is to keep growing in our appreciation of and in our responsiveness to what Paul calls in today's first reading the good news 'about the Son of God'.

## 15 October, Tuesday, Twenty-Eighth Week in Ordinary Time
*Luke 11:37–41*

We are familiar with the sayings, 'don't judge a book by its cover', and 'all that glitters is not gold'. Both sayings express the truth that what is visible to the naked eye is not always a good guide to the true reality of something. Image and reality do not always match. When Jesus' host at a meal expressed surprise that Jesus did not first wash his hands in accordance with custom, Jesus declared that Pharisees like him were more concerned with externals than with what was within the human heart. The preoccupation with external, ritual cleanliness, distracted them from that deeper cleanliness, what Jesus calls elsewhere purity of heart. Jesus was very concerned with the core of the person, often referred to as the heart in the Jewish Scriptures and in the Gospels. In that culture, the heart was understood not just as the seat of the emotions but also as the seat of the intellect and of the will. If the heart was right, so much else would be right. In the gospel reading, Jesus declares that the heart of someone can be filled with wickedness and extortion or greed, even though a certain religious preoccupation is visible to all. Jesus encourages us to ask ourselves, 'Where is my heart?' 'What lies at the deepest core of my being?'

Elsewhere Jesus suggests that it is our way of living, our way of relating to others, that reveals what is in our hearts and what lies at our core. At the end of the gospel reading, he calls on his host to give alms out of what he has. This will show that at his core is not extortion but generosity. We all need to keep working on what is inside ourselves, in the words of the gospel reading. Indeed, more fundamentally, we need the Lord to keep working on what is inside ourselves. We need him to keep creating in us a new heart and a new spirit.

## 16 October, Wednesday, Twenty-Eighth Week in Ordinary Time
*Luke 11:42–46*

In the gospel reading Jesus criticises the lawyers, the interpreters of the Jewish Law, for loading burdens on people's shoulders that are unendurable, and then doing nothing to help people lift those burdens. Jesus saw himself in a very different light. On one occasion, according to Matthew's Gospel, he declared, 'Come to me all you who labour and are overburdened and I will give you rest'. Far from burdening people, Jesus worked to release them from unnecessary burdens. That is not to say that his message was not challenging and demanding; it was. However, his message was essentially good news for people, not bad news. The path he called people to take was the way of life. Jesus came so that people might have life and have it to the full. The Gospel is not a burden; it is a joy because it is good news, the good news of God's enduring love for us in Christ. The Gospel is a light in the darkness, a source of hope when all seems hopeless, a giver of strength when weakness seems to overpower us. If we respond to the Gospel and allow it to shape our lives, we will become more alive, more complete as human beings, more loving. If we really live the Gospel, then, like Jesus, we will bring rest and peace to those who find themselves burdened for whatever reason.

## 17 October, Thursday, Twenty-Eighth Week in Ordinary Time

*Luke 11:47–54*

At one point in today's gospel reading, Jesus is very critical of the lawyers. The lawyer in the time of Jesus was the expert in religious law. He had made a special study of God's Law, both the written law in the Scriptures and also the oral law that had grown up around that written law and that sought to apply the written law to the changing circumstances of people's daily lives. They lawyers were considered experts in the understanding of God's will for people's lives, as that will found expression in God's Laws, both written and oral. They had the potential to penetrate to the truth of what God wants of us. However, Jesus accuses them of failing in their task. Yes, they have the key of knowledge, the key that gives access to God's truth for our lives, but they haven't used this key to gain access to this truth for themselves, and, more seriously, they have become an obstacle to others gaining this truth. Jesus speaks here as the one who is himself the access to God's truth, to God's will for our lives. He is the door; he is the key to the door. In looking at what Jesus does and in listening to what he says we discover God's truth. Elsewhere in the Gospel Jesus declares that it is above all the wise and the intelligent, people like the experts in the Jewish law, who are failing to receive this revelation of God's truth in Jesus, whereas what he calls 'infants' are doing so with ease. Perhaps the gospel reading is suggesting that sometimes learning and intelligence can be a block to faith, in so far as it makes us too sure of our own position. We need to bend low to receive God's visitation in Jesus, to humble ourselves, to become like little children.

## 18 October, Friday, Feast of St Luke, Evangelist

*Luke 10:1–9*

Today we celebrate the feast of the author of nearly a quarter of the New Testament, Luke, who not only wrote a Gospel but also wrote the Acts of the Apostles. He was the only evangelist who was moved to write a work in two parts, the life of Jesus in his Gospel and the life of the early Church in his Acts of the Apostles. He saw great continuity between these two parts of his story. In the first part the main protagonist is Jesus of Nazareth; in the second part, the main protagonist remains Jesus of Nazareth, but now the risen Lord at work through the Holy Spirit. The first part of his work could be understood as the acts of Jesus and the second part as the acts of the Holy Spirit, understood as the Spirit of the risen Jesus. In that sense Luke, perhaps more than any other writer in the New Testament, reminds us that the Lord who lived and worked in Galilee and Judea continues to live and work in his Church, the community of believers, today. Jesus who, in today's gospel reading, sent out seventy-two others ahead of him in pairs, continues to send out his followers today and, as in the gospel reading, he doesn't send us out as lone rangers but in pairs. The ministry to which he calls us is a shared ministry, one in which we give to and receive from each other. The harvest remains as great today as it was in the time of Jesus. It can only be brought in by labourers who work together. The source of our working together is the Holy Spirit. At the first Pentecost, according to the Acts of the Apostles, the Spirit brought together people of different races and languages. There were several pentecosts or comings of the Holy Spirit in Luke's story of the early Church. We need to keep calling for a fresh outpouring of the Spirit upon us, so that we can work together as the Lord's labourers in God's harvest.

## 19 October, Saturday, Twenty-Eighth Week in Ordinary Time

*Luke 12:9–12*

Our faith is very personal to each one of us. It shapes who we are, just as Abraham's faith defined his identity, according to Paul in today's gospel reading. At the heart of our faith is a personal relationship with the Lord. We try to grow into that relationship more fully as we go through life. We strive to allow that relationship to shape all our other relationships, all that we do and say. We try to live our lives 'in Christ', to allow him to live his life in us. Paul could say, 'It is no longer I who live, but Christ who lives in me'.

The more Christ comes to live in us, the more we will witness to him with our lives. That is what Jesus asks of us in today's gospel reading. He calls on us to openly declare ourselves for him in the presence of others. Jesus is suggesting that although our faith may be personal to each one of us, it is not to be a private matter with no reference to others. There is a certain social pressure nowadays to keep our faith in the private domain. It is a pressure we have to resist. If we witness to the Lord with sureness and courage, then, as Jesus declares at the end of the gospel reading, the Holy Spirit will be with us. 'Do not worry,' Jesus says, 'the Holy Spirit will teach you what you must say.' When we bear witness to our faith, declaring ourselves publicly for the Lord, we create an opening for the Holy Spirit to work within and through us.

## 21 October, Monday, Twenty-Ninth Week in Ordinary Time
*Luke 12:13–21*
The parable Jesus tells in today's gospel reading is the story of a man who sought to make his life secure by holding on to and enhancing what he owns. At the beginning of the story he is already a rich man; he has more than he needs. When he has an even bigger harvest than expected, his only problem is how to store this unexpected bonus. The answer he comes up with is to tear down his perfectly good barns and build bigger ones. His preoccupation with storing his surplus blinds him to other more important considerations, such as, 'What might God be asking me to do with my surplus?' 'How can I serve others with this surplus?' He was looking for security in the wrong place.

He thought that a greater abundance of possessions would make his life more secure. However, death came to him in the midst of his abundance; his life could not be secured in the way he thought. Jesus is saying to us that what makes our life really secure is making ourselves rich in the sight of God. We become rich in the sight of God by recognising that all we have is ultimately a gift from God to be shared with others. God graces us so that we in turn can grace others. If we make ourselves rich in the sight of God by living generously out of the abundance that God has given us, then our lives will be truly secure with a security that endures beyond this earthly life into eternity.

## 22 October, Tuesday, Twenty-Ninth Week in Ordinary Time
*Luke 12:35–38*

In the Gospels Jesus is often presented as doing something that is completely at odds with the prevailing culture. A very clear example of that is to be found in John's Gospel, when, at the Last Supper, Jesus washes the feet of his disciples. The Word who was God and who became flesh performs a task that only slaves would be expected to do, washing the feet of others. In today's gospel reading from Luke, Jesus uses an image that would have been just as shocking. It is the image of a rich man who, on returning from a wedding feast, shows his appreciation for his faithful servants by sitting them down at table and waiting on them. This is the kind of role reversal that would never have happened in real life. Yet, Jesus seems to be saying that life in the kingdom of God is not like real life. As he will say a little later in Luke's Gospel, 'I am among you as one who serves', not as one who sits at table. He has come to reveal the hospitality of God, to invite people to his table where they can have an experience of God's welcoming and hospitable love, and through that experience allow themselves to be transformed. The Lord does call us to be his faithful servants, faithful to the end, awake and alert to the Lord's coming whenever that happens. More fundamentally, the Lord calls on us to receive his service of us. It is in learning to receive his service of us that we are empowered to become his faithful servants in today's world.

## 23 October, Wednesday, Twenty-Ninth Week in Ordinary Time

*Luke 12:39–48*

As well as the group of Beatitudes that are well known to us, there are single beatitudes scattered throughout the gospels. One such beatitude is to be found in today's gospel reading. Jesus declares, 'happy that servant if his master's arrival finds him at his employment'. This is the 'faithful and wise' servant who provides for the needs of the members of the household while the master of the household is away from the house. The master/slave relationship is not one that we are comfortable with today. Yet, it was an integral part of the world in which Jesus lived. In sharing his vision for human life, Jesus regularly drew on the day-to-day experience of the people amongst whom he was moving. Although the social world presupposed by Jesus' image may be foreign to most of us, the message it embodies retains its validity for disciples of every age. We all seek to be the Lord's faithful and wise servants. He needs such servants, people he can trust to provide for the needs of all the members of his household, all who have been created in God's image and likeness and whom the risen Lord desires to draw to himself. We are all servants of one Lord, which means that none of us can set ourselves up as lord of others. Rather, our task is to care faithfully and wisely for the needs of those alongside us. We are called to embody the Lord's concern for the members of the family of God. If we are faithful to that calling, we too will be embraced by the Lord's beatitude in today's gospel reading.

## 24 October, Thursday, Twenty-Ninth Week in Ordinary Time

*Luke 12:49–53*

When Jesus says in today's gospel reading that he has come to bring fire to the Earth, he is referring to the fire of the Holy Spirit. At the beginning of Luke's Gospel, John the Baptist said that whereas he baptises with water, Jesus would baptise with the Holy Spirit and fire. This prophecy is fulfilled at Pentecost when the Holy Spirit comes down upon the disciples in the form of tongues of fire. Yet, before Jesus can pour out the Spirit on his followers, he must first undergo what he refers to in the gospel reading as a baptism. This is a reference to his death, when he will be plunged into great suffering. He speaks of his distress until this baptism is over. The Spirit Jesus will pour out is the Spirit of his risen life, but before entering into glory he must first undergo the cross. Jesus had to go through his own baptism of fire for us to receive the fire of the Spirit. That realisation helps us to appreciate the gift of the Holy Spirit all the more. The Holy Spirit that is poured into our hearts is not only the Spirit of the risen Lord but the Spirit of the crucified and risen Lord. In the first reading Paul reminds us just what a wonderful gift the Holy Spirit is. He refers to the Holy Spirit there as God's power working in us that can do immeasurably more than we can ask or imagine. What we cannot do on our own, we can do in the power of the Spirit that has been given to us at such a cost by Jesus.

## 25 October, Friday, Twenty-Ninth Week in Ordinary Time

*Luke 12:54–59*

Irish people often talk about the weather. That's probably because we get a lot of weather, different kinds of weather. We often watch the sky to see what kind of weather might be coming along in the next few minutes. The sky can tell us that there is a shower on the way or that a clearance is coming over us. In the gospel reading, Jesus acknowledges that his own contemporaries were good at interpreting the signs in the sky and recognising the weather that was coming, but they were not so good at interpreting the times in which they lived and recognising that someone greater than Solomon, greater than Jonah, was standing among them. We can all fail to interpret the signs of the time in that sense. We can fail to recognise the Lord who stands among us and who calls out to us in and through the various circumstances of our lives. To recognise the Lord among us and to hear his voice we need eyes that see and ears that hear. We need to develop a kind of contemplative attitude, an attentiveness of mind and heart. We also need an expectant faith, a faith that fully expects the Lord to be present wherever we find ourselves, a faith that expects the Lord to speak a word that addresses our own particular situation in life. We pray for that contemplative attitude and expectant faith this day.

## 26 October, Saturday, Twenty-Ninth Week in Ordinary Time

*Luke 13:1–9*

In the parable that concludes today's gospel reading I am struck by the contrasting reactions of the vineyard owner and the man who worked in the vineyard to the plight of the fig tree that had borne no fruit for three years. The vineyard owner wanted the fig tree cut down. As far as he was concerned it was taking up space that could be used in a more profitable way, perhaps by planting a more productive tree. However, the man who worked in the vineyard, who got his hands dirty day in and day out and who knew the fig tree, had a different perception. He felt it should be given another year, and during that year he would do all he could to help it finally to bear fruit. I suspect that Jesus would have seen himself much more in the man who worked in the vineyard than in the vineyard owner. Jesus was very patient with people whose lives were far from perfect but who were aware of their failings and wanted to do better. Zacchaeus comes to mind. He was someone many people would have written off, just as the vineyard owner had written off the fig tree. However, Jesus saw the desire in Zacchaeus to move beyond where he was and, addressing him by name, invited himself into Zacchaeus' home: 'I must stay at your house today'. Just as the man who worked in the vineyard wanted to invest in the fig tree rather than cut it down, Jesus wanted to invest in Zacchaeus, and his loving investment brought about a transformation in Zacchaeus. The Lord relates to all of us in a similar way. He keeps investing in us, especially at those moments when we are tempted to give up on ourselves and others are tempted to do the same. The Lord never gives up on us, and all he needs is a little opening in our hearts for his investment to bear rich fruit.

## 28 October, Monday, Ss Simon and Jude, Apostles

*Luke 6:12–19*

The two saints whose feast we celebrate today are listed as among the list of twelve apostles in today's gospel reading from Luke. Simon is referred to as 'the Zealot', and Jude or Judas is identified as the son of James. We know very little about either of these two close associates of Jesus. Jude or Judas has the misfortune to share the same name as the member of the Twelve who betrayed Jesus, Judas Iscariot. When the fourth evangelist refers to Judas or Jude on one occasion he qualifies the name immediately as 'not Iscariot'. If Jude or Judas has the same name as the member of the Twelve who betrayed Jesus, Simon has the same name as the leader of the Twelve, Simon, son of John, who became known as Peter or 'Rock'. Luke refers to the Simon whose feast we celebrate today as 'the Zealot'. This would suggest that he was zealous for God's Law. In one of his letters Paul refers to himself as 'zealous for the traditions of my fathers', by which he meant the Jewish Law and the traditions that had grown up around it. Simon, like Paul, must have been able to channel his zeal for the

Jewish Law into a zeal for Jesus who came to fulfil the true meaning of the Jewish Law. We know all too well today that religious zeal is not always a blessing; it can be violently destructive. However, when our religious or spiritual zeal is focused on Jesus, it will always be creative and life-giving. Zeal for the Lord will show itself in a zeal or an enthusiasm for all that the Lord values. This will be a zeal driven by love, by the Lord's love for all of humankind. The world is always in need of such loving zeal, the zeal of the Holy Spirit, the Spirit of God's love that has been poured into our hearts.

## 29 October, Tuesday, Thirtieth Week in Ordinary Time
*Luke 13:18–21*

In today's second reading, Paul declares that 'we are not saved yet'. Yes, he says, we possess the Holy Spirit, but this Spirit is only the first fruit of final and full salvation. That is why, Paul goes on to say, that we who possess the first fruits of the Spirit groan inwardly as we wait for our bodies to be set free. We know that we are not yet all that God intends us to be. God has begun a good work in our lives through the Holy Spirit, but that good work has yet to be brought to completion and it will only be brought to completion in eternity. Our faith is always a hopeful faith. On the basis of what God has already done and is doing in our lives, we hope to be saved, in the words of Paul in today's reading. We are always on the way; we have not yet arrived. That message of Paul ties in with the teaching of Jesus in the gospel reading. He speaks of the dynamic nature of the kingdom of God by means of two parables. The kingdom of God is like a mustard seed which a man took and threw into his garden; it is like leaven which a woman took and mixed in with flour. The mustard seed has not yet grown into a tree; the flour is not yet leavened all through. Yet, because of the life, death and resurrection of Jesus, a process has been set in motion in our own lives and in our world. This is God's process, with which we are asked to cooperate. It is God's work and we are asked to give ourselves over to it. If we keep surrendering to this continuing work of the Lord among us and within us, then we and our world will experience the fullness of God's salvation and the full coming of his kingdom.

## 30 October, Wednesday, Thirtieth Week in Ordinary Time
*Luke 13:22–30*

In the Gospels people often asks questions of Jesus and when they do so he generally responds to their question. However, occasionally he is portrayed by the evangelists as not responding to a question. We find an example of that at the beginning of today's gospel reading. Someone asks Jesus, 'Will only a few be saved?' Jesus refuses to respond directly to that kind of speculation – 'How many will be saved?' Instead he takes the question as an opportunity to call on people to strive to enter by the narrow door. Jesus implies that the way towards salvation, fullness of life, requires effort and focus on our part, just as entering through a narrow door requires a certain amount of focus and concentration. The narrowness of the door does not imply that only a few will get through it.

In fact, at the end of the gospel reading Jesus says that people from east and west, from north and south, will come to take their places at the feast in the kingdom of God. Beyond the door there is a vast multitude. There is an implicit answer there to the question, 'Will only a few be saved?' Jesus says, 'No, not a few, but many'. Yet, that broad hospitality of God, Jesus implies, is not a reason for complacency. We still have to strive to enter by the narrow door, and we do that by following behind Jesus, walking in his way, hearing God's word and keeping it, as he did.

## 31 October, Thursday, Thirtieth Week in Ordinary Time

*Luke 13:31–35*

In the course of the Gospels, Jesus uses many images to describe his ministry. He is the flute player who invites people to dance to the tune that he plays. In today's gospel reading, he compares his ministry to that of a hen who gathers her brood of chicks under her wings for their protection. Jesus came to gather people to himself so that we might be protected from evil and become fully alive with the life of God, which is a life of love. Yet, the tragedy for Jesus was that many people seemed unwilling to be gathered, in particular the people of Jerusalem. As Jesus declares, 'you refused'. Jesus was standing before the mystery of human freedom; his loving outreach was being rendered powerless by it. We can use our freedom to reject the love and life that God is offering us through Jesus. The Lord is always doing his work of gathering, but at some level of our being we need to cooperate with the Lord's work if it is to be effective for us. Yet, in the first reading today, Paul sounds a powerful triumphant note in this regard. He declares that 'nothing can come between us and the love of Christ'. How extraordinarily reassuring is that word 'nothing'. Paul seems to be saying that the Lord's love will somehow find a way to break through to us, even if we are doing our best to resist it. Clearly Paul believes that the Lord is very reluctant to take 'no' for an answer. The Lord is a persistent lover. He will do his utmost to gather us to himself, sometimes in spite of ourselves. All he needs is the smallest chink in our armour.

## 1 November, Friday, Feast of All Saints

*Matthew 5:1–12*

A lot of people do not like large gatherings. They find big crowds exhausting. Today's feast, however, is precisely about crowds of people. The first reading expresses it well, 'a huge number, impossible to count, of people from every nation, race, tribe and language'. Today is the feast not just of a few chosen saints but of all saints. Today we honour all the saints, those who are formally canonised and those who are not. If our vision of humanity is shaped exclusively by the media we might be tempted to think that there are a lot more villains out there than saints. It is reassuring to be reminded by today's feast that there exists a huge number of saints, impossible to count. In the words of the letter to the Hebrews, we are surrounded by a 'great cloud of witnesses'. None of us can live as the Lord wants us to live purely on our own. We need the good example of others to inspire us and to show us what is possible. Today's feast declares that we are surrounded by such a cloud of witnesses, if only we could recognise them. Some of these people have already passed beyond us and are now 'standing in front of the throne of the Lamb', in the words of today's first reading. Many of them, however, are our companions on the journey of life. They do not look at all like the statues in our churches. They are very ordinary, yet they are also very special. These are the people we are grateful to have met and to have around.

The feast of All Saints encourages us to believe that any one of us could be part of that huge number, impossible to count. In that sense, today's feast is about every one of us. John, in today's second reading, is speaking about all of us when he declares that 'we are already the children of God', and that, in the future, 'we shall be like' God. We are all destined for sainthood. God intends that all of us would be conformed to the image of God's Son. For most of us, that will only come to pass fully beyond this life. Yet, because we are already sons and daughters of God through Baptism, we are called to grow now towards that wonderful transformation that awaits us. The road to sainthood begins here, wherever we happen to find ourselves. In today's gospel reading, Jesus shows us what that road to sainthood looks like. In the Beatitudes, Jesus painted a portrait of himself, the living saint par excellence. He was also painting a portrait of the person that we are all called to become. The Beatitudes give us different facets of the person of Jesus, while at the same time showing us different ways in which we might reflect the person of Jesus.

## 2 November, Saturday, Commemoration of all the Faithful Departed
*Matthew 11:25–30*

I always find November a somewhat sombre and difficult month. The golden colours of autumn are quickly giving way to the barrenness of winter. As the month progresses, the days will get gradually shorter and darkness will increasingly make its presence felt. We lose the colours of nature and the life-giving quality of light. It is a month I associate with loss. It is perhaps fitting, then, that November is the month when we reflect upon more personal experiences of loss, the loss of significant people in our lives, people who have journeyed with us, who gave us love and whom we loved in return. The commemoration of All Souls is a day when we do that in a special way. On this day, we feel a sense of communion with our faithful departed. As followers of a risen Lord, we believe that our faithful have not just departed from us but have also returned to God, from whom they came. We understand death as a door through which we pass back to the source of our being, the Creator of all life. We also believe that our loved ones, in passing over into God, do not break their communion with us. Even though they have departed from us, they remain in communion with us and we remain in communion with them. A vital stream of life continues to flow between our deceased loved ones and ourselves.

The faith and love that bound us together in this life still binds us to them when they pass over into the next life. In the gospel reading, Jesus gives her son back to the grieving widow. One of the ways we expressed our love for our loved ones in this life was by praying for them. Our loved ones who have died can still be touched by the love that finds its voice in prayer. Prayerful remembrance is one of the ways we continue to give expression to our loving communion with them. Such prayer helps them and can also help us. None of us will have had a perfect relationship even with those we have loved the most. When someone close to us dies, there is always some unfinished business. Praying for our loved ones can help to heal whatever may need healing in our relationship with them. As a result, our communion with them can deepen after their death until it comes to fullness at the moment when we too pass over from this life and are united with them in God's love at that great banquet of life portrayed in today's first reading.

Although nothing is more painful than the loss of a loved one in death, our faith gives us this hope-filled vision in the face of death. In today's second reading, Paul says that 'hope is not deceptive, because the love of God has been poured into our hearts by the Holy Spirit which has been given to us'. Our hope is grounded in God's love for us now, a very personal love that is poured into the hearts of each one of us through the Holy Spirit. God's love, revealed in Jesus and poured into our hearts through the Spirit, continues to hold on to us when we pass through the door of death. As all authentic human love is always life-giving for the one loved, God's love is supremely life-giving for us, even in the face of our bodily death. What God's love has already done for us through his Son and the Spirit in this life is the assurance of what God's love will do for us in eternity. As Paul says in the second reading, 'Now that we have been reconciled [to God], surely we may count on being saved by the life of his Son'.

## 4 November, Monday, Thirty-First Week in Ordinary Time

*Luke 14:12–14*

In today's gospel reading Jesus addresses himself to a wealthy Pharisee who was his host at a meal. The Pharisees tended to eat only with their own kind. Jesus challenges his host to invite to his table those he would not normally invite, people beyond his circle. Jesus, in contrast to his host, shared table with all sorts of people, with the rich and the poor, with the educated and uneducated, with the religious and those considered sinners, with men and with women. His very broad table was a symbol of his whole ministry. He did not exclude anyone from his outreach. He wanted to reveal the year of the Lord's favour to everyone, especially to those who would have considered themselves outside of God's favour. By his whole way of life, including his style of eating, Jesus was revealing the broad hospitality of God. In contrast, the God whom the Pharisees revealed was a God who wanted to exclude more than include. The gospel reading calls on all of us to reveal something of the hospitality of God by our whole way of life. We can all be tempted to exclude others, even whole groups of people. It is very easy to move purely within a circle of people whose outlook, attitudes and social class are like our own. The gospel reading invites us to keep widening our circle so that it reveals more and more of the expansive heart of God revealed for us in the life of Jesus.

## 5 November, Tuesday, Thirty-First Week in Ordinary Time

*Luke 14:15–24*

Not all of the beatitudes in the Gospels are spoken by Jesus. Today's gospel reading opens with a beatitude spoken by one of Jesus' fellow guests at a banquet to which Jesus had been invited: 'Happy the one who will be at the feast in the kingdom of God!' Perhaps he imagined that the meal at which he was present, hosted by a leading Pharisee, with other Pharisees present, was a kind of foretaste of the banquet of eternal life. The parable Jesus spoke in response to this guest's beatitude suggests otherwise. It is a story about a man who gave a great banquet at which those expected to be there failed to turn up. Instead the banquet was filled with people who would never have been invited to the kind of banquet at which Jesus was a guest – the poor, the crippled, the blind, the lame, and those who were to be found by the open roads and hedgerows. Jesus was portraying a banquet that was very far removed from the one to which he had been invited. It is as if Jesus was saying to the guest who pronounced the beatitude, 'Don't think that this rather exclusive banquet is in any way like the banquet in the kingdom of God'. There is nothing selective about God's guest list. However, the parable warns than we can exclude ourselves from God's banquet by allowing ourselves to become overly absorbed by the attachments of this life. God wants a full and varied table. There can be no doubting God's desire. It is our desire to be at God's table that is the only issue. We are to seek the Lord with something of that earnestness with which the Lord seeks us, or in that striking image in today's responsorial psalm, with the same earnestness as a child seeks its mother. 'A weaned child on its mother's breast, even so is my soul'.

## 6 November, Wednesday, All the Saints of Ireland
*Luke 6:20–26*

Just under a week ago we celebrated the feast of All Saints. Today, we celebrate the feast of All the Saints of Ireland. We know the names of some of those saints, like Patrick, Brigid, Columcille, Ita and many others. It is striking how many of the stained-glass windows in our churches depict Irish saints. However, today we also remember those saintly men and women of our land of whom we have little or no record. In the words of today's first reading, 'some of them left a name behind them, so that their praises are still sung. While others have left no memory, and disappeared as though they had not existed, they are now as though they had never been'. Yet, the impact for good of this second group, those who have left no memory, could have been just as powerful as the impact for good of the well-known Irish saints. The saints are those whose lives are transparent before God; the light of God's love shines through them. They are always a power for good, whether or not they leave a memory. When a child in school was asked, 'Who are the saints?', she thought of the stained-glass windows in her parish church and said, 'the saints are those who let the light in'. Before we can allow the light of the Lord to shine through us, we first have to be aware of our need of his light. In today's gospel reading, Luke tells us that people were drawn to Jesus from near and far, Jerusalem, Tyre and Sidon. They came out of a sense of their need of God's life-giving and healing light. They were poor, hungry, distressed and needy, and they knew it, and Jesus says to them, 'Happy are you … '. He declared this mass of broken humanity to be happy, because they knew their need of what Jesus could offer them. The first step on the road to sanctity is that awareness of our need of the Lord for what only the Lord can give us. As we come before the Lord in our poverty, we open ourselves to his coming. We make it possible for him to work in and through us. It is our awareness of our need of the Lord which makes us transparent before the light of his love, enabling that light to shine through us into our often-dark world.

## 6 November, Wednesday, Thirty-First Week in Ordinary Time
*Luke 14:25–33*

The language at the beginning of today's gospel reading about the need to hate family members to become a follower of Jesus seems very strange to our ears. It is a Semitic idiom of expressing preference, whereby if someone prefers one thing or one person over another, they are said to love the one and hate the other. The Jesus who said, 'love your enemies', is not asking us to hate our own flesh and blood. Yet, he is calling for a level of allegiance that takes priority over even the most cherished of human allegiances. He is to be the primary love in our lives. That doesn't mean that we will love others less, including the members of our family. Rather, if the Lord is the first love in our lives, then our natural loves will be enhanced; we will be empowered to love others in the way the Lord loves them. When we love the Lord with all our heart, soul, mind and strength, we will be caught up into the Lord's love for others. The more we give ourselves to the Lord, the freer we are to give ourselves to others in the way the Lord gives himself to them. Jesus is aware that he is asking a lot of us, which is why the parable he speaks calls on us to think seriously about our response to his call, just as a builder has to think things through before he starts to build and a king has to think carefully before he goes to war. Yet, elsewhere in the Gospels, Jesus assures us that if we respond to his call, all embracing as it is, we will receive from the Lord far more than we give him.

## 7 November, Thursday, Thirty-First Week in Ordinary Time
*Luke 15:1–10*
We spend a certain amount of our time looking for something, and that is certainly true if you are as prone to loosing things as often as I am. We also find ourselves looking for people in various ways. Parents look for their children if they ramble off. Men and women look for someone they can share their lives with. We all look for friends, people with whom we can journey and who want to journey with us. Underneath all this searching and longing is a more fundamental search for God, who alone can satisfy the deepest longings in our hearts. St Augustine wrote that our hearts are restless until they rest in God. Even more fundamental than our search for God is God's search for us. God's search for us took flesh in the person of Jesus. He said of himself that he came to seek and to save the lost; Jesus gave expression to God's longing to be in communion with us. The shepherd who searches for his lost sheep and the woman who searches for her lost coin in today's two parables are images of Jesus' search for us, of God's search for us in Jesus. God never ceases to seek us out because we are all lost in different ways. Our search for God is always in response to God's search for us. In the words of the first letter of St John, 'We love

because God first loved us'. If we open our hearts to God's searching love for us in Jesus, then we will be moved to search for God.

## 8 November, Friday, Thirty-First Week in Ordinary Time

*Luke 16:1–8*

The parables Jesus spoke were all drawn from the experience of life with which he and his hearers would have been familiar. All of human life is in these stories, what we might call the good, the bad and the ugly. Many of the characters in the stories that Jesus told leave a lot to be desired. That is certainly true of the parable in today's gospel reading. A wealthy landlord entrusted the care of his estate to a steward or a manager. We are aware of the figure of the absentee landlord from our own history. This particular steward took advantage of the absence of the landlord to enrich himself dishonestly. Eventually, as often happens, his dishonesty caught up with him. The landlord came to hear of what was happening and called him in and gave him his notice. What the dishonest steward does next showed that he had some redeeming feature. He called in the landlord's debtors who worked the land and he reduced their debt to the landlord by cancelling what he had planned to take for himself. In that way he hoped to make friends with these tenants, so that when he lost his job they might look favourably upon him. He was still acting out of self-interest, but in a slightly more enlightened way. Jesus saw something of merit in the actions of this rather shady character. A moment of crisis brought home to him that some things were more important than acquiring wealth for himself, such as the friendship and hospitality of others. The landlord ends up praising his dishonest steward for his astuteness, his wisdom. What is Jesus saying to us through this story? The crisis that the steward found himself in brought about a shift in his values. Jesus is calling on us to value people more than possessions, and to use our material resources in the service of others, especially those in greatest need. Our values are to be in line with the Lord's values, and it is people he values more than anything else.

## 9 November, Saturday, The Dedication of the Lateran Basilica

*John 2:13–22*

In the early fourth century AD the first Christian emperor, Constantine, had a church built on land that once belonged to the Laterani family. That church of Constantine was the precursor of the present Lateran Basilica. This basilica is the cathedral of the diocese of Rome. It is the church of the pope in his capacity as bishop of Rome. For that reason, it has the title, 'mother and head of all the churches of the city and the world'. Our local parish churches are much more modest buildings than the Basilica of St John Lateran in Rome, yet they are equally monuments to people's faith. In today's first reading Paul tells the Christians in Corinth, 'you are God's building ... you are God's temple'. Paul is reminding us that more fundamental than the building we call church are the people we call Church. The church building is there to help us to express our identity as a people of faith, called to worship God through Christ in the Spirit. If our worship is to be authentic, the shape of our worship must become the shape of our lives. Our whole lives are to be a movement towards God, through Christ and in the Spirit. This is what it means to be Church, to be the temple of God in the world, the living sign of God's presence. In the gospel reading Jesus points to himself as the temple of God in the world, the one through whom God is present in the world. This is the heart of our own baptismal calling, to become temples of God through whom God's loving presence touches the lives of others.

## 11 November, Monday, Thirty-Second Week in Ordinary Time

*Luke 17:1–6*

In the gospel reading Jesus is very critical of those who lead others in the community astray, or 'cause them to stumble', in another translation. He was aware that his followers could become an obstacle to other people coming to faith. On several occasions in the Gospels, the disciples are portrayed as trying to block people, including children, from coming in contact with Jesus. Those in positions of leadership in the Church have a special responsibility to ensure that they don't become obstacles to people coming to faith in Jesus or to believers growing in their faith in Jesus. We have all become very aware in recent years of the great harm that can be done to the Church, the believing community, by the giving of scandal. Our English word 'scandal' comes from the Greek word that stands behind the word 'obstacle' in today's gospel reading. When Jesus says in today's gospel reading, 'Watch yourselves', we are being reminded that the way to nurture the faith of others is to nurture our own faith first, whereas if we fail to nurture our faith or if we fail to live in accordance with our faith, the faith of others is undermined. We all have an influence for good or otherwise on each other's relationship with the Lord. We can be an obstacle on the faith journey of others or we can help to bring each other to the Lord. If we are to lead each other to the Lord, we need to keep making our own the prayer of the disciples in today's gospel reading, 'Increase our faith'.

## 12 November, Tuesday, Thirty-Second Week in Ordinary Time
*Luke 17:7–10*

When a loved one dies, family members will take care to choose readings for the funeral mass that in some way reflect the life of the person who has died. Today's first reading from the Book of Wisdom is a reading that is often chosen for a funeral mass. It is easy to understand why. The Book of Wisdom from which the reading comes was written within a 100 years of the birth of Jesus. It anticipates Jesus' message about eternal life. It declares that the virtuous or the faithful are at peace beyond death, that they will live with God in love, and that grace and mercy await them. Death is a door through which the faithful enter into God's peace, love, grace and mercy. It is a very hopeful vision of life beyond death. Jesus declares, some years after this book was written, that those who believe in him will never die, in the sense that they will come to share in his own risen life. Sharing in his risen life will be an experience of peace, love, grace and mercy.

The parable that Jesus speaks in today's gospel reading suggests that such a life, for which we long and hope, will always be the Lord's gift to us. It is not something we earn or can lay claim to in some kind of deserving way. Just as the servant in Jesus' culture had no claim on his master for doing his duty, so we have no claim on God, even after we have done all that God asks of us. We live as God wants us to live not because we think it entitles us to something from God, but simply out of gratitude to God for all that he has already given us through Jesus and for all that he has yet to give us beyond this earthly life.

## 13 November, Wednesday, Thirty-Second Week in Ordinary Time
*Luke 17:11–19*

There are 150 prayers in the Book of Psalms, and the prayer of petition, the prayer for help, is the prayer that occurs most frequently in that collection. From our own experience we may be aware that the prayer that comes most naturally and easily to us is the prayer of petition. We turn to God above all when we sense the need of God's help, when we are made aware of our own vulnerability. We find an example of that prayer of petition, that prayer out of the depths, at the beginning of today's gospel reading. Ten lepers cry out in unison to Jesus, standing at a distance, 'Jesus! Master! Take pity on us.' Jesus responds to their prayer, curing their leprosy and sending them to the priest to authenticate their healing. However, only one of the ten moves beyond the prayer of petition to the prayer of praise and thanksgiving. The gospel reading says that this man 'turned back praising God', and 'threw himself at the feet of Jesus and thanked him'. He praised God and thanked Jesus. He recognised that it was God working through Jesus that was the reason for his healing. It was only to this man that Jesus said, 'your faith has saved you'. This man's response to the gift he had received was the response of faith, and it brought him a deeper healing beyond his physical healing, what Jesus calls 'salvation'. He was the least likely to make this model response to the gift he had received from God through Jesus. He was a foreigner, a non-Jew, a Samaritan. Yet, Jesus holds him up as a model of faith for us all. The response of faith to being blessed by God is always one of praise and thanksgiving. We need to allow this prayer of praise and thanksgiving to rise up within us on a regular basis, because we are all being continuously graced by God. Paul puts it very simply in one of his letters: 'Give thanks in all circumstances; for this is the will of God in Christ Jesus for you'.

## 14 November, Thursday, Thirty-Second Week in Ordinary Time

*Luke 17:20–25*

Many people ask questions of Jesus in the course of the Gospels. Jesus does not always answer the questions in the way that people might expect. In today's gospel reading, the Pharisees ask Jesus when the kingdom of God is to come. They heard him proclaim, 'the kingdom of God is at hand', and they wanted him to set a date for its coming. It was a 'when' question, but Jesus did not give a 'when' answer. Yes, there will be a time in the future when the kingdom of God will come in all its fullness, when the Son of Man will come in great power and glory. However, Jesus does not go down the road of calculating the timing of this future event. Rather, he draws attention to the here and now. The kingdom of God in all its fullness may be a future reality, but there is a sense in which it is already a present reality. As Jesus says to his questioners, 'the kingdom of God is among you'. The kingdom of God is in your midst, if only you had eyes to see it. It is present in what Jesus is saying and doing. The kingdom of God is present among us today, because Jesus, now in his risen form, continues to move among us, in word and in deed. The kingdom of God may be hidden, like the mustard seed in the soil or the leaven in the flour, but it is here among us in all its transforming power. When we feel low in ourselves or we feel discouraged about the state of the Church, we need to repeat to ourselves those words of Jesus in today's gospel reading, 'the kingdom of God is among you'.

## 15 November, Friday, Thirty-Second Week in Ordinary Time
*Luke 17:26–37*

Today's first reading speaks about 'the good things that are seen'. It celebrates 'the grandeur and beauty' of our world. However, the author criticises those who fail to recognise the One who stands behind all this goodness, grandeur and beauty, the Creator or Author. The world points beyond itself to the God who made it. Yet, the author recognises that it is easy to become absorbed in God's world and never acknowledge God. In the gospel reading, Jesus speaks about the ordinary and good human activities of eating and drinking, marrying, buying and selling, planting and building. Yet, he also acknowledges that these good, wholesome human activities can so hold our attention that we never look beyond them to what he calls 'the days of the Son of Man'.

We already live in those days. The Son of Man, the risen Lord, stands among us. He calls out to us every day. God calls out to us through his risen Son. We can fail to notice the presence of the Lord at the heart of all our day-to-day activities. We can fail to hear God's call amid the attractiveness and the busyness of God's world. The readings today encourage us to be alert to the Lord's presence in both the natural world and our own personal world. There is a sense in which the ground on which we stand, wherever it is, is always holy ground.

## 16 November, Saturday, Thirty-Second Week in Ordinary Time
*Luke 18:1–8*

The depiction of the widow in today's parable is of a very strong woman who will stop at nothing to get justice for herself. When an injustice is done to us or to someone else, it will often galvanise us into taking action on our own behalf or on behalf of others. People will fight tooth and nail to get justice for themselves and for those who are dear to them. The widow in the parable is clearly a fighter. She is up against an unjust judge, which is a contradiction in terms. She is a vulnerable woman, a widow, who takes on a powerful man, a judge. Yet, in this unequal contest, it is the widow who emerges victorious. She wears down the unjust judge until he gives her what she wants, what she is entitled to. While the judge is depicted in our gospel reading as saying, 'I must give this widow her just rights, or she will persist in coming and worry me to death', the more literal translation of 'worry me to death' would be 'give me a black eye'. Jesus sees in this feisty widow a quality that his disciples need. They will need something of her persevering and trusting faith, the kind of faith that remains strong in the face of injustice and rejection. When Jesus asks in his comment on the parable, 'When the Son of Man comes, will he find any faith on earth?', he wonders aloud whether he will find people of such combative and enduring faith when he comes at the end of time. Luke's introduction to Jesus' parable suggests that such persevering faith, a faith that doesn't lose heart, is the fruit of continual prayer. The faith that endures to the end is ultimately a gift from God that is given to those who keep opening themselves to receive it in prayer.

## 18 November, Monday, Thirty-Third Week in Ordinary Time
*Luke 18:35–43*

There can be a lot of pressure on people nowadays not to witness to their faith. We can sometimes feel cowed into keeping our faith to ourselves. This is probably especially true of young people at school. Many of them would be slow to show their faith publicly for fear of ridicule by their peers. That kind of peer pressure can be insidious. In today's gospel reading, the blind man who sat at the roadside begging clearly had some kind of faith in Jesus. When people told him, in answer to his question, that Jesus of Nazareth was passing by, he immediately gave public expression to his faith, crying aloud, 'Jesus, Son of David, take pity on me'. One of the ways we all give expression to our faith is through such prayers of petition. However, the blind man immediately encountered a hostile response to this public expression of his faith. People scolded him and told him to keep quiet. Yet, here was a man whose faith would not be forced into the shadows. In response to this hostile response, he shouted all the louder. His prayer became more intense. As a result, he received from the Lord the encouragement and respect that others denied him, 'What do you want me to do for you?' In a similar way, the Lord will always be alongside us, supporting us, when our public witness to our faith leaves us isolated. The man's persistent faith brought him into a greater light, as his sight was restored to him by Jesus. His persistent prayer of faith also led him to become a public disciple of Jesus; he immediately followed Jesus, praising God. Our own persistent faith in the face of opposition will bring us into a greater light too. Through such enduring faith we too will become more fully the Lord's disciples who follow him along his way.

## 19 November, Tuesday, Thirty-Third Week in Ordinary Time
*Luke 19:1–10*

Whatever else can be said about Zacchaeus, we can certainly say of him that he was a seeker, a searcher. The gospel reading says that 'he was anxious to see what kind of man Jesus was'. In his search to know Jesus, he was prepared, quite literally, to go out on a limb, the limb of a tree. This would have been considered a rather undignified place to be for a man of his status. Zacchaeus does something extravagant in order to see Jesus, to come to know him. In the course of his search he discovered that the one he was searching for was also searching for him. 'I must stay at your house today,' said Jesus, who came to seek out and to save the lost. Zacchaeus, who was searching, discovered that he was the object of a greater search. When Zacchaeus then offered Jesus hospitality, he discovered that a greater hospitality was being offered to him, the hospitality of God through Jesus. 'Today, salvation has come to his house, because this man too is a son of Abraham.' Zacchaeus belonged to God's people; there was room for him at God's table, in spite of the murmuring of the crowd. The story we have just heard reminds us all that our movement towards

God is always overshadowed by God's movement towards us. When we take a small step towards the Lord, we discover that he has already taken a giant step towards us.

## 20 November, Wednesday, Thirty-Third Week in Ordinary Time
*Luke 19:11–28*

The stories Jesus told often draw upon familiar aspects of daily life, without condoning them or even challenging them. This is true of the parable in today's gospel reading. It is the kind of thing that happened in Jesus' time. A rich man goes abroad and entrusts his servants with responsibility in his absence. He expects them to use the resources he has given them creatively. It wouldn't be a good interpretation of the parable to simply identify the rich man with God. According to the gospel reading, Jesus spoke this parable to those who thought that because Jesus was approaching Jerusalem, the kingdom of God was going to show itself there and then. To correct that impression, Jesus speaks a parable which suggests there will be an interval of time before the full coming of the kingdom of God. In that interval the Lord wants us to make creative use of the resources and gifts that he has given us. He doesn't want us to do nothing, out of fear, which was the case with the third servant in the parable. Fear can be very immobilizing, the fear of failure, the fear of getting it wrong, the fear of being misunderstood. Pope Francis comes across as someone who is not held back by fear. He is prepared to take a risk in the service of the Lord and his Gospel, to do something that has not been done before. We need something of that fearless, and adventurous spirit today. We learn more by trying something and failing than by doing nothing. The Lord wants to work through us, but we need to give him scope to do so. We need to recognise the resources the Lord has given us and then place them at his disposal by being creative and courageous in our use of them.

## 21 November, Thursday, Presentation of the Blessed Virgin Mary

*Matthew 12:46–50*

There is no scene in the Gospels corresponding to today's memorial, yet there is a presumption that Mary's parents would have presented her to the Lord in the Temple of Jerusalem when she was a child. Christian tradition has understood that Mary's presentation to the Lord by her parents symbolised the consecration of her life to the Lord. As her parents presented her to the Lord, Mary as an adult presented herself to the Lord, made herself available for God's purpose, as expressed in her response to the angel Gabriel, 'Let what you have said be done to me'. In a similar way, our parents presented us to the Lord on the day of our Baptism. As we grow towards adulthood, we then confirm for ourselves what happened for us on the day of our Baptism. Our Confirmation is our personal confirming of our Baptism, which we try to live out every day. Mary's giving of herself over to God's purpose for her life did not always come easily to her, because God's ways are not our ways. In today's gospel she and other members of her family approached where Jesus was teaching and stood outside, anxious to have a word with him. However, rather than just going out to his mother, Jesus sent back word to her that he now had a new family. His disciples, those who did the will of God as Jesus revealed it, were now his brother and sister and mother. Mary had to learn to let go of her son to God's purpose for his life. When we enter into a personal relationship with God, it is always God who does the leading and we who try to follow. God's purposes are always greater and more mysterious than ours, and so there is always a letting-go to God on our part. That doesn't come easily to us, no more than it came easily to Mary, but if we allow God to have God's way in our life, we can be assured that it will be the way of life for us and for all we influence.

## 22 November, Friday, Thirty-Third Week in Ordinary Time
*Luke 19:45–48*

According to our first reading, it was on the twenty-fifth day of the Jewish month of Chislev that Judas Maccabeus and his associates purified the Temple in Jerusalem, which had become contaminated by pagan images and practices. This happened a little over 150 years before the birth of Jesus. The twenty-fifty of Chislev remains an important feastday for Jews today. It is usually celebrated in November/December, the Feast of the Rededication of the Temple. In the gospel reading Jesus is also portrayed as purifying the Temple in Jerusalem. On this occasion it wasn't non-Jewish people who were responsible for the unsatisfactory state of the Temple but other Jews, in particular the priests who were responsible for the Temple. They had allowed people to sell goods in one of the courts of the Temple, the court reserved for non-Jewish people. As a result, non-Jewish people could not pray in the area reserved for them. The Temple was meant to be a house of prayer for Jewish and non-Jewish people. Jesus saw that the Temple was not conducting its business in accordance with God's purpose. It had become, according to Jesus, a 'robber's den' rather than a 'house of prayer'. According to Luke, Jesus had referred to the Temple, when a twelve-year-old, as 'my Father's house'. Jesus, the Son of God, acted authoritatively to purify and renew his Father's house. Every institution stands in need of continuing renewal, including religious institutions, of which the most sacred in Jesus' day was the Temple in Jerusalem. The Church, likewise, is always in need of reform. We who comprise the Church are always in need of the Lord's reforming and renewing zeal. It is a zeal that is born of love, because the Lord wants us to become all that God desires for us. Each day we try to open ourselves anew to the Lord's continuing work of renewal in our lives.

## 23 November, Saturday, Thirty-Third Week in Ordinary Time
*Luke 20:27–40*

In his first letter to the Corinthians, Paul declares, 'no eye has seen, nor ear heard, nor human heart conceived, what God has prepared for those who love him'. The eternal life God has prepared for us is beyond our seeing, hearing and conceiving. Yet when Jesus speaks of life beyond this earthly life, life in the kingdom of God, he uses a variety of images drawn from this earthly life to convey some sense of this life which eye has not seen. He speaks of a great banquet at which people from north, south, east and west will gather; he refers to the many-roomed house of God his Father; he uses the term 'Paradise', with its overtones of a beautiful garden. All these images are suggestive, not descriptive. The life of heaven cannot be described in human language; it is not just an extension of this earthly life. It is of a different, more wonderful, quality. In today's gospel reading, the Sadducees, who did not believe in life beyond this earthly life, imagine the life of the resurrection to be an extension of this earthly life and ridicule it accordingly. A man has seven wives in this life, which of them will be his wife in the life of the resurrection? In his reply to their question, Jesus suggests that what he calls life 'in the other world' will be very different from life in this world, because in this other world, people will never die. They will share in the life of God, and will truly be sons and daughters of God. Without saying clearly what life beyond this earthly life is like, he states clearly what it is not like. Perhaps when it comes to the life of heaven we can only say what it is not, rather than what it is. Yet, Jesus does imply in his answer to the Sadducees' question that the essence of life in this other world will be a new and closer relationship with the 'God of the living'. The deeper our relationship with the God of the living, the more alive we will be and, therein, lies our hope.

## 25 November, Monday, Thirty-Fourth Week in Ordinary Time
*Luke 21:1–4*

The Gospels suggest that Jesus was very observant of life, and, in particular, of people. In today's gospel reading he notices someone that would have gone unnoticed by others. Among the rich people putting offerings into the Temple treasury, Jesus notices a poor widow putting in two small coins. Socially speaking, she was insignificant, and her contribution was insignificant compared to that of others. Yet, Jesus noticed a quality of generosity in her that was truly praiseworthy. In giving her little, she was, in reality, giving everything, all she had to live on. I am reminded of a verse in the Jewish Scriptures, 'Humans look at appearances, but God looks at the heart'. In her tiny contribution to the Temple treasury, Jesus recognised an extraordinary generosity of heart. Perhaps Jesus recognised something of himself in her. She gave her all, and Jesus was about to give his all as he faced into his passion and death. There are times in all our lives when we are very aware that we have very little to give, for whatever reason. It might be due to ill health or advancing years or some personal circumstance which is taking its toll on us. We may feel that we are contributing little to others. Yet, the little we give in those circumstances can reveal a great generosity of spirit. We may not always recognise that in ourselves; others may not recognise it. Yet, today's gospel reading suggests that the Lord certainly does. The Lord always notices the little we give, when a little is all we have

## 26 November, Tuesday, Thirty-Fourth Week in Ordinary Time
*Luke 21:5–11*

Pilgrims who go to the Holy Land today will invariably visit the Wailing Wall in Jerusalem. It is the western wall of the platform on which the great Temple of King Herod rested. It is the most public remnant of what is left of that great building, which in its day was considered one of the wonders of the world. At the beginning of today's gospel reading, people speak in admiration of this wonderful building, remarking on its fine stonework. It must have seemed very strange to those people's ears when Jesus interjected, 'the time will come when not a single stone will be left on another; everything will be destroyed'. Forty years later, the Roman legions under the command of the emperor Titus would indeed destroy the Temple, dismantling what had taken nearly sixty years to complete. Today's gospel reading reminds us that everything passes, even what seems indestructible and permanent. Jesus will go on to say on this same occasion, 'Heaven and earth will pass away', but then immediately qualifies this all-encompassing statement, 'but my words will not pass away'. In the midst of monumental change, the words of Jesus endure. Jesus himself endures and his relationship with us and ours with him endures, even into eternity. This is why it is worth investing in this relationship. It is the one fixed point in the midst of all change. It is our relationship with the Lord which allows us to endure through all the changes that come our way, including that most profound change that is associated with the ending of our earthly life.

## 27 November, Wednesday, Thirty-Fourth Week in Ordinary Time
*Luke 21:12–19*

There are times in our lives when what we perceive to be great setbacks can turn out to be great opportunities. What is initially experienced as a very negative event can bring us some unexpected blessing. In today's gospel reading, Jesus paints a stark picture of the future for his disciples. They will be seized, persecuted and imprisoned, and some will even be put to death. Yet, Jesus declares that this dark experience will also be a great opportunity. It will be an opportunity for his disciples to bear witness to their faith in Jesus. Paul, writing to the Church in Philippi from his prison, declared to them that 'what has happened to me has actually helped to spread the Gospel, so that it has become known throughout the whole imperial guard and to everyone else that my imprisonment is for Christ'. This was Paul's opportunity to bear witness. The dark experience that Jesus predicts for his disciples will be an opportunity in another sense too. Their vulnerability at this time will be an opportunity for the Lord to work powerfully in and through them. 'I will give you an eloquence and a wisdom that none of your opponents will be able to resist or contradict.' In a similar way, Paul in that same letter tells the Church in Philippi, 'I can do all things through him who strengthens me'. Difficult times for the Church, times of hostility and opposition, can be great opportunities. It is an opportunity for us to be courageous in our witness to our faith, and an opportunity for the Lord to show that he is capable of working powerfully in and through our frailty and weakness.

## 28 November, Thursday, Thirty-Fourth Week in Ordinary Time
*Luke 21:20–28*

The gospel readings at this time of the year tend to be rather gloomy, at least on first hearing them. We are in the last days of the Church's liturgical year; the new liturgical year begins on Sunday, the first Sunday of Advent. As the Church's year end, we hear of cataclysmic endings in the gospel reading, the ending of Jerusalem, and, even, the ending of the cosmos as we know it. Yet, as well as talking about endings in our gospel reading, Jesus also speaks about comings. More especially, he speaks about his own coming as the glorious Son of Man, bringing liberation to those who await his coming. At the very moment when everything appears to be disappearing, a new reality begins to dawn. The final chapter will not be one of death and de-struction, but one of new beginning and a new liberation for all. This is but one expression of the basic message of the Gospels, that the Lord works in life-giving ways in the midst of death and destruction. There may be great darkness in the world, the darkness of evil and suffering, but the Lord's light shines within it and the darkness will not overcome the light. It is this conviction which keeps us hopeful even in the midst of pain, loss and death. That is why in the words of the gospel reading, we can always stand erect and hold our heads high, not in a spirit of arrogance but in a spirit of hopeful conviction that the Lord's liberating coming is assured, no matter how dark and distressing the moment.

## 29 November, Friday, Thirty-Fourth Week in Ordinary Time

*Luke 21:29–33*

The gospel reading speaks about trees budding as a sign of the nearness of summer. We are many months away from that happening here. The trees are shedding the last of their leaves as winter takes a grip. However, Sunday is the first Sunday of Advent and before Advent is finished the days will begin to get longer and the gradual return of the light will herald the coming of spring in a couple of months. Regardless of whatever season we are in, another statement of Jesus in today's gospel reading will always hold true: 'the kingdom of God is near'. The reign of God through Jesus, our risen Lord, is always near to us. The Lord is constantly present among us and within each of us. One of the ways the Lord is present to us is through his word. His presence in and through his word is constant. The concluding words of Jesus in our gospel reading are, 'Heaven and earth will pass away, but my words will never pass away'. The Lord's life-giving word accompanies us not just through all four seasons of the year, but through all the seasons of our life. The seasons of our life are not as regular as the seasons of nature. We can find ourselves in a personal winter at any time of our lives. We can suddenly enter a time when signs of light and life are difficult to find. It is at such times above all that we need to keep reminding ourselves of what Jesus says in today's gospel reading, 'the kingdom of God is near ... my words will never pass away'.

## 30 November, Saturday, St Andrew, Apostle

*Matthew 4:18–22*

In the first reading, Paul declares that 'faith comes from what is preached, and what is preached comes from the word of God'. Good preaching is rooted in God's word and nurtures faith. The preacher needs to be a good listener to God's word if his or her preaching is to generate and nurture faith. As Christians, we recognise the New Testament as the privileged place where we hear God's word. The Lord speaks to us through the inspired writings of what has come to be known as the New Testament. In the gospel reading, Peter and Andrew, James and John, hear the Lord's word as they engage in their daily work as fishermen. It was while they were casting or mending their nets that they heard the Lord's call to become his followers. The Lord speaks to us all from within the heart of our daily experience. What we might think of as purely secular activities can have a truly sacred quality. Our attentiveness to the Lord's word in the Scriptures can make us more attuned to the many ways he communicates with us in the bits and pieces of life. According to today's responsorial psalm, the heavens proclaim the glory of God, as does the firmament; day unto day takes up the story; night unto night makes known the message. The Lord's glory, story, message can be heard in all of life, if we have ears to hear. Andrew, whose feast we celebrate today, had ears to hear the Lord's word to him as he immersed himself in his day's work. He inspires us to have something of the same contemplative attitude to life that allows us to be sensitive to what the Lord may be saying to us in all of life's situations.